EatingWell™
Fast & Flavorful
Meatless Meals

Jessie Price & the EatingWell Test Kitchen | Introduction by Rachael Moeller Gorman
Foreword by Daphne Oz | Photography by Ken Burris

150 Healthy Recipes
Everyone Will Love

Library of Congress Cataloging-in-Publication Data
has been applied for.

ISBN 978-0-88150-943-4

Published by The Countryman Press,
P.O. Box 748, Woodstock, VT 05091

Distributed by W.W. Norton & Company, Inc.,
500 Fifth Avenue, New York, NY 10110
Printed in China by R.R. Donnelley

Photography by Ken Burris
Cover recipe: Tomato-Corn Pie (*page 179*)

10 9 8 7 6 5 4 3 2 1

AUTHORS | Jessie Price & the EATINGWELL Test Kitchen

TEST KITCHEN
TEST KITCHEN MANAGER | Stacy Fraser
ASSOCIATE EDITOR | Hilary Meyer
RECIPE DEVELOPER, TESTER | Carolyn Casner
RECIPE DEVELOPER, FOOD STYLIST | Katie Webster
FOOD STYLISTS | Patsy Jamieson, Susan Herr
FOOD STYLING ASSISTANT | Elizabeth Neily

ART DIRECTOR | Michael J. Balzano
PHOTOGRAPHER | Ken Burris
DESIGNER | Amanda Coyle
MANAGING EDITOR | Wendy S. Ruopp
ASSISTANT MANAGING EDITOR | Alesia Depot
PRODUCTION MANAGER | Jennifer B. Brown
CONTRIBUTING EDITORS | Carolyn Malcoun, Nicci Micco, M.S.
INTRODUCTION | Rachael Moeller Gorman
CONTRIBUTING WRITERS | Chris Elam, Daphne Oz,
Amy Paturel, M.S., M.P.H., Jim Romanoff
NUTRITION EDITOR | Brierley Wright, M.S., R.D.
DIETITIAN & NUTRITION ADVISOR | Sylvia Geiger, M.S., R.D.
RESEARCH EDITOR | Anne Bliss
EDITORIAL INTERNS | JP Dubuque, Emilie Stigliani,
Jordan Werner, Amelia Wurzburg
INDEXER | Amy Novick, BackSpace Indexing

EATINGWELL MEDIA GROUP
CEO | Tom Witschi
EDITORIAL DIRECTOR | Lisa Gosselin

Garden-Fresh Stir-Fry with Seitan (*p. 136*)

CONTENTS

FOREWORD

By Daphne Oz

For me, eating meatless did not start off as a choice. Back in the 1970s, my maternal grandmother decided to pack away her Spam and Canadian bacon in favor of a new eating regime—no more red, white or even barely pink meat. She inflicted this new regime on her very unhappy six children and even more dejected surgeon husband—the son of an Irish-Italian, meat-loving family, no less!

What began out of a love for her many animals, including horses, sheep, goats and a cow (she lives on the same farm near Philadelphia today), grew into a passion for the pursuit of health knowledge. As meat became part of every "square" meal around the country, she looked for balance through a diet of whole, unprocessed, natural foods. It surely took some getting used to, but my grandmother is an excellent cook and was able to sate her family's palates with plenty of delectable, meat-free dishes…and this was long before the advent of texturized soy protein and wheat gluten that taste and look like beef, pork and turkey.

My mother was a product of this environment, and by the time I came around in 1986, she had already persuaded my Turkish father, Dr. Mehmet Oz, to give up his daily meat fix. As a kid, I regularly noshed on tabouli, roasted eggplant, sweet potato casserole and vegetarian chili. When I headed to high school I began to realize how bizarre it was that, as an American teen, I had never tried a hot dog, eaten a hamburger or ordered a steak dinner. Never.

Like most teens, I had my rebellion. When I got to college, I wanted to eat like all the "normal" kids and would order the sirloin when we went out to dinner—but I never loved it. I quickly resumed my almost entirely vegetarian lifestyle, not just because I loved animals (though I do) or because I saw the proof that our overconsumption of animal products dramatically increases the incidence of preventable disease and undermines the viability of our planet (which it does), but because I simply didn't need meat.

Now that I'm an adult with a husband to feed, I find myself eating meat on very rare occasions (maybe five times a year), with fresh fruits, vegetables, whole grains and some fish composing the vast majority of my meals. But, I admit, this can get boring without inspiration. Though my family had years of experience with vegetarian cooking, our palates today crave excitement and adventure. We want to taste the flavors of the world in our own homes as well as enjoy new versions of the comfort foods we grew up with. I was looking for a guide to inject some excitement into the healthful meals on my table. And when I heard that the team behind EATINGWELL Magazine was putting together a vegetarian cookbook, I knew I had found my answer.

The key to their success—and the reason I know this cookbook will open your eyes to a whole new world of decadent vegetarianism—is that the editors of EATINGWELL have been producing great-tasting, healthy vegetarian recipes for years, backed by science-based nutrition and tested in kitchens the country over. And their priority with vegetarian recipes has always been to show us how to make meat-free meals that are not just balanced and healthy, but also full of flavor!

You won't find any bland steamed greens here, no ma'am. Whether it's the Bean Burgers with Spicy Guacamole (I have never made it through an entire one, they are so rich and delicious), the Jícama & Cucumber Salad with Red Chile Dressing (the perfect crunchy and refreshing salad for late-summer picnics), the Goat Cheese Grits with Fresh Corn (nothing says comfort like cheese and corn) or the Glazed Chocolate-Pumpkin Bundt Cake (need I say more?), choosing vegetarianism—and health—does not mean sacrificing the joy of eating.

Now that the experts have done the work for us, all we have to do is flip through the book, pick a recipe and start cooking.

Braised Summer Vegetables with a Green Herb Sauce (*p. 54*)

VEGETARIAN, THE EATINGWELL WAY

By Jessie Price

Here at EATINGWELL our mission is to make great-tasting food that's healthy too. Part of that means we're a bit obsessed with fruits and vegetables. Just take a look at the cover of EATINGWELL Magazine—every issue we feature a mouthwatering image of a whole fruit or vegetable.

But it's not just produce that we get excited about. We love coming up with new ways to cook with whole grains, like our riff on Hoppin' John (*page 123*) that uses wholesome barley instead of the white rice that's traditionally used. We have a million ways to prepare protein-rich beans. Take a look at the smoky pinto beans we serve along with sweet potato fritters (*page 124*). We're always adding heart-healthy nuts to recipes or enjoying a drizzle of peppery olive oil over freshly picked greens. In other words, celebrating inherently nutritious foods is what we do every day.

So creating meatless recipes is a natural for us. The cooks here in the EATINGWELL Test Kitchen are omnivores. Yes, we eat meat and fish, but we also trade stories about our vegetable gardens, CSA shares and weekly trips to the farmers' market. And when we produce vegetarian recipes, we do it with gusto. We elbowed each other out of the way for tastes of the Corn & Basil Cakes (*page 182*) each time we tested them. We marvelled at the Thyme-Braised Brussels Sprouts (*page 187*)—they're so simple, just simmered with shallots, broth and thyme, yet something magical happens in that pot.

For us vegetarian cooking isn't about deprivation. Nor is it just about loading up on processed carbs and cheese or substituting "imitation meats" where we'd normally use chicken or beef. If we want a vegetarian burger, we make our own. It may be quicker to just buy a frozen patty, but we're happy to skip all those processed ingredients, and we're pretty sure our homemade versions are going to be a whole lot better!

We sometimes hear people say vegetarian food's just not delicious or that they're going to be hungry if they skip meat. Those same people may also turn their noses up at tofu or say they "don't eat broccoli." Our guess is they just need a taste of these foods done right. If all you've had is overcooked, mushy broccoli, one taste of Spicy Broccoli Salad (*page 191*), made with perfectly steamed broccoli that still has a touch of crispness and tossed with a zesty vinaigrette, and you'll be a convert. Or instead of plain tofu, try it Tex-Mex style with jalapeños, scallions and cilantro as we do in Vegan Migas (*page 141*).

Many of the recipes in this book were developed by our own team here in the EATINGWELL Test Kitchen. Others come from cookbook authors and recipe developers from around the world, including Deborah Madison, Diane Kochilas, Chris Schlesinger and John Willoughby. All the recipes have been thoroughly tested, on average seven times, on both gas and electric stoves and by different cooks. That means you can trust that these recipes will really work when you make them at home.

Plus each recipe is analyzed and approved by our registered dietitians to make sure that it meets our nutrition guidelines. (*For more on how we analyze recipes, turn to page 220.*) Like all our recipes, the vegetarian recipes in this book follow our guiding principles for healthy cooking. We cook mainly with whole foods, use plenty of fresh fruits, legumes and vegetables. We choose whole grains over refined, steer clear of trans fats and keep an eye on sodium. We also watch out for saturated fats, so we choose low-fat dairy and olive oil or canola oil over butter. And we keep portion sizes in check.

We know that the recipes in this book are going to give you great results every time. And not only are they healthy, you're going to love eating them. Whether you're a devoted vegetarian or just trying to eat less meat, with the recipes in this book you're sure to be eating well.

Quick Cucumber Kimchi (*p. 188*)

THE MEATLESS DIFFERENCE

By Rachael Moeller Gorman

Forget what you might think about vegetarians: going meatless—for a few nights a week or for a lifetime–is not about suffering through rabbit fare. In fact, if you use the recipes in this book, it's not about suffering at all but indulging in the varieties of fresh vegetables and fruits, whole grains and legumes that can bring new flavors and variety into your meals.

But there's another reason to think about changing the way you eat. Science is showing that cutting back on meat is healthier for just about everyone, and more and more people agree: 3 percent of the American adult population—over 7 million people—never eat meat, fish or poultry, up from less than 1 percent as recently as 1994. The U.S. market for processed vegetarian foods (soymilk, veggie burgers and the like) was $1.17 billion in 2006, expected to grow to $1.6 billion by 2011, and there are more and more alternatives to meat out there. In fact, you probably know several people who have decided not to eat meat—perhaps even yourself—and even others who eschew dairy and eggs as well.

More than 7 million

Americans—that's 3 percent of the U.S. adult population—**never eat meat, fish or poultry**.

That's up from less than 1 percent two decades ago.

The decision to pursue a plant-based diet is a very personal one, and each person has his or her own mix of reasons for choosing to live without meat. Religion has been one of the biggest, historically. An estimated 35 percent of the people in India are vegetarian, for example.

In other regions, like certain Mediterranean nations, the semivegetarian lifestyle is cultural. Think of a hearty minestrone soup. It might have a bit of meat for flavor, but the real "meat" of it is the beans and plenty of vegetables. Or think of a typical Chinese beef stir-fry. Sure it has strips of beef, but they're thin and small and far outnumbered by the snow peas, carrots, onions and peppers or, really, whatever brightly colored vegetable happens to be on hand. These ways of cooking are a long way from your prototypical American meat, potatoes and (small!) vegetable serving, where that hunk of meat is the priority and the sides, particularly the vegetables, get short shrift.

Some vegetarians cite animal rights and cruelty concerns as reasons for not eating meat, along with worries about growth stimulants and antibiotics given to the livestock, as well as animal-borne illness. Still others find themselves dairy-free because of an allergy or lactose intolerance.

Concern about the environment is a major reason for giving up meat (*see "Follow a Greener Diet," page 10*). Meat production has increased dramatically over the past 50 years and it's not good for Mother Earth. The United Nations' Food & Agriculture Organization (FAO) determined recently that livestock is one of the top two or three most significant contributors to the most serious environmental problems, on every scale, from local to global.

But perhaps the most compelling reason? Eating meat can affect both how long you live and how well you live. There is no question that the food you eat is linked to the quality of life you lead. Doctors have long told us to eat more fruits and vegetables (the current recommendation stands at 5 to 13 servings a day) and studies are now showing just how much shifting our diets from meat-based to plant-based foods will help us reap the rewards of their sage advice.

Vegetarian diets typically include fewer processed foods and more fruits and vegetables— good news, as the latest research suggests that packing your diet with produce is perhaps one of the best things you can do for your health. People who cut meat from their diet consume less saturated fat and cholesterol, more dietary fiber and higher levels of folate, vitamins C and E, potassium, magnesium and unsaturated fat. Eating a colorful variety of fruits and vegetables provides all sorts of phytochemicals. For example, the beta carotene in orange and dark green vegetables mops up tissue-damaging free radicals. Anthocyanins in blue/purple foods (think: blueberries) are linked with heart health and optimal brain

Follow a Greener Diet

Going meatless even a few days a week may be healthy for you, but, on a grander scale, it may be even healthier for the environment. Meat production has increased dramatically over the past 50 years. In 1967-9, total world meat production stood at 101 million tons/year; in 1997-9, it was 240 million tons per year and it's projected to increase to 414 million tons per year in 2030, driven especially by large increases in Asian countries that have historically eaten little meat. This taxes the Earth's resources. Going meatless can:

▷ SAVE LAND. Livestock use up more land than anything else humans have a hand in. When one accounts for both grazing areas and land used to grow food for animals we eat, they currently take up 70 percent of all agricultural land and 30 percent of all the land on the planet.

▷ SAVE WATER. A vegetarian diet requires 2.9 times less water, 2.5 times less energy, 13 times less fertilizer and 1.4 times less pesticides than a nonvegetarian diet, according to a 2009 study out of Loma Linda University in California.

▷ SAVE FORESTS. As more land is needed for livestock, more forests are cut down: pastures now occupy 70 percent of previously forested land in the Amazon and land for growing animal food takes up much of the rest.

▷ REDUCE TOTAL GREENHOUSE GASES. When you consider the CO_2-absorbing trees that are cleared for grazing and feed-crop production, global livestock production accounts for more total greenhouse-gas emissions than transportation (18 versus 15 percent of the total, respectively).

▷ REDUCE METHANE AND NITROUS OXIDE, PLUS AMMONIA. Some greenhouse gases—ones that are much worse for global warming than CO_2—are produced by the livestock industry: livestock emits 37 percent of the anthropogenic (generated by human activities, such as farming) methane, which causes 23 times the warming of CO_2, and 65 percent of anthropogenic nitrous oxide, mostly from manure (296 times as potent as CO_2). Sixty-four percent of anthropogenic ammonia emissions, which help cause acid rain, also come from livestock.

▷ REDUCE WATER POLLUTION. Livestock are responsible for much of the U.S.'s water pollution, including 55 percent of erosion and sediment, 37 percent of pesticide use, 50 percent of antibiotic use and one-third of the nitrogen and phosphorus loads into fresh water.

▷ FOSTER BIODIVERSITY. Livestock reduce biodiversity: they now account for 20 percent of the world's land animals and the 30 percent of the world's surface that they now live on was once habitat for wildlife. Stated in a report of the United Nations' Food and Agriculture Organization (FAO): "The livestock sector may well be the leading player in the reduction of biodiversity, since it is the major driver of deforestation, as well as one of the leading drivers of land degradation, pollution, climate change, overfishing, sedimentation of coastal areas, and facilitation of invasions by alien species."

▷ SAVE ENERGY. Comparing soy to meat, per gram of protein: meat production requires 6 to 17 times more land, 6 to 20 times more fossil fuel and 4.4 to 26 times more water. (In other words, livestock don't feed nearly as many people, per acre, as other uses of the land, such as soybean production.)

▷ REDUCE WASTE. In the U.S., the livestock population produces 130 times more waste than the human population.

Sources: Chiu et al., *Asia Pac J Clin Nutr* 2009;18 (4):647-653.
Key et al., *Proceedings of the Nutrition Society* (2006); 65, 35–41.
Marlow et al., *Am J Clin Nutr* 2009;89(suppl):1699S–703S.
Reducing Transport Greenhouse Gas Emissions: Trends and Data 2010; International Transport Forum.
Stenfield et al, FAO 2006.

function. Compounds called isothiocyanates in cruciferous vegetables, such as broccoli and Brussels sprouts, help us clear toxins from our bodies.

Given all this, it's not surprising that observational studies have linked vegetarian eating with protection against a variety of chronic conditions, including heart disease, high blood pressure and diabetes.

Here are 8 healthy reasons to skip the meat.

1. LOWER YOUR RISK OF HEART DISEASE

Cardiovascular health, in particular, seems to be better in vegetarians. Back in 1999, researchers at the University of Oxford in the UK pulled together data from five major observational studies that followed the lives of 27,808 vegetarians (here, "vegetarian" is defined as people who either answered "yes" to the question "Are you a vegetarian?" or those who said they don't eat any meat or fish) for an average of 10.6 years. They compared how many vegetarians died from various causes (heart disease, various cancers) to how many nonvegetarians died from the same causes.

These studies amassed huge amounts of information on what these people ate, which diseases they suffered and when and how they died. The results: committed vegetarians—those who had stuck with the lifestyle for more than five years—were 26 percent less likely to die of ischemic heart disease/coronary artery disease than people who regularly ate meat. People who ate meat only occasionally (a few times a month) were 20 percent less likely to die of heart disease: eating even occasional meatless meals seemed to improve health. Interestingly, people who ate fish but not meat or poultry were 34 percent less likely to die from heart disease. Turns out our hearts are happy on veggies.

But why? Interestingly, nuts seem to be one major reason. Some of the most important studies of vegetarians find that those who eat nuts more than four times a week suffer fewer than half as many heart attacks as people who eat nuts less than once a week. One possible reason: many nuts or legumes, such as peanuts, contain little saturated fat and are high in mono- and polyunsaturated fats, which have been shown to lower bad LDL cholesterol.

People who ate meat only occasionally (a few times a month) were

20%

less **likely to die of heart disease.**

2. LOWER YOUR CHOLESTEROL

Vegetarians tend to have lower total and LDL cholesterol levels, and researchers are finding that these lower cholesterol levels probably explain much of vegetarians' protection from heart disease (high cholesterol contributes to plaques in our arteries, increasing the risk of heart attack). In addition to eating more nuts, vegetarians' avoidance of meat—with its often high saturated fat—helps keep cholesterol levels healthy. Higher levels of fiber and plant sterols (cholesterol-like chemicals in plants that block our body's absorption of cholesterol) in vegetarian diets probably also help keep cholesterol at bay. What's more, many vegetarians rely on soy as a protein source—and soy appears to reduce blood cholesterol by helping the liver clear more LDL from the body.

3. IMPROVE YOUR BLOOD PRESSURE

Like high cholesterol, high blood pressure (a.k.a., hypertension) is a risk for cardiovascular disease and it, too, seems to benefit from a meat-free, vegetable-rich lifestyle. In the Inland Empire region of Southern California, in the city of Loma Linda, the Seventh-Day Adventist Church flourishes. Adventists often avoid meat, alcohol and cigarettes and since the 1950s studies have been watching these folks to see how their choices affect their health. In a 2009 report on a study of 89,224 Adventists, semi-vegetarians (people who eat red meat, poultry and fish less than once a week) had a 23 percent reduction in relative risk of hypertension when compared to people who ate red meat, poultry and fish more than once a week. The more restrictive a person's diet was (*see page 12*), the lower his chance of developing high blood pressure. Vegans—who don't consume any animal products at all—showed a risk reduction that was an amazing 75 percent lower than meat-eaters' risk. These findings could be the result of the high levels of potassium (potassium works with sodium to maintain fluid levels in the body and thus impacts blood pressure), magnesium, antioxidants and fiber inherent in a vegetable-rich diet, all of which have been linked to lower blood pressure.

4. GET LEANER

Lower blood pressure might be the product of something else altogether: lower weight. The same 2009 Seventh-Day Adventist study found that the amount of meat in one's diet was directly related to that person's body mass index (BMI), an estimate of body fat calculated from height and weight. In short, the less meat someone ate, the lower his or her BMI was. (Shockingly, the only average BMI that fell into the healthy range was that of the vegan

The Vegetarian Spectrum

While there are many different ways to pursue a partial or wholly vegetarian diet, people who avoid meat can generally be grouped into four main types. Here, we've outlined the common categories of vegetarian eating and what nutrients people in each category need to be concerned about.

SEMI-MEATLESS

Eats: Some meat, poultry and fish; milk, eggs, fruits, vegetables, legumes, whole grains.

Avoids: Meat several days a week.

Needs plenty of: Iron, via either red meat or dark poultry meat or plant-based sources like legumes and spinach, plus vitamin C-rich foods like orange juice to boost iron absorption; salmon and tuna for omega-3 fats; soy products, peanuts and legumes for zinc.

Should consider these supplements: One-a-day-type multivitamin if you want extra insurance.

PESCO-VEGETARIAN

Eats: Fish, milk, eggs, fruits, vegetables, legumes, whole grains.

Avoids: Meat, poultry.

Needs plenty of: Fortified foods, such as cereals, to supplement nutrients that meat typically provides, such as iron; in addition, plant-based iron sources like legumes and spinach and vitamin C-rich foods like orange juice; soy products, peanuts and legumes for adequate zinc.

Should consider these supplements: One-a-day-type multivitamin to ensure adequate iron.

LACTO-OVO-VEGETARIAN

Eats: Milk, eggs, fruits, vegetables, legumes, whole grains.

Avoids: Meat, poultry, fish.

Needs plenty of: Fortified foods, such as cereals, to supplement certain nutrients that meat typically provides, such as vitamin B_{12} and iron; milk or fortified soymilk for calcium and vitamin D; soy products, peanuts and legumes for zinc; plant sources of iron—dried fruits, legumes, seeds, vegetables like broccoli and spinach, and whole grains eaten along with sources of vitamin C, such as orange juice; use iodized salt.

Should consider these supplements: One-a-day-type multivitamin to ensure adequate vitamin B_{12} and iron; omega-3 fats (DHA/EPA derived from algae).

VEGAN

Eats: Fruits, vegetables, legumes, whole grains.

Avoids: Meat, dairy, fish, eggs and sometimes other animal-derived foods, such as honey and gelatin.

Needs plenty of: Fortified foods, such as soymilk and breakfast cereals fortified with calcium, vitamin D and vitamin B_{12}; an assortment of soy, grains and beans (for protein); plant sources of iron—dried fruits, legumes, seeds, vegetables like broccoli and spinach, and whole grains eaten along with sources of vitamin C, such as orange juice; soy products, peanuts and legumes for zinc; use iodized salt.

Should consider these supplements: One-a-day-type multivitamin to ensure adequate B_{12} and iron, calcium and vitamin D; omega-3 fats (DHA/EPA derived from algae).

For an index of vegan recipes, see page 221.

28%
How much you can **lower your risk of diabetes** by going meatless just a couple times a week (versus a regular meat-eating diet), according to one study.

Illustrations by Michael J. Balzano

time may overwork and injure the kidneys), dementia (perhaps due to the lower blood pressure or higher antioxidant intake of vegetarians), diverticulitis (fiber is most likely the key protective factor) and gallstones (which can be caused by too much cholesterol).

Not every study on vegetarian diets supports all of the health benefits mentioned above—partly because it's tricky to study vegetarians, as they're defined by what they don't eat and what they do eat is purely a matter of personal choice.

---

7. KEEP YOUR WHOLE FAMILY HEALTHY

When a family sits down at the dinner table for the evening meal, there's no menu. There's no buffet. Every member of the family eats the same food, which begs the question: are vegetarian diets good for everyone, even young children? Indeed they are, says the American Dietetic Association, which states in its position paper on vegetarian diets: "Well-planned vegetarian diets are appropriate for individuals during all stages of the life cycle, including pregnancy, lactation, infancy, childhood and adolescence." As long as meal planning is thoughtful and thorough, lacto-vegetarian, lacto-ovo-vegetarian and vegan diets can fill all the nutrient needs of every family member.

Research suggests growth and development of vegetarians are similar to nonvegetarians: in a British study, 390 lifelong vegetarians grew just as tall as people who became vegetarian after age 20 and women first menstruated at the same age as well (thus, physical development was not delayed in vegetarians). Lacto-ovo-vegetarian kids are about the same size as meat-eaters, though some studies suggest that younger vegan kids are a bit shorter, though still within normal range. On the plus side, studies have shown that vegetarian children and adolescents consume less saturated fat and cholesterol, and have higher intakes of fruits, vegetables and fiber, than nonvegetarians. They are also slimmer and have lower cholesterol levels. It is important for these kids to focus on getting enough calcium, vitamin D, iron, zinc and vitamin B_{12}.

Even if you're pregnant or breast-feeding, eating vegetarian can be healthy, as long as you give it careful consideration. Iron is a nutrient of particular concern—iron deficiency is common in any pregnancy, especially so in vegetarian women, and can cause harm to developing fetal organs. Some research has shown that vitamin B_{12}, calcium and zinc can also be lower in vegetarians. But of the few studies that have been conducted, babies born to vegetarians and those born to meat-eaters are equally healthy (there's no research on pregnant vegans).

DHA—an omega-3 fat found mostly in fatty fish, important for brain development—is another concern. Some studies have shown that infants of vegetarian mothers have less DHA in their umbilical-cord blood and that the breast

Q&A Can I get enough protein if I eat a vegetarian diet?

Not a problem, say doctors. "Protein is not a major concern for a vegetarian who's eating a wide diversity of food, particularly one who's using milk and eggs," says Winston Craig, Ph.D., M.P.H., of Andrews University in Michigan.

In general, the recommended daily intake for protein is 0.8 gram per kilogram of body weight, or 0.36 gram per pound. To account for differences in the way the body processes plant proteins, nutrition experts sometimes up this a bit—to 1 g/kg or 0.45 g/lb—for vegans. (One can easily meet these needs by including some source of protein—beans and other legumes, whole grains, nuts, fortified "milks"—at every meal and snack.)

Proteins are chains of amino acids, some of which the body can't make and must get from food, called "essential" amino acids. Protein is found in almost every food we eat, including plant foods like beans, grains, seeds and nuts (as well as vegetables, to a lesser degree), but most plant proteins are "incomplete" proteins, meaning that they contain some, but not all, of these essential amino acids in adequate amounts; eating a variety of plant foods usually ensures all essential proteins are consumed.

Soybeans, on the other hand, contain all the essential amino acids at high levels. Doctors used to think that you needed to eat adequate amounts of all the essential amino acids together in the same meal to get a complete protein. But research has shown that as long as you get all the amino acids at some point during the day, you'll undoubtedly get all the protein your body needs.

"Unless a vegan is eating cucumber and white rice and that's about all he's eating, protein is typically not a concern," says Craig.

milk they drink is also lower in DHA. (*Find suggestions for food sources from which pregnant women—and everyone else—can get adequate amounts of iron, B_{12}, vitamin D and omega-3s, on pages 12-13.*)

Even older adults can thrive on a meatless regime. Though older people need fewer calories, they need more calcium, vitamin D and vitamin B_6. And, as in all vegetarians, especially vegans, vitamin B_{12}, which you get mainly from animal-based foods, remains a priority, since our ability to absorb B_{12} from food declines as we age, as does our ability to produce vitamin D from the sun.

---

8. SAVE MONEY

Although meat is relatively inexpensive at the supermarket (due to government subsidies), a thoughtful vegetarian diet full of whole foods can be much cheaper. A pound of flank steak, about 200 grams of protein, costs about $6.99. A pound of black beans plus about 2½ pounds of brown rice, which together contain about 200 grams of complete vegetarian protein, costs about $5.60—20 percent less. Indeed, a study comparing a week's worth of family vegetarian meals to a week's worth of non-vegetarian meals found that the vegetarian meals cost 20 percent less than the meat-based ones. (If you choose processed meat substitutes, like veggie burgers, however, you'll spend more, so stick to whole foods.)

Healthy vegetarian meals are easy and affordable, as long as you plan carefully. Just as an omnivore must consider the foods he or she buys to make sure his or her family is eating a well-balanced diet, so must a vegetarian, who must make an effort to obtain certain nutrients. Replacing saturated-fat-packed meats with saturated-fat-packed dairy and eggs won't help your health, and piling on the refined carbohydrates will only make you hungry sooner. A bad vegetarian diet is just as unhealthy as any other unhealthy diet.

This book will help you to plan well, using whole foods, lots of produce and constant variety. And by adding some meatless meals, you might just lower your risk of heart disease and lose some weight.

> A study comparing a week's worth of vegetarian meals to a week's worth of nonvegetarian meals found that **the vegetarian meals cost**
>
> # 20%
>
> **less than the meat-based ones.**

Make Your Mondays Meatless

In 2003, Sid Lerner, an advertising executive who worked on such famous campaigns as "Please Don't Squeeze the Charmin," was talking with several members of the Johns Hopkins Bloomberg School of Public Health faculty. They were discussing the Surgeon General's recommendation to cut saturated fat intake by 15 percent when they figured that it basically worked out to one day's worth of fat a week. Lerner thought back on the World War I rationing programs of Meatless Mondays and Wheatless Wednesdays and, with a veteran ad man's unerring vision, the modern Meatless Monday movement was born.

The goal of going meatless one day a week is to cut saturated-fat intake from meat consumption by 15 percent to reduce our risk of chronic preventable conditions like heart disease, cancer, diabetes and stroke. In the intervening years, with the growing concern over the environmental costs of industrialized farming practices, and aided by the vocal support of thought leaders like Michael Pollan and Al Gore, Meatless Mondays has grown into a movement.

Currently, there are 14 international Meatless Monday programs, from Korea to Brazil, Croatia to Canada; cities like San Francisco and Cape Town have made official proclamations; the entire public school systems of Baltimore, Oakland and New Haven have adopted Meatless Monday; huge universities to small community colleges have updated their dining hall options; and celebrity chef supporters like Mario Batali and Katie Lee are encouraging restaurants around the country to follow their lead.

Meatless Monday is a campaign of moderation. It's just one day. And it's about choice. Ultimately, it's about adding options—trying new veggie dishes—not subtracting them.

Whether your agenda is public health, improving the environment, fiscal responsibility, animal rights, veggie activism or just tasty food, going meatless one day a week can help. It's easy, it's fun and it's delicious. Plus, small steps, over time, can make a huge difference globally. And if you miss a Monday, don't worry—there's always another one just around the corner.

—Chris Elam, program director of the Meatless Monday campaign, meatlessmonday.com

22

23

20

24

APPETIZERS

Here's a collection of small, savory bites to whet your appetite. The key when you include appetizers in your menu is to keep them not-too-filling, so that you still have room for dinner. We like appetizers with big bold flavors, like the Herbed Yogurt Spread (*opposite*) that's full of parsley, basil and garlic or the polenta wedges topped with a simple sun-dried tomato tapenade (*bottom left*), so that you're satisfied with just a taste or two.

▶ Green Olive & Almond Spread

ACTIVE TIME: 10 minutes
TOTAL: 40 minutes

TO MAKE AHEAD: Cover and refrigerate for up to 1 day.

MAKES: 1/2 cup, for 6 appetizer servings

PER SERVING: 70 calories; 7 g fat (1 g sat, 5 g mono); 0 mg cholesterol; 2 g carbohydrate; 0 g added sugars; 1 g protein; 1 g fiber; 149 mg sodium; 48 mg potassium.

NOTE: Spanish **Marcona almonds** are a little flatter than ordinary almonds, with a richer flavor. Always skinned, most Marcona almonds have already been sautéed in oil and lightly salted.

Olives and almonds make this unique vegan spread luxurious and rich, with heart-healthy monounsaturated fats. Sweet-fleshed, delicate Spanish Marcona almonds have grown in popularity in recent years, so don't be surprised to find them in bulk at natural-foods markets as well as some of the major warehouse club stores. Serve with zucchini or cucumber rounds, whole-grain crackers or slices of baguette.

1/2 **cup pitted briny green olives**
1/4 **cup Marcona almonds (*see Note*) *or* other whole almonds, toasted**
1 **teaspoon fresh tarragon *or* 1/2 teaspoon dried**
1 **teaspoon lemon juice**
1 **tablespoon extra-virgin olive oil**

Combine olives, almonds, tarragon and lemon juice in a food processor. Pulse until roughly chopped. Add oil in a steady stream and process just until the oil is absorbed. (*Alternatively, finely chop the olives, almonds and tarragon by hand and combine with lemon juice and oil in a medium bowl.*) The spread should have a coarse but easily spoonable texture. Let stand for about 30 minutes for the flavor to develop.

Feta, White Bean & Herb Dip

ACTIVE TIME: 30 minutes
TOTAL: 30 minutes

TO MAKE AHEAD: Cover and refrigerate for up to 2 days.

MAKES: 8 servings, 1/4 cup each

PER SERVING: 68 calories; 2 g fat (1 g sat, 0 g mono); 9 mg cholesterol; 9 g carbohydrate; 0 g added sugars; 5 g protein; 2 g fiber; 341 mg sodium; 216 mg potassium.

Nutritious, delicious canned beans are so versatile that they should be at the top of the essentials list for any healthy pantry. Here, they are pureed until smooth and used as the velvety base for a zesty, herbalicious dip that stretches a little bit of cheese a long, long way. Serve with assorted vegetables, such as baby carrots, bell pepper strips, radishes, snow peas, broccoli and cauliflower florets, or use as a spread for crostini or a sandwich.

1 **15-ounce can white beans, rinsed**
3/4 **cup nonfat plain yogurt**
1/2 **cup crumbled feta cheese**
1 **tablespoon lemon juice**
1 **teaspoon garlic salt**
1 **teaspoon freshly ground pepper**
1 **cup chopped fresh mixed herbs, such as parsley, dill, mint *and/or* chives**

Puree beans, yogurt, feta, lemon juice, garlic salt and pepper in a food processor until smooth. Add herbs; process until incorporated. Chill until ready to serve.

Herbed Yogurt Spread

ACTIVE TIME: 10 minutes
TOTAL: 10 minutes

TO MAKE AHEAD: Cover and refrigerate for up to 2 days.

MAKES: 8 servings, ¼ cup each

PER SERVING: 33 calories; 0 g fat (0 g sat, 0 g mono); 0 mg cholesterol; 3 g carbohydrate; 0 g added sugars; 5 g protein; 0 g fiber; 241 mg sodium; 26 mg potassium.

Tangy Greek yogurt blended with fresh herbs and garlic makes an easy spread that's similar to Boursin, but without all the fat. It's perfect for spreading on crackers or slices of baguette, or serve it with crudités for dipping. (Photograph: page 18.)

2 **cups nonfat plain Greek yogurt**
2 **scallions, trimmed and minced**
2 **tablespoons chopped fresh parsley, plus additional leaves for garnish**
1 **tablespoon chopped fresh basil *or* ½ teaspoon dried**
1 **clove garlic, minced**
¾ **teaspoon salt**
¼ **teaspoon freshly ground pepper**

Blend yogurt, scallions, chopped parsley, basil, garlic, salt and pepper in a medium bowl with a wooden spoon. Garnish with parsley leaves and serve.

Chewy Cheese Puffs

ACTIVE TIME: 20 minutes
TOTAL: 50 minutes

MAKES: about 30 puffs

PER PUFF: 59 calories; 2 g fat (0 g sat, 1 g mono); 8 mg cholesterol; 11 g carbohydrate; 0 g added sugars; 1 g protein; 0 g fiber; 104 mg sodium; 14 mg potassium.

NOTE: Tapioca starch, also called sweet manioc starch or tapioca flour, creates a pleasing chewiness when baked. **Potato starch** is an acceptable substitute. Both can usually be found with gluten-free products in most health-food stores or large supermarkets. Tapioca starch is also available in most Asian markets.

These Parmesan-infused puffs have a South American lineage and unlike their French pastry counterparts aren't loaded with butter and all the saturated fat that comes along with it. Instead, these irresistible morsels get their texture from manioc (tapioca) or potato starch, so they're slightly chewy and much more satisfying.

3 **cups tapioca starch *or* 2 cups potato starch (*see Note*)**
²/₃ **cup low-fat milk**
2 **tablespoons extra-virgin olive oil**
1 **teaspoon kosher salt**
1 **large egg**
1 **large egg white**
½ **cup grated Parmesan cheese**

1. Position rack in center of oven; preheat to 350°F. Coat a baking sheet with cooking spray.
2. Place starch in a medium bowl. Combine milk, oil and salt in a small saucepan and bring to a boil over high heat. Pour over the starch and stir until crumbly and blended. When the mixture has cooled slightly, stir in egg, egg white and cheese. Knead the dough in the bowl until smooth, 3 to 5 minutes. (It will be dry, yet hold together.)
3. Pinch off 1 tablespoon of dough at a time and roll into a ball. Place 20 balls on the prepared baking sheet. Bake the balls until puffed and golden on the bottom, about 20 minutes. Repeat with the remaining dough. Let the cheese puffs cool for a minute or so before serving warm.

Salsa Ranchera

There are a lot of great salsas available, but the fresh taste of this one makes it worth the small effort involved. The leftovers won't likely go to waste.

- **6** large ripe tomatoes
- **2** large cloves garlic, unpeeled
- **2-4** jalapeño *or* serrano chiles
- **2** tablespoons sunflower seed oil *or* canola oil
- **½** teaspoon salt

1. Heat a cast-iron skillet over medium heat. Add tomatoes, garlic and chiles to taste; cook, turning every few minutes, until the skins are blistered and charred in places, 15 to 20 minutes. The vegetables will cook at different rates. Remove each when it is charred or browned; allow to cool slightly. Peel the garlic, core the tomatoes and stem the peppers.
2. Transfer the vegetables to a blender and puree until smooth.
3. Heat oil in the same pan over medium-high heat. Carefully pour in the puree, season with salt and cook, stirring and scraping up any bits in the pan, until the sauce has thickened somewhat, 10 to 15 minutes. Serve hot or cold.

ACTIVE TIME: 30 minutes
TOTAL: 30 minutes

TO MAKE AHEAD: Cover and refrigerate for up to 1 week or freeze for up to 2 months.

MAKES: 12 servings, about ¼ cup each

PER SERVING: 38 calories; 3 g fat (0 g sat, 2 g mono); 0 mg cholesterol; 4 g carbohydrate; 0 g added sugars; 1 g protein; 1 fiber; 102 mg sodium; 223 mg potassium.
NUTRITION BONUS: Vitamin C (22% daily value), Vitamin A (16% dv).

Polenta Wedges with Tomato Tapenade

Crispy pieces of polenta topped with a tangy sun-dried tomato tapenade make a pretty and tasty appetizer. (Photograph: page 18.)

- **1** 16- to 18-ounce tube prepared polenta, ends trimmed and cut into **12** slices
  Canola *or* olive oil cooking spray
- **⅔** cup soft sun-dried tomatoes (*see Note*)
- **4** teaspoons extra-virgin olive oil
- **1** tablespoon lightly packed flat-leaf parsley leaves
- **2** teaspoons rinsed capers
- **1** small clove garlic, chopped
  Pinch of freshly ground pepper

1. Preheat broiler. Coat a baking sheet with cooking spray.
2. Place polenta slices on the prepared baking sheet and coat with cooking spray. Broil in upper third of oven until starting to brown, 8 to 12 minutes. Turn and broil until lightly browned, 3 to 5 minutes more.
3. Meanwhile, pulse sun-dried tomatoes, oil, parsley, capers, garlic and pepper in a food processor (a mini food processor works well), scraping down the sides as needed, until coarsely chopped.
4. Transfer the polenta slices to a clean cutting board and cut each into quarters. Top each wedge of polenta with about ¼ teaspoon of the tapenade.

ACTIVE TIME: 30 minutes
TOTAL: 30 minutes

TO MAKE AHEAD: Cover and refrigerate the tapenade for up to 3 days.

MAKES: 48 pieces

PER PIECE: 15 calories; 0 g fat (0 g sat, 0 g mono); 0 mg cholesterol; 2 g carbohydrate; 0 g added sugars; 0 g protein; 0 g fiber; 68 mg sodium; 61 mg potassium.

NOTE: For this recipe, look for soft **sun-dried tomatoes** (*not* packed in oil). If you can only find tomatoes that are very dry (and hard), soak in boiling water for about 20 minutes, then drain and chop them before using.

Mini Brie & Apple Quiches

ACTIVE TIME: 15 minutes
TOTAL: 30 minutes

MAKES: 30 quiches

PER QUICHE: 39 calories; 2 g fat (1 g sat, 1 g mono); 39 mg cholesterol; 3 g carbohydrate; 0 g added sugars; 2 g protein; 0 g fiber; 65 mg sodium; 20 mg potassium.

NOTE: Mini phyllo (or fillo) shells are available in the freezer section near other frozen appetizers. They do not need to be defrosted before filling and baking.

Store-bought mini phyllo shells are the secret to being able to make 30 elegant little appetizers in 30 minutes or less. Sweet Golden Delicious apple makes an excellent partner for the creamy Brie and egg custard, but if you want to mix it up, you can prepare half (or all) of the batch with diced Bosc pear instead.

30   **mini phyllo shells (two 1.9-ounce packages;** *see Note*)
½   **medium apple, such as Golden Delicious, peeled and finely diced**
5   **large eggs**
1   **teaspoon Dijon mustard**
¼   **teaspoon salt**
    Pinch of freshly ground pepper
    Pinch of ground nutmeg
4   **ounces Brie (½ small wheel), cut into 30 squares**

1. Preheat oven to 350°F. Line a large baking sheet with parchment paper.
2. Arrange phyllo shells on the prepared baking sheet. Divide apple among the shells.
3. Whisk eggs, mustard, salt, pepper and nutmeg in a large measuring cup. Pour the egg mixture over the apple (do not overfill the shells). Place a Brie square in each shell.
4. Bake the mini quiches until the egg is set, the Brie is melted and the phyllo is starting to brown around the edges, about 15 minutes. Let cool slightly before serving.

Pickled Eggs

ACTIVE TIME: 20 minutes

TOTAL: 1 hour 20 minutes (plus 24 hours pickling time)

TO MAKE AHEAD: Once removed from the pickling liquid, the eggs will keep, in an airtight container, in the refrigerator for up to 3 days.

MAKES: 6 servings

PER SERVING: 87 calories; 5 g fat (2 g sat, 2 g mono); 212 mg cholesterol; 5 g carbohydrate; 1 g added sugars; 7 g protein; 1 g fiber; 104 mg sodium; 125 mg potassium.

Not to knock the kind that you pull out of a jar at your local bar or convenience store, but this homemade version of pickled eggs is downright artistic by comparison. Apple cider vinegar and beet juice dye the egg whites fuchsia to surround the bright yellow yolks. Eat one of these eggs out of hand with your favorite cold ale or sliced with some of the pickled onions in a flatbread for a deluxe snack.

- 1 **15-ounce can beets**
- 1 **cup cider vinegar**
- 1/2 **cup sugar**
- 2 **teaspoons salt**
- 2 **bay leaves**
- 4 **whole cloves**
- 1 **medium onion, sliced into rings**
- 6 **large eggs**

1. Drain liquid from beets into a small saucepan, reserving the beets for another use. Add vinegar, sugar, salt, bay leaves and cloves to the pan. Bring to a boil over medium-high heat, stirring occasionally, until the sugar dissolves. Pour the pickling liquid into a large deep bowl and stir in onions; set aside to cool for 1 hour.

2. Meanwhile, place eggs in a single layer in a saucepan; cover with water. Bring to a simmer over medium-high heat. Reduce heat to low and cook at the barest simmer for 10 minutes. Remove from heat, pour out hot water and cover with ice-cold water. Let stand until cool enough to handle before peeling.

3. When the pickling liquid is cool, place the peeled eggs in a 4-cup container; pour the pickling liquid over the eggs, then spoon the onions on top. (The onions should hold the eggs under the liquid.) Cover and refrigerate for 24 hours.

4. Remove the eggs and onions from the pickling liquid. Refrigerate in an airtight container. Serve the onions alongside the eggs, if desired.

Spinach with Chickpeas

Infused with a decidedly Spanish blend of herbs and spices, this spinach-and-bean mixture works well as a tapa, served on rounds of lightly toasted bread, or in larger portions as a side dish. For a more rustic-flavored variation, try preparing it with smoked paprika.

2 pounds baby spinach
3 tablespoons extra-virgin olive oil, divided
1 medium red onion, finely chopped
5 cloves garlic, minced
1 19-ounce can chickpeas, rinsed
1 1/2 teaspoons dried thyme
1 1/2 teaspoons dried oregano
1 1/2 teaspoons ground cumin
1 teaspoon kosher salt
1/2 teaspoon hot paprika
1/2 cup golden raisins
1/2 cup vegetable broth

1. Rinse spinach and let drain in a colander. With water still clinging to it, place half the spinach in a Dutch oven over medium heat. Cook, tossing with tongs and adding the remaining spinach by the handful until all is added and wilted, 6 to 8 minutes. Drain in the colander. Let cool slightly, then coarsely chop.
2. Wipe out the pan, then heat 1 tablespoon oil over medium heat. Add onion and garlic and cook, stirring, until the onion is tender and lightly browned, 8 to 10 minutes. Stir in chickpeas, thyme, oregano, cumin, salt and paprika. Using a potato masher, mash some of the chickpeas; cook, stirring, for 3 minutes. Stir in raisins and broth, scraping up any browned bits. Add the chopped spinach and stir gently to combine. Remove from the heat; let stand 10 minutes. Drizzle with the remaining 2 tablespoons oil just before serving.

ACTIVE TIME: 35 minutes
TOTAL: 45 minutes

TO MAKE AHEAD: Cover and refrigerate for up to 2 days. Bring to room temperature or reheat over medium-low heat before serving.

MAKES: 12 servings, about 1/2 cup each

H❋W H⬆F H♥H

PER SERVING: 116 calories; 4 g fat (1 g sat, 3 g mono); 0 mg cholesterol; 17 g carbohydrate; 0 g added sugars; 4 g protein; 4 g fiber; 239 mg sodium; 546 mg potassium.

NUTRITION BONUS: Vitamin A (143% daily value), Folate (43% dv), Vitamin C (40% dv), Magnesium (18% dv), Iron & Potassium (16% dv).

Jalapeño Poppers

ACTIVE TIME: 40 minutes
TOTAL: 40 minutes

TO MAKE AHEAD: Cover and refrigerate the filling (Step 2) for up to 1 day.

MAKES: 12-18 poppers

PER POPPER: 87 calories; 4 g fat (2 g sat, 1 g mono); 39 mg cholesterol; 8 g carbohydrate; 0 g added sugars; 5 g protein; 2 g fiber; 419 mg sodium; 119 mg potassium.

NOTE: Touching **hot peppers** can "burn" your hands. Wear rubber gloves or wash your hands thoroughly after handling them.

The creamy bean-and-cheese filling in our take on jalapeño poppers makes them more satisfying and a whole lot healthier than the typical bar-food version. Plus, ours are rolled in cornmeal and "oven-fried" to crispy perfection rather than being saturated with grease in a deep fryer, so you can feel free to pop a few without any guilt. The amount of filling in this recipe is enough to stuff about 12 large jalapeños. Buy a few extra if the peppers at your market are small.

12	large *or* 18 small whole fresh jalapeño peppers (*see Note*)
1	cup nonfat refried beans
1	cup shredded Monterey Jack *or* extra-sharp Cheddar cheese
1	scallion, sliced
1	teaspoon salt, divided
¼	cup all-purpose flour
2	large eggs
½	cup fine cornmeal
	Olive oil *or* canola oil cooking spray

1. Make a slit down the length of one side of each pepper. Place the peppers in a large microwave-safe dish. Cover and microwave on High until just softened, about 5 minutes. Transfer to a clean cutting board to cool.
2. Meanwhile, combine refried beans, cheese, scallion and ½ teaspoon salt in a small bowl.
3. When the peppers are cool enough to handle, scrape out the seeds with a small spoon (a ¼-teaspoon measuring spoon works well). Fill each pepper with about 1 tablespoon of the bean filling, or until the pepper is full but not overstuffed (the amount will depend on the size of the pepper). Close the pepper around the filling.
4. Preheat oven to 450°F. Coat a large rimmed baking sheet with cooking spray.
5. Place flour in a shallow dish. Lightly beat eggs in another shallow dish. Combine cornmeal and the remaining ½ teaspoon salt in a third shallow dish. Roll each stuffed pepper in flour, shaking off any excess. Dip in egg and let any excess drip off. Then roll in the cornmeal mixture. Place the peppers on the prepared baking sheet. Generously coat all sides of each pepper with cooking spray.
6. Bake for 5 minutes. Turn each pepper over and continue baking until hot and the filling starts to ooze in a few spots, about 5 minutes more.

37

36

42

SALADS

Salads, whether sides or main courses, are a great way to get the recommended 5 to 13 servings a day of vegetables and fruits. (In fact, fewer than one in three Americans currently meets these standards.) It's easy to get several produce servings with an array of leafy greens and colorful vegetables and fruits in your salads—and they're packed with phytochemicals, which can help with everything from boosting the immune system to protecting against cancer.

Jícama & Cucumber Salad with Red Chile Dressing

Mildly sweet and very crunchy, jícama is a light brown-skinned tuber popular in Latin American countries. They range in size from a half pound to several pounds and can be eaten raw or cooked. Here jícama is combined with cucumber and dressed in a slightly spicy vinaigrette to make a salad that's a refreshing start to any Mexican-inspired meal.

¼	cup cider vinegar
1½	tablespoons mild-flavored honey *or* agave syrup
1	tablespoon canola oil
2	teaspoons minced onion
1-1½	teaspoons mild-to-medium-hot New Mexican red chile powder (*see Notes*), plus more for garnish
¼	teaspoon salt
2	cups diced peeled jícama (about ½ medium; *see Notes*)
1	medium English cucumber, peeled, seeded and diced
2	tablespoons chopped fresh mint

1. Puree vinegar, honey (or agave syrup), oil, onion, chile powder to taste and salt in a blender until smooth.
2. Toss jícama and cucumber with the dressing in a large bowl; stir in mint. Refrigerate for about 30 minutes.
3. Sprinkle the salad with more chile powder before serving, if desired.

ACTIVE TIME: 20 minutes
TOTAL: 50 minutes

MAKES: 6 servings, ²/3 cup each

H✖W   H↑F   H♥H
PER SERVING: 63 calories; 3 g fat (0 g sat, 2 g mono); 0 mg cholesterol; 10 g carbohydrate; 4 g added sugars; 1 g protein; 3 g fiber; 105 mg sodium; 157 mg potassium.
NUTRITION BONUS: Vitamin C (18% daily value).

NOTES:
Unlike most commercial chili powder, which is a blend of spices, **New Mexican ground red chile** is just straight ground New Mexican chile—available in different heat levels. Ancho chile powder or regular chili powder can be used as a substitute in this recipe.

Jícama is a round root vegetable with thin brown skin and white crunchy flesh. It has a slightly sweet and nutty flavor. To peel it, use a small, sharp knife or vegetable peeler, making sure to remove both the papery brown skin and the layer of fibrous flesh just underneath.

Green Salad with Strawberries & Goat Cheese

ACTIVE TIME: 20 minutes
TOTAL: 20 minutes

MAKES: 4 servings, about 1½ cups each

H✂W   H↑F   H♥H

PER SERVING: 206 calories; 16 g fat
(3 g sat, 9 g mono); 4 mg cholesterol;
15 g carbohydrate; 3 g added sugars;
5 g protein; 4 g fiber; 209 mg sodium;
449 mg potassium.
NUTRITION BONUS: Vitamin C (135% daily
value), Vitamin A (64% dv), Folate
(20% dv).

NOTE: **To toast chopped or sliced nuts,**
stir constantly in a small dry skillet
over medium-low heat until fragrant
and lightly browned, 2 to 4 minutes.

This green salad is packed with the essence of early summer. Sweet, ripe strawberries provide a delicious contrast to spicy watercress and the green, fresh taste of baby spinach. The sweet-and-sour vinaigrette pulls all the flavors into harmony.

1	tablespoon pure maple syrup *or* brown sugar
2	tablespoons red-wine vinegar
1	tablespoon extra-virgin olive oil
¼	teaspoon salt
	Freshly ground pepper to taste
3	cups baby spinach
3	cups watercress, tough stems removed
2½	cups sliced fresh strawberries (about 12 ounces)
⅓	cup fresh chives, cut into 2-inch pieces
½	cup toasted chopped pecans (*see Note*)
¼	cup crumbled goat cheese

Whisk maple syrup (or brown sugar), vinegar, oil, salt and pepper in a large bowl. Add spinach, watercress, strawberries and chives; toss to coat. Divide the salad among 4 plates and top with pecans and goat cheese.

Mixed Green Salad with Grapefruit & Cranberries

ACTIVE TIME: 25 minutes
TOTAL: 25 minutes

TO MAKE AHEAD: Cover and refrigerate the dressing (Steps 1-2) for up to 2 days. Refrigerate the grapefruit segments for up to 2 days. Assemble and refrigerate the undressed salad for up to 4 hours. Toss with the dressing and top with cranberries and pine nuts just before serving.

MAKES: 12 servings, about 1 cup each

H✖W   H↑F   H♥H
PER SERVING: 162 calories; 11 g fat (1 g sat, 6 g mono); 0 mg cholesterol; 15 g carbohydrate; 1 g added sugars; 3 g protein; 3 g fiber; 205 mg sodium; 425 mg potassium.
NUTRITION BONUS: Vitamin A (93% daily value), Vitamin C (50% dv), Folate (26% dv).

NOTES:

Hearts of palm are the tender inner stem portion of certain species of palm trees. Their flavor and texture is reminiscent of artichoke. Look for canned hearts of palm near other canned vegetables in most supermarkets.

To toast chopped nuts, small nuts and seeds, place in a small dry skillet and cook over medium-low heat, stirring constantly, until fragrant and lightly browned, 2 to 4 minutes.

Grapefruit juice is the base for the tangy vinaigrette on this salad studded with grapefruit segments and dried cranberries. It serves 12 as a starter or about six if you'd like a larger portion per person. (Photograph: page 30.)

- **2** red grapefruit
- **¼** cup extra-virgin olive oil
- **2** tablespoons minced scallions
- **1** tablespoon white-wine vinegar
- **¼** teaspoon salt
- **¼** teaspoon freshly ground pepper
- **8** cups torn butter lettuce
- **6** cups baby spinach
- **1** 14-ounce can hearts of palm (*see Notes*), drained and cut into bite-size pieces
- **⅓** cup dried cranberries
- **⅓** cup toasted pine nuts (*see Notes*)

1. Remove the skin and white pith from grapefruit with a sharp knife. Working over a bowl, cut the segments from their surrounding membranes. Cut the segments in half on a cutting board and transfer to a large salad bowl. Squeeze the grapefruit peel and membranes over the original bowl to extract ¼ cup grapefruit juice.
2. Whisk oil, scallions, vinegar, salt and pepper into the bowl with the grapefruit juice.
3. Add lettuce, spinach and hearts of palm to the salad bowl with the grapefruit segments. Just before serving, toss the salad with the dressing until well coated. Sprinkle cranberries and pine nuts on top.

Warm Beet & Spinach Salad

Beets are absolutely at their best in fall, right about the time that the last crop of spinach is ready to harvest. This warm salad combines both with sharp red onion and salty Kalamata olives all dressed in a warm balsamic vinaigrette. To add a creamy, tangy layer, top with some crumbles of mild chevre. (Photograph: page 30.)

1 tablespoon extra-virgin olive oil	1 clove garlic, minced
1 cup thinly sliced red onion	2 cups steamed beet wedges *or*
2 plum tomatoes, chopped	slices (*see Note, page 218*)
2 tablespoons sliced pitted Kalamata olives	2 tablespoons balsamic vinegar
	¼ teaspoon salt
2 tablespoons chopped fresh parsley	¼ teaspoon freshly ground pepper
	8 cups baby spinach

Heat oil in a large nonstick skillet over medium heat. Add onion and cook, stirring, until starting to soften, about 2 minutes. Add tomatoes, olives, parsley and garlic and cook, stirring, until the tomatoes begin to break down, about 3 minutes. Add beets, vinegar, salt and pepper and cook, stirring, until the beets are heated through, about 1 minute more. Place spinach in a large bowl. Add the beet mixture and toss to combine. Serve warm.

ACTIVE TIME: 20 minutes
TOTAL: 20 minutes

MAKES: 4 servings, about 2 cups each

H✕W   H↑F   H♥H
PER SERVING: 122 calories; 5 g fat (1 g sat, 4 g mono); 0 mg cholesterol; 17 g carbohydrate; 0 g added sugars; 4 g protein; 4 g fiber; 351 mg sodium; 731 mg potassium.
NUTRITION BONUS: Vitamin A (122% daily value), Folate (49% dv), Vitamin C (48% dv), Potassium (21% dv), Magnesium (19% dv), Iron (15% dv).

Islander Salad

Along with tomatoes, capers and fresh basil, cubed new potatoes, Sicilian olives and crumbles of ricotta salata give this salad more heft than your average tossed affair. Add some grilled slices of whole-grain country bread and you've got a great light supper or lunch. (Photograph: page 30.)

1 small red onion, thinly sliced	1 tablespoon capers, rinsed and chopped
1 head crisp lettuce, such as romaine *or* iceberg, washed and torn into bite-size pieces	½ cup crumbled ricotta salata (*see Note*) *or* feta cheese (2 ounces)
1 large tomato, cut into wedges	2 tablespoons tomato juice
2 small new potatoes, cooked and cubed	1 tablespoon extra-virgin olive oil
	1 tablespoon red-wine vinegar
6 black olives, preferably Sicilian, pitted and chopped	¼ teaspoon salt
	Freshly ground pepper to taste
1 tablespoon chopped fresh basil	

Cover onion with very cold water in a small bowl and let soak for 10 minutes. Drain and transfer to a salad bowl. Add lettuce, tomato, potatoes, olives, basil, capers and cheese. Whisk tomato juice, oil and vinegar in a small bowl. Season with salt and pepper. Pour over the salad and toss.

ACTIVE TIME: 20 minutes
TOTAL: 30 minutes

MAKES: 6 servings

H✕W   H↑F   H♥H
PER SERVING: 130 calories; 6 g fat (2 g sat, 3 g mono); 11 mg cholesterol; 15 g carbohydrate; 0 g added sugars; 4 g protein; 3 g fiber; 340 mg sodium; 555 mg potassium.
NUTRITION BONUS: Vitamin A (144% daily value), Vitamin C (50% dv), Folate (33% dv), Potassium (16% dv).

NOTE: **Ricotta salata**, a firm, salted ricotta, can be found at well-stocked cheese shops and Italian markets.

The Big Salad

ACTIVE TIME: 20 minutes
TOTAL: 20 minutes

MAKES: 4 servings, 3½ cups each

H↑F

PER SERVING: 400 calories; 24 g fat
(5 g sat, 12 g mono); 17 mg cholesterol;
39 g carbohydrate; 1 g added sugars;
12 g protein; 10 g fiber; 713 mg sodium;
1,007 mg potassium.
NUTRITION BONUS: Vitamin A (203% daily
value), Vitamin C (142% dv), Folate
(74% dv), Potassium (29% dv), Calcium
(25% dv), Iron & Magnesium (23% dv),
Zinc (17% dv).

All the color, crunch and great tastes of this salad let you know that it's loaded with vitamins and minerals, antioxidants and fiber. The recipe is substantial enough to make four main dishes or, if you like, eight little "big" salads that work as starters or sides.

½	cup Mustard-Balsamic Vinaigrette (*recipe follows*), divided
1	15-ounce can chickpeas, rinsed
1	cup thinly sliced red onion
1	red bell pepper, sliced
1	cup shredded carrots
1	cup cauliflower florets, coarsely chopped
12	Kalamata olives, pitted and finely chopped
12	cups mixed salad greens
½	cup crumbled feta cheese
3	tablespoons coarsely chopped walnuts, toasted (*see Note, page 219*)

1. Prepare Mustard-Balsamic Vinaigrette.
2. Combine chickpeas, onion, bell pepper, carrots, cauliflower and olives in a medium bowl. Add ¼ cup vinaigrette; toss to coat. Toss greens with the remaining ¼ cup vinaigrette in a large bowl. Divide among 4 plates and top with the vegetable mixture. Sprinkle with feta and the walnuts. Serve immediately.

Mustard-Balsamic Vinaigrette

ACTIVE TIME: 5 minutes | **TOTAL:** 5 minutes
TO MAKE AHEAD: Cover and refrigerate for up to 1 week. | **MAKES:** 1¼ cups

½	cup balsamic vinegar
¼	cup extra-virgin olive oil
¼	cup canola oil
2	tablespoons coarse-grained mustard
1	tablespoon pure maple syrup *or* 1½ teaspoons brown sugar
1	teaspoon dried basil
⅛	teaspoon salt
	Freshly ground pepper to taste

Combine vinegar, olive oil, canola oil, mustard, maple syrup (or brown sugar), basil, salt and pepper in a jar with a tight-fitting lid and shake well.
PER TABLESPOON: 59 calories; 6 g fat (1 g sat, 4 g mono); 0 mg cholesterol; 2 g carbohydrate; 1 g added sugars; 0 g protein; 0 g fiber; 47 mg sodium; 11 mg potassium.

Spiced Eggplant-Lentil Salad with Mango

This Indian-inspired salad has a complex taste that comes from convenient ingredients, such as prepared salsa, chili powder and curry powder, that each offer multiple layers of flavor. Add ready-to-use canned lentils and you have a dish that tastes like it should take a long time to prepare ready to serve in 45 minutes.

ACTIVE TIME: 45 minutes
TOTAL: 45 minutes

TO MAKE AHEAD: Prepare through Step 3, cover and refrigerate for up to 1 day.

MAKES. 4 servings, about 2 cups each

H⬆F   H♥H

PER SERVING: 485 calories, 20 g fat (3 g sat, 9 g mono); 0 mg cholesterol; 75 g carbohydrate; 17 g added sugars; 13 g protein; 16 g fiber; 275 mg sodium; 1,053 mg potassium.
NUTRITION BONUS: Vitamin A (119% daily value), Vitamin C (102% dv), Folate (70% dv), Potassium (30% dv), Iron (28% dv), Magnesium (24% dv).

4	tablespoons peanut oil *or* extra-virgin olive oil, divided
2½	teaspoons chili powder, divided
2½	teaspoons curry powder, divided
2	medium eggplants (¾ pound each), trimmed and cut into 1-inch cubes
⅓	cup lemon *or* lime juice, plus more to taste
¼	cup prepared salsa
¼	cup honey *or* agave syrup (*see Note, page 218*)
¼	teaspoon salt
¼	teaspoon freshly ground pepper, plus more to taste
1½	cups cooked lentils (*see Notes*) *or* one 15-ounce can, rinsed
2	bunches scallions, coarsely chopped (reserve 2 tablespoons for garnish)
4	cups torn romaine lettuce
2	large ripe mangoes, peeled and diced (*see Notes*)
¼	cup coarsely chopped roasted peanuts *or* cashews
¼	cup chopped fresh cilantro

1. Preheat oven to 500°F.
2. Combine 1 tablespoon oil with 2 teaspoons each chili powder and curry powder in a large bowl. Add eggplant and toss well. Spread the eggplant on a large, rimmed baking sheet. Roast, stirring once halfway through, until tender, about 15 minutes.
3. Thoroughly combine the remaining 3 tablespoons oil, remaining ½ teaspoon each chili powder and curry powder, lemon (or lime) juice, salsa, honey (or agave syrup), salt and pepper in a large bowl. Add the roasted eggplant, lentils and scallions; gently toss to combine. Adjust seasonings with more lemon (or lime) juice and/or pepper, if desired.
4. Serve the salad on a bed of romaine, topped with mango, nuts, cilantro and the reserved 2 tablespoons scallions.

NOTES:

To cook lentils, combine ½ cup red or brown lentils in a medium saucepan with 1½ cups water. Bring to a boil over medium-high heat; reduce heat so the lentils boil gently, cover and cook, stirring occasionally, until just tender, 12 to 18 minutes (red lentils cook more quickly than brown). Makes 1½ cups.

To peel and dice a mango, slice both ends off the mango, revealing the long, slender seed inside. Set the fruit upright on a work surface and remove the skin with a sharp knife. With the seed perpendicular to you, slice the fruit from both sides of the seed, yielding two large pieces. Turn the seed parallel to you and slice the two smaller pieces of fruit from each side. Dice into desired size.

Toasted Pita & Bean Salad

ACTIVE TIME: 30 minutes
TOTAL: 30 minutes

TO MAKE AHEAD: Cover and refrigerate the dressing (Step 3) for up to 3 days.

MAKES: 4 servings, about 2 cups each

H↑F

PER SERVING: 430 calories; 21 g fat (7 g sat, 10 g mono); 33 mg cholesterol; 46 g carbohydrate; 0 g added sugars; 17 g protein; 12 g fiber; 735 mg sodium; 626 mg potassium.
NUTRITION BONUS: Folate (50% daily value), Vitamin A (38% dv), Calcium, Iron & Vitamin C (28% dv), Magnesium (21% dv), Potassium (18% dv), Zinc (17% dv).

NOTE: Toast cumin seeds in a small skillet over medium heat, stirring occasionally, until very fragrant, 2 to 5 minutes. Let cool. Grind into a powder in a spice mill or blender.

This salad is inspired by fattoush, *a Middle Eastern salad made with pita bread and tomatoes. This version has the added benefits of whole-grain pita breads and beans for a burst of protein. If you can get them, use convenient canned Middle Eastern fava beans (called* ful *or* foul*) to make the dish even more authentic (and tasty).*

- 2 6-inch whole-wheat pita breads, cut or torn into bite-size pieces
- 2 cloves garlic, peeled
- 1/8 teaspoon salt
- 2 tablespoons lemon juice
- 2 tablespoons ground toasted cumin seeds (*see Note*)
- 3 tablespoons extra-virgin olive oil
     Freshly ground pepper to taste
- 2 cups cooked (*or* canned) pinto beans (*see "How to Cook Beans," page 127*), well drained and slightly warmed
- 1 cup diced plum tomatoes *or* 1/2 pint cherry tomatoes, quartered
- 1/2 cucumber, peeled and diced
- 1 cup sliced romaine lettuce
- 1 cup crumbled feta cheese
- 3 tablespoons chopped fresh parsley
- 3 tablespoons chopped fresh mint

1. Preheat oven to 400°F.
2. Spread pita pieces out on a large baking sheet. Bake until crisp and beginning to brown, 5 to 7 minutes. Let cool on the pan.
3. Mash garlic and salt with the back of a chef's knife or a spoon to form a paste. Transfer to a salad bowl, add lemon juice and ground cumin and whisk to blend. Add oil in a slow, steady stream, whisking constantly. Season with pepper.
4. Place beans, tomatoes and cucumber in the bowl. Add the toasted pita, lettuce, feta, parsley and mint; toss to mix. Season with pepper to taste. Serve immediately.

Asparagus Salad Topped with Poached Eggs

ACTIVE TIME: 30 minutes
TOTAL: 30 minutes

TO MAKE AHEAD: Cover and refrigerate the dressing (Step 3) for up to 1 day.

MAKES: 4 servings

H✖W

PER SERVING: 239 calories; 18 g fat (4 g sat, 11 g mono); 217 mg cholesterol; 9 g carbohydrate; 0 g added sugars; 13 g protein; 3 g fiber; 360 mg sodium; 534 mg potassium.
NUTRITION BONUS: Folate (60% daily value), Vitamin A (53% dv), Vitamin C (38% dv), Calcium (23% dv), Iron (16% dv), Potassium (15% dv).

NOTE: Use a vegetable peeler to thinly shave curls off a block of hard cheese.

This salad is satisfying yet light, making it a nice option for lunch, brunch or even dinner with some crusty bread. Roasting brings out a toasty flavor in the asparagus. We like this salad with medium-set poached eggs so the yolks are still a little runny, but poach your eggs for the full 8 minutes if you prefer hard-set yolks. (Photograph: page 30.)

2	**bunches asparagus (about 1 pound each), trimmed**
3	**tablespoons extra-virgin olive oil, divided**
½	**teaspoon kosher salt, divided**
½	**teaspoon freshly ground pepper, divided**
	Zest of 1 lemon
2	**tablespoons lemon juice**
1	**tablespoon minced shallot**
½	**teaspoon dry mustard**
4	**large eggs**
¼	**cup distilled white vinegar**
1	**7-ounce bag baby arugula (about 10 cups)**
½	**cup thinly shaved Parmigiano-Reggiano cheese (*see Note*)**

1. Preheat oven to 450°F.
2. Toss asparagus with 2 teaspoons oil and ¼ teaspoon each salt and pepper in a large bowl. Transfer to a large rimmed baking sheet. Roast, stirring once, until very tender, 15 to 20 minutes.
3. Meanwhile, whisk the remaining 2 tablespoons plus 1 teaspoon oil, the remaining ¼ teaspoon each salt and pepper, lemon zest, lemon juice, shallot and dry mustard in the bowl. Set aside 4 teaspoons of the dressing in a small bowl.
4. When the asparagus is done, set aside to cool while you poach the eggs.
5. Break each egg into its own small bowl. Fill a large, straight-sided skillet or Dutch oven with 2 inches of water; bring to a boil. Add vinegar. Reduce to a gentle simmer: the water should be steaming and small bubbles should come up from the bottom of the pan. Submerging the lip of each bowl into the simmering water, gently add the eggs, one at a time. Cook 4 minutes for soft set, 5 minutes for medium set and 8 minutes for hard set. Using a slotted spoon, transfer the eggs to a clean kitchen towel to drain for a minute.
6. Toss arugula with the dressing in the large bowl. Divide the salad among 4 plates. Top with asparagus and a poached egg and drizzle with 1 teaspoon of the reserved dressing. Garnish with cheese.

Vegetarian Taco Salad

Taco salads have become all the rage, but they have a dark secret: some chain-restaurant versions can pack as much fat as a stick of butter—no kidding. This healthy take on the crowd-pleaser is built on a foundation of crunchy lettuce, fresh corn, chopped tomatoes, ready-to-use canned beans and whole-grain brown rice. Tossed with fresh herbs and spices, along with convenient jarred salsa, this meal-in-a-salad-bowl won't disappoint.

2	tablespoons extra-virgin olive oil
1	large onion, chopped
1 1/2	cups fresh corn kernels (*see Note, page 218*) *or* frozen, thawed
4	large tomatoes, divided
1 1/2	cups cooked long-grain brown rice (*see Note*)
1	15-ounce can black, kidney *or* pinto beans, rinsed
1	tablespoon chili powder
1 1/2	teaspoons dried oregano, divided
1/4	teaspoon salt
1/2	cup chopped fresh cilantro
1/3	cup prepared salsa
2	cups shredded iceberg *or* romaine lettuce
1	cup shredded pepper Jack cheese, divided
2 1/2	cups coarsely crumbled tortilla chips
	Lime wedges for garnish

1. Heat oil in a large nonstick skillet over medium heat. Add onion and corn; cook, stirring, until the onion begins to brown, about 5 minutes. Coarsely chop 1 tomato. Add it to the pan along with rice, beans, chili powder, 1 teaspoon oregano and salt. Cook, stirring frequently, until the tomato cooks down, about 5 minutes. Let cool slightly.
2. Coarsely chop the remaining 3 tomatoes. Combine with cilantro, salsa and the remaining 1/2 teaspoon oregano in a medium bowl.
3. Toss lettuce in a large bowl with the bean mixture, half the fresh salsa and 2/3 cup cheese. Serve sprinkled with tortilla chips and the remaining cheese, passing lime wedges and the remaining fresh salsa at the table.

ACTIVE TIME: 40 minutes
TOTAL: 40 minutes

TO MAKE AHEAD: Prepare through Step 1, cover and refrigerate for up to 3 days; reheat slightly before serving.

MAKES: 6 servings, about 1 1/2 cups each

H✕W   H↑F   H❤H
PER SERVING: 395 calories; 17 g fat (5 g sat, 5 g mono); 20 mg cholesterol; 52 g carbohydrate; 0 g added sugars; 14 g protein; 9 g fiber; 459 mg sodium; 774 mg potassium.
NUTRITION BONUS: Vitamin A & Vitamin C (38% daily value), Calcium & Folate (23% dv), Potassium (22% dv), Magnesium (21% dv), Iron (15% dv).

NOTE: To cook long-grain brown rice, bring 1 cup water and 1/2 cup long-grain brown rice to a boil in a small saucepan. Reduce heat to low, cover, and simmer at the lowest bubble until the water is absorbed and the rice is tender, about 40 minutes. Remove from the heat and let stand, covered, for 10 minutes. Makes 1 1/2 cups.

Miso-Garlic-Roasted Tofu Caesar Salad

In this hearty version of the classic romaine salad, miso does double duty as a marinade for the roasted tofu and a rich, savory layer in the dressing. There are several varieties of miso available, but the mellow, subtle sweetness of brown rice miso is just unobtrusive enough to blend into the lemony dressing while letting the flavors of the olive oil come through, and just rich enough to add character to otherwise plain-Jane tofu.

TOFU

- 1 14-ounce package extra-firm tofu, drained
- 2 tablespoons lemon juice
- 2 tablespoons miso (*see Note*)
- 2 cloves garlic, minced

CROUTONS

- 2 slices country-style bread, crusts removed, cut into ½-inch cubes
- 2 teaspoons extra-virgin olive oil
- ¼ teaspoon freshly ground pepper
- ⅛ teaspoon salt

DRESSING & SALAD

- ⅓ cup extra-virgin olive oil
- 3 tablespoons lemon juice
- 4 teaspoons miso
- 1 clove garlic, minced
- 8 cups torn, bite-size romaine lettuce
- 2 cups torn, bite-size radicchio
- ½ cup grated Parmesan cheese

1. Position racks in upper and lower thirds of oven; preheat to 425°F. Coat a large rimmed baking sheet with cooking spray.
2. **To prepare tofu:** Pat tofu dry and cut into ¾-inch cubes. Combine lemon juice, miso and garlic in a large bowl. Add the tofu and gently toss to coat. Spread the tofu in a single layer on the prepared baking sheet. Bake on the upper oven rack, turning two or three times during baking, until browned, for 18 to 20 minutes.
3. **To prepare croutons:** Toss bread with oil, pepper and salt in a medium bowl. Spread in a single layer on a rimmed baking sheet. Bake on the lower oven rack, turning two or three times during baking, until browned and crisp, for 12 to 14 minutes.
4. **To prepare dressing & assemble salad:** Whisk oil, lemon juice, miso and garlic in a large bowl. Add lettuce and radicchio; toss to coat. Serve the salad topped with the roasted tofu and croutons.

ACTIVE TIME: 45 minutes
TOTAL: 45 minutes

TO MAKE AHEAD: Prepare through Step 3; cover and refrigerate tofu and store croutons airtight at room temperature for up to 2 days.

MAKES: 4 servings, about 2¾ cups each

PER SERVING: 389 calories; 29 g fat (6 g sat, 18 g mono); 9 mg cholesterol; 18 g carbohydrate; 0 g added sugars; 15 g protein; 4 g fiber; 755 mg sodium; 512 mg potassium.
NUTRITION BONUS: Vitamin A (166% daily value), Folate (43% dv), Calcium (36% dv), Vitamin C (23% dv), Iron & Magnesium (17% dv).

NOTE: **Miso** is a fermented soybean paste that adds flavor to dishes such as soups, sauces and salad dressings. It is available in different colors, depending on whether it's made with barley-, rice- or soy-based mold and how long it's been fermented. In general, the lighter the color, the milder the flavor. It will keep, in the refrigerator, for at least a year. Any type of miso will work in this recipe.

51

62

56

55

SOUPS & STEWS

Soups and stews are wonderfully homey and comforting food and, when made right, satisfying and healthy too. Our secrets to making delicious soups and stews without loading them up with cream, butter or sodium? Start with quality broth, plenty of vegetables, fresh herbs and spices. Adding whole grains like barley or brown rice and convenient canned beans makes these dishes hearty enough for dinner. (If you are ambitious enough to want to make vegetable broth from scratch, turn to page 217 for a recipe.)

Creamy Cucumber Soup

Here, creamy avocado is pureed with cucumber to create a beautifully verdant, silken-textured soup that's packed with nutrients and rich with healthful mono-unsaturated fats. Serve warm or cold with a zesty arugula salad and some crunchy seeded breadsticks.

1	tablespoon extra-virgin olive oil
2	cloves garlic, minced
1	small onion, diced
1	tablespoon lemon juice
4	cups peeled, seeded and thinly sliced cucumbers, divided
1½	cups vegetable broth
½	teaspoon salt
¼	teaspoon freshly ground pepper
	Pinch of cayenne pepper
1	ripe avocado, diced
¼	cup chopped fresh parsley, plus more for garnish
½	cup low-fat plain yogurt

1. Heat oil in a large saucepan over medium-high heat. Add garlic and onion; cook, stirring occasionally, until tender, 1 to 4 minutes. Add lemon juice and cook for 1 minute. Add 3¾ cups cucumber slices, broth, salt, pepper and cayenne; bring to a simmer. Reduce heat and cook at a gentle simmer until the cucumbers are soft, 6 to 8 minutes.

2. Transfer the soup to a blender. Add avocado and ¼ cup parsley; blend on low speed until smooth. (Use caution when pureeing hot liquids; *see Note.*) Pour into a serving bowl. Stir in yogurt. Chop the remaining ¼ cup cucumber slices. Serve the soup warm or refrigerate and serve it chilled. Just before serving, garnish with the chopped cucumber and more chopped parsley, if desired.

ACTIVE TIME: 35 minutes
TOTAL: 35 minutes

TO MAKE AHEAD: Cover and refrigerate for up to 4 hours.

MAKES: 4 servings, about 1 cup each

H✕W   H↑F   H♥H
PER SERVING: 169 calories; 12 g fat (2 g sat, 8 g mono); 2 mg cholesterol; 14 g carbohydrate; 0 g added sugars; 4 g protein; 5 g fiber; 494 mg sodium; 537 mg potassium.
NUTRITION BONUS: Vitamin C (30% daily value), Folate & Vitamin A (18% dv), Potassium (15% dv).

NOTE: Hot liquids can splatter out of a **blender** when it's turned on. To avoid this, remove the center piece of the lid. Loosely cover the hole with a folded kitchen towel and turn the blender on. Better airflow will keep the contents from spewing all over the kitchen.

Creamy Watercress Soup

ACTIVE TIME: 40 minutes
TOTAL: 40 minutes

MAKES: 4 servings, about 1½ cups each

H✳W   H⬆F

PER SERVING: 237 calories; 12 g fat
(3 g sat, 6 g mono); 11 mg cholesterol;
27 g carbohydrate; 0 g added sugars;
7 g protein; 3 g fiber; 736 mg sodium;
354 mg potassium.
NUTRITION BONUS: Vitamin A (66% daily
value), Vitamin C (57% dv), Folate
(20% dv), Calcium (16% dv).

NOTE: Look for **fresh horseradish root**
in the produce section of well-stocked
supermarkets. Peel with a paring knife
or vegetable peeler before grating.

*Not many flavors can stand up to peppery watercress, but fresh horseradish more
than holds its own. Here the two are brought together in an intensely flavored
soup with a mellow, creamy texture. For the perfect finishing contrasts, the soup is
garnished with crispy, golden breadcrumbs and, if you like, some crumbles of pungent
blue cheese.*

- 2 tablespoons extra-virgin olive oil, divided
- 1 small onion, diced
- 4 cloves garlic, minced
- 4 cups vegetable broth, divided
- 3 tablespoons all-purpose flour
- ⅛ teaspoon salt
- 8 cups chopped watercress, any tough stems removed, plus ½ cup leaves
    for garnish
- 2 tablespoons shredded fresh horseradish (*see Note*) or prepared
    horseradish, or to taste
- ½ cup half-and-half
    Freshly ground pepper to taste
- 2 slices day-old sourdough bread, crusts removed, finely chopped
- 2 tablespoons crumbled blue cheese (optional)

1. Heat 1 tablespoon oil in a large Dutch oven over medium heat. Add onion
and garlic and cook, stirring often, until the vegetables start to soften and
brown, 3 to 5 minutes. Meanwhile, whisk 1 cup broth and flour in a small
bowl until completely smooth. Set aside. Add the remaining 3 cups broth and
salt to the pot and bring to a boil. Reduce heat to maintain a simmer and cook,
stirring often, until the onion is very tender, about 5 minutes.
2. Stir chopped watercress into the pot and cook, stirring often, until tender,
about 5 minutes. Stirring constantly, add the flour mixture and horseradish.
Bring to a simmer and cook until thickened, 1 to 3 minutes.
3. Puree the soup in a blender in batches until smooth. (Use caution when
pureeing hot liquids.) Return to the pot, stir in half-and-half and season with
pepper; keep warm.
4. Heat the remaining 1 tablespoon oil in a medium skillet over medium-low
heat. Add breadcrumbs and cook, stirring often, until golden and crispy, 3 to
5 minutes.
5. Ladle soup into 4 bowls. Garnish with the breadcrumbs, watercress leaves and
blue cheese, if desired.

White Bean Soup

Creamy white beans provide the heft and protein to this simple, flavorful soup. The recipe calls for dried beans, but to make this recipe in under 30 minutes, you can use four 15-ounce cans of your favorite white beans (rinse well to cut the sodium in the canning liquid). Top with whole-grain croutons or a sprinkling of shredded cheese. (Photograph: page 46.)

ACTIVE TIME: 30 minutes
TOTAL: 2 1/2 hours

MAKES: 8 servings, about 1 1/2 cups each

H⟩⟨W   H↑F   H♥H

PER SERVING: 258 calories; 5 g fat (1 g sat, 3 g mono); 0 mg cholesterol; 43 g carbohydrate; 0 g added sugars; 13 g protein; 16 g fiber; 326 mg sodium; 894 mg potassium.
NUTRITION BONUS: Vitamin A (70% daily value), Folate (52% dv), Magnesium (27% dv), Potassium (26% dv), Iron (24% dv), Vitamin C (17% dv).

- **1** pound dried white beans, soaked overnight *or* quick-soaked (*see "How to Cook Beans," page 127*)
- **2** tablespoons extra-virgin olive oil
- **2** large onions, finely chopped
- **2** large carrots, finely chopped
- **2** stalks celery, finely chopped
- **4** cups water
- **2** large tomatoes, peeled and mashed, *or* 1 tablespoon tomato paste
- **2** teaspoons dried oregano
- **1** teaspoon salt
- **1/8** teaspoon cayenne pepper
- Freshly ground pepper to taste

1. Drain the soaked beans. Rinse and transfer to a Dutch oven. Add enough cold water to cover them by 2 inches (about 2 quarts of water for 1 pound of beans). Bring to a boil, skimming off any foam that rises to the surface. Reduce the heat to low and simmer gently, stirring occasionally, until the beans are tender, about 1½ hours. Drain in a colander; wipe the pot dry.
2. Heat oil in the pot over medium heat. Add onions, carrots and celery; cook, stirring often, until slightly softened, 4 to 8 minutes. Add the cooked beans, water, tomatoes (or tomato paste), oregano, salt, cayenne and pepper. Simmer until the vegetables are tender, about 20 minutes.

Roasted Tomato-Bread Soup

Roasting caramelizes the natural sugars in the tomatoes, onions and garlic for this richly flavored soup. Garlic-rubbed rafts of toasted whole-grain country bread make it more of a meal than your average bowl of tomato soup.

4	cups thinly sliced onions
2	tablespoons extra-virgin olive oil
1/4	teaspoon salt
1/4	teaspoon freshly ground pepper
4	cups cherry tomatoes, halved
1/2	cup thinly sliced garlic, plus 1 whole clove, peeled and halved
3	cups vegetable broth
6	slices whole-grain country bread
2/3	cup chopped fresh basil
6	tablespoons finely shredded Parmesan cheese

1. Preheat oven to 450°F.
2. Toss onions, oil, salt and pepper in a 9-by-13-inch pan. Roast the onions, stirring once or twice, until starting to brown, about 20 minutes.
3. Stir in tomatoes and 1/2 cup sliced garlic and continue roasting, stirring once, until the tomatoes are falling apart and beginning to brown in spots, about 20 minutes more.
4. Transfer the onion-tomato mixture to a large saucepan. Add broth. Bring to a simmer over medium-high heat. Remove from the heat and cover to keep warm.
5. Meanwhile, place bread on a large baking sheet and bake until toasted, about 10 minutes. Rub both sides of the toasted bread with the halved garlic clove. (Discard remaining garlic.)
6. To serve, place a piece of toasted bread in a shallow soup bowl. Ladle about 1 cup soup over the bread. Sprinkle with basil and cheese; serve immediately.

ACTIVE TIME: 30 minutes
TOTAL: 1 hour

TO MAKE AHEAD: Prepare through Step 1, cover and refrigerate for up to 2 days.

MAKES: 6 servings, about 1 cup each

H❯❮W   H↑F   H♥H
PER SERVING: 221 calories; 8 g fat (2 g sat, 4 g mono); 4 mg cholesterol; 29 g carbohydrate; 2 g added sugars; 9 g protein; 6 g fiber; 547 mg sodium; 462 mg potassium.
NUTRITION BONUS: Vitamin C (35% daily value), Vitamin A (32% dv).

Braised Summer Vegetables with a Green Herb Sauce

ACTIVE TIME: 55 minutes
TOTAL: 1½ hours

TO MAKE AHEAD: Cover and refrigerate for up to 3 days. Reheat in the microwave or on the stovetop over low heat.

MAKES: 6 servings, 2 cups vegetables each

H✕W H↑F H♥H

PER SERVING: 247 calories; 12 g fat (2 g sat, 9 g mono); 0 mg cholesterol; 32 g carbohydrate; 0 g added sugars; 5 g protein; 7 g fiber; 346 mg sodium; 1,103 mg potassium.
NUTRITION BONUS: Vitamin C (180% daily value), Vitamin A (151% dv), Potassium (32% dv), Folate (24% dv), Magnesium (17% dv).

A scrumptious mélange of summer vegetables braised and topped with a drizzle of an intensely green, pestolike sauce made from garden-fresh herbs was inspired by a summer stroll through the farmers' market. Feel free to mix up the produce based on what you have on hand, and make extra sauce since it freezes well and is perfect for tossing with pasta or swirling into soups. If they're available, try adding fresh fava or other shell beans to bump up the protein in this quintessentially summery dish. (Photograph: page 6.)

VEGETABLE BRAISE

- **2** tablespoons extra-virgin olive oil
- **2** bay leaves
- **6** small onions, halved, *or* 2 large onions, cut into 2-inch pieces
- **7** large cloves garlic, peeled and halved
- **3** sprigs fresh thyme
- **6** fresh sage leaves
- **12** small *or* 3 large carrots, peeled and cut into 3-inch lengths
- **12** ounces small new potatoes, scrubbed and cut into 1½-inch wedges
- **8** ounces yellow wax beans *or* a mixture of beans, trimmed and cut in half
- **5** medium tomatoes, peeled (*see Note, page 219*), seeded and quartered, juice reserved
- **1** large yellow *or* orange bell pepper, cut into strips
- **1** pound summer squash, cut into 2-inch pieces
- **½** teaspoon salt
- **¼** teaspoon freshly ground pepper

GREEN HERB SAUCE

- **⅓** cup packed fresh basil leaves
- **⅓** cup flat-leaf parsley leaves
- **2** tablespoons fresh marjoram leaves
- **1** small clove garlic
- **3** tablespoons extra-virgin olive oil
- **3** tablespoons water, or more if necessary
- **2** tablespoons capers, rinsed
-     Pinch of salt

1. **To prepare vegetable braise:** Heat oil and bay leaves in a large Dutch oven over medium-low heat until fragrant, about 1 minute. Stir in onions, garlic, thyme and sage; cover and cook, without stirring, 3 minutes. Layer carrots, potatoes, beans, tomatoes, bell pepper and squash on top without stirring. Season with salt and pepper, and pour the reserved tomato juice over the vegetables. Cover and cook until the vegetables are tender and juicy, 40 to 60 minutes. After 30 minutes, if the pot seems dry, add a few tablespoons water.
2. **To prepare green herb sauce:** Puree basil, parsley, marjoram, garlic and oil in a food processor or blender. With the motor running, add water and process until the sauce is smooth and creamy. Transfer the sauce to a bowl, stir in capers and season with salt.
3. Remove the bay leaves and thyme sprigs from the vegetables. Serve drizzled with the green herb sauce.

Egyptian Edamame Stew

Frozen shelled edamame, available in most supermarkets, bring convenience and the cholesterol-lowering power of soy to this quick and satisfying stew. The recipe is inspired by the Middle Eastern dish ful medames, *a highly seasoned fava bean stew, so it's well suited to be accompanied by couscous, bulgur or warm whole-wheat pita bread to soak up the aromatic sauce.* (Photograph: page 46.)

- 1   16-ounce package frozen shelled edamame (about 3 cups)
- 1   tablespoon extra-virgin olive oil
- 1   large onion, chopped
- 1   large zucchini, diced
- 2   tablespoons minced garlic
- 2   teaspoons ground cumin
- 1   teaspoon ground coriander
- 1/8 teaspoon cayenne pepper, or to taste
- 1   28-ounce can diced tomatoes
- 1/4 cup chopped fresh cilantro *or* mint
- 3   tablespoons lemon juice

1. Bring a large saucepan of water to a boil. Add edamame and cook until tender, 4 to 5 minutes or according to package directions. Drain.
2. Heat oil in a large saucepan over medium heat. Add onion and cook, covered, stirring occasionally, until starting to soften, about 3 minutes. Add zucchini and cook, covered, until the onion is starting to brown, about 3 minutes more. Add garlic, cumin, coriander and cayenne and cook, stirring, until fragrant, about 30 seconds. Stir in tomatoes and bring to a boil; reduce heat to a simmer and cook until slightly reduced, about 5 minutes.
3. Stir in the edamame and cook until heated through, about 2 minutes more. Remove from the heat and stir in cilantro (or mint) and lemon juice.

ACTIVE TIME: 30 minutes
TOTAL: 30 minutes

MAKES: 4 servings, about 2 cups each

H✖W   H⬆F   H♥H
PER SERVING: 282 calories; 9 g fat (1 g sat, 3 g mono); 0 mg cholesterol; 36 g carbohydrate; 0 g added sugars; 17 g protein; 12 g fiber; 316 mg sodium; 1,289 mg potassium.
NUTRITION BONUS: Vitamin C (83% daily value), Folate (77% dv), Vitamin A (46% dv), Potassium (37% dv), Iron (32% dv), Magnesium (28% dv), Calcium (18% dv).

Red Wine Braised Roots

ACTIVE TIME: 30 minutes
TOTAL: 2 1/2 hours

TO MAKE AHEAD: Cover and refrigerate for up to 1 day. Reheat in a 250°F oven or on the stovetop over low heat.

MAKES: 8 servings, about 1 1/3 cups each

H✂W   H⬆F   H❤H

PER SERVING: 151 calories; 1 g fat (0 g sat, 0 g mono); 0 mg cholesterol; 26 g carbohydrate; 0 g added sugars; 4 g protein; 7 g fiber; 695 mg sodium; 871 mg potassium.
NUTRITION BONUS: Vitamin A (191% daily value), Vitamin C (62% dv), Folate (26% dv), Potassium (25% dv).

NOTES:
You can **peel root vegetables,** such as beets, carrots and parsnips, with a vegetable peeler, but for tougher-skinned roots like celeriac, rutabaga and turnips, removing the peel with a knife can be easier. Cut off one end of the root to create a flat surface to keep it steady on the cutting board. Follow the contour of the vegetable with your knife. If you use a vegetable peeler on the tougher roots, peel around each vegetable at least three times to ensure all the fibrous skin has been removed.

Mushroom broth can be found in the natural-foods section of large supermarkets and in natural-foods stores.

Red wine, mushrooms and thyme bring a deep richness to this braise of mixed root vegetables. The earthy dish makes a great autumnal side, but can also be served over egg noodles, whole-wheat couscous or even garlicky mashed potatoes as a hearty entree.

1 1/2	**cups red wine**
1/4	**ounce dried mushrooms, such as porcini**
4	**pounds assorted root vegetables, peeled (*see Notes*)**
8	**ounces white mushrooms, halved if large**
2	**large onions, sliced**
2	**tablespoons chopped fresh thyme *or* 2 teaspoons dried**
1	**tablespoon tomato paste**
1	**teaspoon salt**
1/4	**teaspoon freshly ground pepper**
4	**cups mushroom broth (*see Notes*)**
4	**bay leaves**

1. Preheat oven to 350°F.
2. Place wine in a small saucepan and heat until steaming. Remove from the heat, add dried mushrooms and let stand while you prepare the vegetables.
3. If using carrots, cut into 3-inch pieces. If using parsnips, quarter lengthwise and remove the woody core, then cut into 3-inch pieces. Cut any round roots (beets, turnips, rutabaga and/or celeriac) into 1-inch-wide wedges. Place the roots, white mushrooms and onions in a large (12-by-15-inch) roasting pan.
4. Line a sieve with cheesecloth or a coffee filter and place over a measuring cup or small bowl. Strain the wine-mushroom mixture through the sieve, reserving the wine. Coarsely chop the mushrooms and whisk them into the wine along with thyme, tomato paste, salt and pepper. Pour over the vegetables; add broth and bay leaves. Cover the roasting pan with foil.
5. Bake, stirring occasionally, for 1 1/2 hours. Uncover and continuing baking, stirring occasionally, until the vegetables are very tender, about 30 minutes more. Discard bay leaves.

Red Lentil & Caramelized Onion Soup

ACTIVE TIME: 30 minutes
TOTAL: 45 minutes

MAKES: 4 servings, 2¼ cups each

H⬆F   H♥H

PER SERVING: 449 calories; 7 g fat (2 g sat, 4 g mono); 106 mg cholesterol; 70 g carbohydrate; 0 g added sugars; 30 g protein; 25 g fiber; 243 mg sodium; 1,394 mg potassium.
NUTRITION BONUS: Vitamin A (220% daily value), Folate (136% dv), Iron (57% dv), Potassium (40% dv), Vitamin C (38% dv), Magnesium (31% dv), Zinc (27% dv).

NOTE: To hard-boil eggs, place in a single layer in a saucepan; cover with water. Bring to a simmer over medium-high heat. Reduce heat to low and cook at the barest simmer for 10 minutes. Remove from heat, pour out hot water and cover with ice-cold water. Let stand until cool enough to handle before peeling.

Fresh lime juice balances out the creamy, mellow sweetness of the pureed lentil-carrot base of this colorful, hearty soup. Caramelized onions, crisp snow peas, cilantro and sliced hard-boiled eggs are a flavorful and beautiful topping. Serve with warm whole-wheat naan or roti bread.

- 3 teaspoons extra-virgin olive oil, divided
- 2 onions (1 chopped and 1 thinly sliced)
- 1 jalapeño pepper, seeded and finely chopped
- 2 cups chopped carrots (about 4 carrots)
- 2 cups red lentils
- 8 cups water
- ½ teaspoon ground turmeric
- ¼ cup lime juice
- ¼ teaspoon salt
  Freshly ground pepper to taste
- 2 hard-boiled eggs (*see Note*), sliced
- 10 snow peas, blanched and cut into thin strips
- 1 tablespoon chopped fresh cilantro

1. Heat 1½ teaspoons oil in a Dutch oven over medium-high heat. Add chopped onion and jalapeño; cook, stirring often, until the onion starts to turn golden, about 5 minutes. Add carrots, lentils and water. Bring to a boil. Add turmeric, cover and simmer until the carrots and lentils are tender, 15 to 20 minutes.
2. Meanwhile, heat the remaining 1½ teaspoons oil in a small skillet over medium heat. Add sliced onion and cook, stirring often, until it turns medium brown, about 10 minutes.
3. Transfer the lentil mixture to a food processor or blender and puree, in batches if necessary, until smooth. Add a little water if necessary. (Use caution when pureeing hot liquids.) Return the puree to the pot. Stir in lime juice and season with salt and pepper.
4. Ladle the soup into bowls. Top each serving with sautéed onions, egg slices and snow peas and sprinkle with cilantro.

Sweet & Sour Barley-Bean Stew

A touch of honey, lemon juice and chopped fresh basil give a sophisticated sweet-and-sour profile to this satisfying bean-and-barley stew. The classic pairing of eggplant and tomato gives the dish a summery feel, but it freezes well so you might want to make extra for an easy meal during the colder months.

2/3	cup pearl barley
1	large eggplant, cut into 1-inch cubes
1 1/4	teaspoons salt, divided
2	teaspoons extra-virgin olive oil
1	medium onion, slivered
1	clove garlic, minced
1	15-ounce can crushed tomatoes
4	tablespoons finely chopped fresh basil, divided, plus extra sliced leaves for garnish
1/4	cup lemon juice
3	tablespoons mild honey *or* agave syrup
1	15-ounce can cannellini beans, rinsed
	Freshly ground pepper to taste

1. Cook barley in a large saucepan of boiling water until just tender, 30 to 35 minutes. Drain and rinse.

2. Meanwhile, place eggplant in a large colander and sprinkle with 1 teaspoon salt. Let stand for 30 minutes. Rinse with cold water and squeeze firmly to remove excess moisture.

3. Heat oil in a large nonstick skillet over medium heat. Add onion and garlic and cook, stirring often, until beginning to brown, 6 to 8 minutes. Stir in the eggplant, tomatoes, 2 tablespoons basil, lemon juice and honey (or agave syrup). Cover, reduce heat to low and simmer until the eggplant is tender, 10 to 15 minutes.

4. Stir in reserved barley and beans and heat for 2 minutes. Season with the remaining 1/4 teaspoon salt and pepper and stir in the remaining 2 tablespoons chopped basil. Serve hot, garnished with sliced basil leaves.

ACTIVE TIME: 30 minutes

TOTAL: 1 hour

TO MAKE AHEAD: Cover and refrigerate for up to 2 days or freeze for up to 2 months.

MAKES: 4 servings, 1½ cups each

H✖W   H↑F   H♥H

PER SERVING: 330 calories; 3 g fat (1 g sat, 2 g mono); 0 mg cholesterol; 72 g carbohydrate; 13 g added sugars; 11 g protein; 18 g fiber; 629 mg sodium; 799 mg potassium.

NUTRITION BONUS: Vitamin C (38% daily value), Potassium (28% dv), Vitamin A (19% dv), Magnesium (18% dv), Iron (16% dv), Folate (15% dv).

Spicy Tofu Hotpot

The ginger-infused, spicy broth for this satisfying one-pot meal adds all the flavor you need to otherwise-humble firm tofu. NOTE: *Look for fresh Chinese-style noodles in the refrigerated case of your supermarket alongside wonton wrappers; in a pinch, use regular whole-grain spaghetti and increase the noodle-cooking time accordingly.*

14	ounces firm tofu, preferably water-packed
2	teaspoons canola oil
2	tablespoons grated fresh ginger
6	cloves garlic, minced
4	ounces fresh shiitake mushrooms, stemmed and sliced (about 2 cups)
1	tablespoon brown sugar
4	cups vegetable broth
¼	cup reduced-sodium soy sauce
2	teaspoons chile-garlic sauce (*see Note*), or to taste
4	cups thinly sliced bok choy greens
8	ounces fresh Chinese-style (lo mein) noodles (*see Note, above*)
½	cup chopped fresh cilantro

1. Drain and rinse tofu; pat dry. Cut into 1-inch cubes.
2. Heat oil in a Dutch oven over medium heat. Add ginger and garlic; cook, stirring, until fragrant, about 1 minute. Add mushrooms and cook until slightly soft, 2 to 3 minutes. Stir in sugar, broth, soy sauce and chile-garlic sauce; cover and bring to a boil. Add bok choy and tofu, cover and simmer until the bok choy is wilted, about 2 minutes. Increase heat to high and add noodles, pushing them down into the broth. Cook, covered, until the noodles are tender, 2 to 3 minutes. Remove from the heat and stir in cilantro.

ACTIVE TIME: 20 minutes
TOTAL: 30 minutes

MAKES: 6 servings, 1½ cups each

H⧓W   H♥H
PER SERVING: 221 calories; 6 g fat (1 g sat, 2 g mono); 28 mg cholesterol; 32 g carbohydrate; 2 g added sugars; 12 g protein; 4 g fiber; 734 mg sodium; 389 mg potassium.
NUTRITION BONUS: Vitamin A (57% daily value), Folate & Vitamin C (38% dv), Calcium (21% dv), Iron (19% dv), Magnesium (15% dv).

NOTE: **Chile-garlic sauce**, a blend of ground chiles, garlic and vinegar, is commonly used to add heat and flavor to Asian soups, sauces and stir-fries. It can be found in the Asian section of large supermarkets (sometimes labeled as chili-garlic sauce or paste) and keeps up to 1 year in the refrigerator.

Vegetarian Tortilla Soup

ACTIVE TIME: 1 hour
TOTAL: 1 1/2 hours

MAKES: 8 servings, 1 generous cup each

H✖W   H↑F   H❤H

PER SERVING: 209 calories; 13 g fat
(2 g sat, 7 g mono); 0 mg cholesterol;
18 g carbohydrate; 0 g added sugars;
7 g protein; 5 g fiber; 545 mg sodium;
400 mg potassium.
NUTRITION BONUS: Vitamin A (44% daily
value), Vitamin C (28% dv), Calcium
(16% dv).

NOTES:

Pasilla chiles, sometimes called
negro chiles, are medium-hot dried
peppers with a flavor that defines
tortilla soup in central Mexico. Find
them and other dried chiles in the
produce section of large supermarkets
or online at *melissas.com*.

Epazote, an herb used in Mexican
cooking, has a pungent, distinctive
flavor unlike any other herb. Look for
it fresh at farmers' markets or find it
dried at Latin markets or online from
melissas.com.

*Toasted dried chiles are key to the complex flavors at the foundation of this meatless
version of the traditional Mexican soup* sopa de tortilla. *Pan-seared tofu, plenty of
hearty greens, creamy diced avocado and shredded Mexican cheese enrich the tasty
soup to make a one-dish meal that will leave you feeling as if you'd dined south of the
border.* (Photograph: page 46.)

3   large dried pasilla (*negro*), ancho *or* New Mexico chiles (*see Notes*)
1   15-ounce can diced tomatoes, preferably fire-roasted
2   tablespoons plus 2 teaspoons canola oil *or* extra-virgin olive oil, divided
1   medium white onion, sliced 1/4 inch thick
3   cloves garlic, peeled
4   cups vegetable broth *or* "no-chicken" broth (*see Note, page 218*)
4   cups water
1   large sprig epazote (optional; *see Notes*)
1   14-ounce package extra-firm tofu
4   cups chopped chard, spinach *or* kale leaves
1/4-1/2   teaspoon salt
1   ripe large avocado, cut into 1/4-inch cubes
2   cups roughly broken tortilla chips
3/4   cup shredded Mexican melting cheese, such as Chihuahua *or* asadero,
      or Monterey Jack *or* mild Cheddar (optional)
1   large lime, cut into 8 wedges

1. Holding the chiles one at a time with metal tongs, quickly toast them by turning them an inch or two above an open flame for a few seconds until the
   aroma fills the kitchen. (*Alternatively, toast chiles in a dry pan over medium heat,
   pressing them flat for a few seconds then flipping them over and pressing again.*)
2. When cool enough to handle, stem and seed the chiles, break them into
   pieces and put them in a blender along with tomatoes and their juice. (A food
   processor will work, though it won't completely puree the chiles.)
3. Heat 2 tablespoons oil in a Dutch oven over medium heat. Add onion and
   garlic and cook, stirring frequently, until golden, 6 to 9 minutes. Scoop up
   the onion and garlic with a slotted spoon and transfer to the blender with the
   tomato mixture. Process until smooth.
4. Return the pot to medium heat. When quite hot, add the puree and stir
   nearly constantly until thickened to the consistency of tomato paste, about
   6 minutes. Add broth, water and epazote (if using). Bring to a boil, then adjust
   heat to maintain a simmer.
5. Drain tofu, rinse and pat dry; cut into 1/2- to 3/4-inch cubes. Heat the remaining
   2 teaspoons oil in a large nonstick skillet over medium heat. Add the tofu and
   cook in a single layer, stirring every 2 to 3 minutes, until beginning to brown,
   6 to 8 minutes total. Add the tofu to the soup and simmer for 30 minutes.
6. Add chard (or spinach or kale) to the soup and season with salt to taste.
   Cook, stirring, until the greens are wilted, about 2 minutes, depending on the
   type of greens.
7. Ladle the soup into 8 soup bowls. Divide avocado, tortilla chips and cheese
   (if using) among the bowls. Serve warm, with lime wedges.

Spicy Chickpea-Potato Stew

Ready-to-use canned chickpeas and chunks of Yukon Gold potatoes make this Indian-spiced stew hearty and quick enough to prepare on a weeknight. To round out the meal, add brown basmati rice and roasted carrots.

ACTIVE TIME: 25 minutes
TOTAL: 45 minutes

MAKES: 4 servings, 1½ cups each

H✕W   H↑F   H❤H
PER SERVING: 347 calories; 6 g fat
(1 g sat, 3 g mono); 0 mg cholesterol;
64 g carbohydrate; 0 g added sugars;
12 g protein; 12 g fiber; 473 mg
sodium; 1,082 mg potassium.
NUTRITION BONUS: Vitamin C (77% daily
value), Folate (39% dv), Potassium
(31% dv), Magnesium (23% dv),
Iron (20% dv), Vitamin A (17% dv),
Zinc (16% dv).

2	15-ounce cans chickpeas, rinsed, divided
¾	cup water
1	tablespoon extra-virgin olive oil
1	medium onion, finely chopped
3	cloves garlic, finely chopped (1 tablespoon)
1	jalapeño pepper, seeded and finely chopped
1½	teaspoons ground cumin
¼	teaspoon ground turmeric
12	ounces tomatoes, preferably plum tomatoes, seeded and coarsely chopped
1	pound potatoes, preferably Yukon Gold, peeled and cut into 1½-inch cubes (4-5 potatoes)
¼	teaspoon salt
	Freshly ground pepper to taste
	Cayenne pepper to taste
1	small cucumber, peeled and sliced
1	small red onion, thinly sliced and separated into rings
1	tablespoon chopped fresh cilantro

1. Puree ¾ cup of the chickpeas and water in a blender or food processor until smooth.
2. Heat oil in a large skillet over medium-high heat. Add onion, garlic and jalapeño and cook, stirring often, until the onion is lightly browned, about 5 minutes. Stir in cumin and turmeric. Add tomatoes and the chickpea puree; bring to a boil. Add potatoes, reduce heat, cover, and simmer until the potatoes are barely tender, 15 to 20 minutes.
3. Stir in the remaining chickpeas. Simmer, covered, until the potatoes are tender (but not mushy) and the stew is heated through, 5 to 10 minutes more. Season with salt, pepper and cayenne. Serve topped with cucumber slices, red onion rings and cilantro.

Half-Hour Chili

Awesome chili needn't simmer in a pot all day long. Behold a truly tasty half-hour chili made possible by using convenient canned beans and tomatoes (no pantry should be without them). Whole-grain bulgur adds another layer of toothsome texture and nutritional heft. This chili is relatively mild, so it's a good crowd pleaser. If you like it spicy, add extra chili powder or serve with hot sauce.

1	tablespoon canola oil
3	medium onions, chopped
1	carrot, chopped
1	tablespoon finely chopped jalapeño pepper
2	cloves garlic, finely chopped
1-2	tablespoons chili powder
1	teaspoon ground cumin
1	28-ounce can plus one 14-ounce can whole tomatoes, chopped, with juices
1	teaspoon brown sugar
¼	teaspoon salt
2	15-ounce cans red kidney beans, rinsed
⅓	cup bulgur (*see Note*)
½	cup nonfat plain yogurt for garnish
⅓	cup chopped scallions for garnish
¼	cup chopped fresh cilantro for garnish

1. Heat oil in a Dutch oven over medium heat. Add onions, carrot, jalapeño, garlic, chili powder to taste and cumin. Cook, stirring often, until the onions and carrot are soft, 5 to 7 minutes.
2. Add tomatoes with their juices, sugar and salt; cook for 5 minutes over high heat. Reduce heat to low; stir in beans and bulgur. Simmer until the chili is thickened, about 15 minutes.
3. Garnish with yogurt, scallions and cilantro, if desired.

ACTIVE TIME: 15 minutes
TOTAL: 30 minutes

MAKES: 6 servings, about 1⅓ cups each

H✗W   H↑F   H♥H
PER SERVING: 218 calories; 4 g fat (0 g sat, 2 g mono); 0 mg cholesterol; 40 g carbohydrate; 1 g added sugars; 10 g protein; 13 g fiber; 688 mg sodium; 852 mg potassium.
NUTRITION BONUS: Vitamin A (49% daily value), Vitamin C (43% dv), Potassium (25% dv), Folate & Iron (24% dv), Magnesium (20% dv).

NOTE: **Bulgur** is made by parboiling, drying and coarsely grinding or cracking wheat berries. Don't confuse bulgur with cracked wheat, which is simply that—cracked wheat. Since the parboiling step is skipped, cracked wheat must be cooked for up to an hour whereas bulgur simply needs a quick soak in hot water for most uses. Look for it in the natural-foods section of large supermarkets, near other grains, or online at *kalustyans.com, buylebanese.com*.

81

70

83

77

SANDWICHES, WRAPS & BURGERS

Our sandwiches, wraps and burgers aren't just for lunch. The ones on the next few pages are also perfect for easy, casual dinners. If you have a choice at the supermarket, choose *whole-grain* breads, tortillas, pitas, wraps or buns. We like to make our own veggie burgers, rather than use store-bought. They take a little longer, but you get to control the taste and what goes into them. Make extras and freeze them so you have them on hand when you're in a hurry.

Hot Chile Grilled Cheese

ACTIVE TIME: 30 minutes
TOTAL: 30 minutes

MAKES: 4 servings

H✕W   H↑F   H♥H

PER SERVING: 415 calories; 6 g fat
(3 g sat, 1 g mono); 13 mg cholesterol;
70 g carbohydrate; 0 g added sugars;
19 g protein; 9 g fiber; 761 mg sodium;
307 mg potassium.
NUTRITION BONUS: Vitamin C (163% daily
value), Folate (39% dv), Iron (20% dv).

NOTE: Dark green **poblano peppers**,
smaller than a bell pepper but larger
than a jalapeño, can be fiery or relatively
mild; there's no way to tell until you
taste them. Find them near other fresh
peppers at most large supermarkets.

STOVETOP VARIATION: Place four 15-ounce
cans and a medium skillet (not nonstick)
by the stove. Heat 1 teaspoon canola oil
in a large nonstick skillet over medium
heat. Place 2 sandwiches in the pan.
Place the medium skillet on top of the
sandwiches, then weight it down with
the cans. Cook the sandwiches until
golden on one side, about 2 minutes.
Reduce the heat to medium-low, flip the
sandwiches, replace the top skillet and
cans, and cook until the second side is
golden, 1 to 3 minutes more. Repeat
with another 1 teaspoon oil and the
remaining 2 sandwiches.

Here's everything there is to love about a chile relleno turned into a deluxe Mexican-style grilled cheese sandwich. And even better, a mashed-up salsa and pinto bean spread adds the heft and protein to make it a satisfying meal. To change things up, use the same fillings on flour tortillas and griddle until crispy to make a bean quesadilla.

- **4** poblano peppers (*see Note*)
- **1** 15-ounce can pinto beans, preferably low-sodium, rinsed
- **3** tablespoons prepared salsa
- **⅛** teaspoon salt
- **½** cup shredded Monterey Jack *or* Cheddar cheese
- **2** tablespoons low-fat plain yogurt
- **3** scallions, sliced
- **2** tablespoons chopped fresh cilantro
- **8** slices sourdough bread

1. Place peppers in a microwave-safe bowl, cover with plastic wrap and micro-wave on High until soft, 3 to 4 minutes. Let stand, covered, until cool enough to handle.
2. Meanwhile, combine beans, salsa and salt in a medium bowl. Mash the beans with a fork until they begin to form a paste (some can remain whole). Combine cheese, yogurt, scallions and cilantro in a small bowl.
3. When the peppers are cool enough to handle, slice each one in half lengthwise and remove the stem and seeds.
4. Heat a panini maker to high. (*No panini maker? See Stovetop Variation, left.*)
5. Spread ⅓ cup of the bean mixture on each of 4 slices of bread. Top with a heaping tablespoon of the cheese mixture. Place 2 pepper halves over the cheese. Cover with the remaining slices of bread.
6. Grill the sandwiches in the panini maker until golden brown, about 4 minutes. Cut in half and serve immediately.

Grilled Eggplant & Portobello Sandwich

ACTIVE TIME: 25 minutes
TOTAL: 25 minutes

MAKES: 4 servings

H✕W   H↑F   H♥H
PER SERVING: 232 calories; 5 g fat
(1 g sat, 2 g mono); 4 mg cholesterol;
38 g carbohydrate; 4 g added sugars;
10 g protein; 9 g fiber; 666 mg sodium;
788 mg potassium.
NUTRITION BONUS: Potassium (22% daily
value), Folate (20% dv), Magnesium &
Vitamin C (18% dv).

NOTE: The dark gills found on the
underside of a **portobello mushroom
cap** are edible, but can turn a dish an
unappealing gray/black color. Gently
scrape the gills off with a spoon.

*Toothsome portobello mushroom caps and thick rounds of eggplant were made for
grilling; they hold up well over the fire and take on lots of good smoky flavor. Here,
eggplant and mushrooms become the foundation for a hearty sandwich, layered with
peppery arugula and slices of ripe tomato—but cut them into julienne slices, lay them
on a platter, drizzle with good olive oil and vinegar and they become an excellent
antipasto as well. (Photograph: page 66.)*

1	**small clove garlic, chopped**
¼	**cup low-fat mayonnaise**
1	**teaspoon lemon juice**
1	**medium eggplant (about 1 pound), sliced into ½-inch rounds**
2	**large *or* 3 medium portobello mushroom caps, gills removed (*see Note*)**
	Canola *or* olive oil cooking spray
½	**teaspoon salt**
½	**teaspoon freshly ground pepper**
8	**slices whole-wheat sandwich bread, lightly grilled *or* toasted**
2	**cups arugula *or* spinach, stemmed and chopped if large**
1	**large tomato, sliced**

1. Preheat grill to medium-high.
2. Mash garlic into a paste on a cutting board with the back of a spoon. Combine
   with mayonnaise and lemon juice in a small bowl. Set aside.
3. Coat both sides of eggplant rounds and mushroom caps with cooking spray
   and season with salt and pepper. Grill the vegetables, turning once, until
   tender and browned on both sides: 2 to 3 minutes per side for eggplant, 3 to 4
   minutes for mushrooms. When cool enough to handle, slice the mushrooms.
4. Spread 1½ teaspoons of the garlic mayonnaise on each piece of bread. Layer
   the eggplant, mushrooms, arugula (or spinach) and tomato slices onto 4 slices
   of bread and top with the remaining bread.

Eggplant Subs with Provolone

A toasted coriander-seed crust gives roasted eggplant slices fantastic flavor that layers exquisitely with spicy greens and a savory tomato-olive relish in these sophisticated Italian-style subs. A thin slice of salty provolone tops it all off, but slivers of Parmigiano Reggiano would be just as tasty.

1/4 cup coriander seeds
1 medium eggplant (about 1 pound), cut into 3/4-inch rounds
1 1/2 tablespoons extra-virgin olive oil
1/4 teaspoon salt
1/4 teaspoon freshly ground pepper
4 6-inch lengths of whole-wheat baguette, split
2 cups arugula *or* watercress, trimmed
Tomato-Olive Relish (*recipe follows*) *or* 1 cup prepared mild salsa
4 thin slices provolone cheese

1. Preheat oven to 450°F. Coat a baking sheet with cooking spray. Coarsely grind coriander seeds in a spice grinder or blender. Transfer to a shallow dish.
2. With a pastry brush, lightly coat both sides of eggplant rounds with oil, then dredge in coriander to lightly coat. Season with salt and pepper. Arrange the eggplant in a single layer on the prepared baking sheet.
3. Bake the eggplant until tender, 20 to 25 minutes.
4. Set the bottom half of each baguette piece on a square of foil. Layer with arugula (or watercress), relish (or salsa), eggplant and cheese and cover with the top half of the baguette. Wrap the sandwiches in foil and bake until heated through, 5 to 7 minutes. Serve immediately.

ACTIVE TIME: 45 minutes (including making Tomato-Olive Relish)
TOTAL: 45 minutes

MAKES: 4 servings

H↑F   H♥H

PER SERVING: 357 calories; 12 g fat (3 g sat, 7 g mono); 10 mg cholesterol; 51 g carbohydrate; 0 g added sugars; 12 g protein; 10 g fiber; 733 mg sodium; 546 mg potassium.
NUTRITION BONUS: Vitamin C (25% daily value), Iron (21% dv), Calcium (19% dv), Potassium (16% dv), Vitamin A (15% dv).

Tomato-Olive Relish

ACTIVE TIME: 10 minutes | **TOTAL:** 10 minutes
TO MAKE AHEAD: Cover and refrigerate for up to 2 hours. | **MAKES:** about 1 cup

This simple relish makes an excellent spread for sandwiches but works equally well folded into an omelet or tossed with whole-grain pasta and some Parmesan cheese.

1 small tomato, finely diced
1 small red onion, finely diced
6 Kalamata olives, pitted and diced
1/4 cup coarsely chopped fresh basil
2 cloves garlic, minced
2 tablespoons balsamic vinegar
1/4 teaspoon freshly ground pepper

Combine tomato, onion, olives, basil, garlic, vinegar and pepper in a small bowl. Taste and adjust seasoning.

PER 1/4-CUP SERVING: 37 calories; 2 g fat (0 g sat, 1 g mono); 0 mg cholesterol; 5 g carbohydrate; 0 g added sugars; 1 g protein; 1 g fiber; 96 mg sodium; 104 mg potassium.

Egg Salad Sandwiches with Watercress

ACTIVE TIME: 10 minutes
TOTAL: 10 minutes

MAKES: 4 servings

H✗W   H♥H

PER SERVING: 315 calories; 14 g fat
(4 g sat, 5 g mono); 429 mg cholesterol;
28 g carbohydrate; 0 g added sugars;
18 g protein; 4 g fiber; 702 mg sodium;
313 mg potassium.
NUTRITION BONUS: Folate (31% daily value),
Vitamin A (18% dv), Iron (16% dv).

NOTE: To hard-boil eggs, place eggs in
a single layer in a saucepan; cover with
water. Bring to a simmer over medium-
high heat. Reduce heat to low and cook
at the barest simmer for 10 minutes.
Remove from heat, pour out hot water
and cover the eggs with ice-cold water.
Let stand until cool enough to handle
before peeling.

No one will call this egg salad sandwich boring, that's for sure. Watercress adds its trademark peppery flavor while reduced-fat sour cream adds tang to this lunch-counter classic. If you like, skip the bread and add more watercress or even some arugula to serve as a plated salad.

8   hard-boiled large eggs (*see Note*)
3   tablespoons reduced-fat sour cream *or* nonfat plain yogurt
1   tablespoon low-fat mayonnaise
1   tablespoon whole-grain mustard
4   scallions, chopped
¼   teaspoon salt
     Freshly ground pepper to taste
¾   cup trimmed watercress
8   slices pumpernickel bread

1. Scoop out egg yolks. Place 2 yolks in a small bowl; reserve the rest for another use. Chop egg whites. Mash the yolks with a fork and stir in sour cream (or yogurt), mayonnaise and mustard. Gently stir in the whites and scallions and season with salt and pepper.
2. Arrange watercress on 4 bread slices. Top with the egg salad and the remaining bread.

Breakfast Burritos

ACTIVE TIME: 25 minutes
TOTAL: 25 minutes

MAKES: 4 servings

H✂W   H⬆F   H♥H

PER SERVING: 231 calories; 7 g fat
(3 g sat, 3 g mono); 113 mg cholesterol;
33 g carbohydrate; 0 g added sugars;
11 g protein; 5 g fiber; 526 mg sodium;
821 mg potassium.
NUTRITION BONUS: Vitamin C (37%
daily value), Potassium (23% dv),
Magnesium & Vitamin A (15% dv).

NOTE: Poke several holes in potatoes
and microwave on High until cooked
through, 8 to 12 minutes.

*Breakfast burritos are a great way to start the day when you have time to sit down to
a real meal, but they also make a fabulous easy dinner. Add a side of black beans
and some corn sautéed with chiles and lime juice, and you have breakfast for dinner,
south-of-the-border style.*

1   teaspoon canola oil
2   red potatoes, cooked (*see Note*), peeled, if desired, and diced (1¹/2 cups)
¹/2 cup chopped scallions (4-6 scallions), divided
1   tomato, seeded and diced
1   4-ounce can chopped green chiles, drained
¹/4 teaspoon salt
    Freshly ground pepper to taste
2   large eggs
2   large egg whites
    Pinch of cayenne pepper
2   tablespoons chopped fresh cilantro
4   corn tortillas *or* small whole-wheat flour tortillas, warmed (*see Note,
     page 219*)
¹/2 cup tomato salsa
¹/4 cup shredded Cheddar *or* Monterey Jack cheese

1. Heat oil in a large nonstick skillet over medium heat. Add potatoes and ¹/3
   cup scallions and cook, stirring, for 1 minute. Add tomato and chiles and
   cook, stirring occasionally, until heated through, about 2 minutes. Season
   with salt and pepper.
2. Beat eggs, egg whites and cayenne with a fork in a small bowl. Push the
   vegetables away from the center of the pan and pour in the egg mixture.
   Cook, stirring the eggs with a wooden spoon, until some curds have formed
   but the mixture is still creamy, 1 to 2 minutes. Sprinkle with cilantro and stir
   the eggs and vegetables together.
3. Divide the egg mixture among warm tortillas and roll each one into a burrito.
   Top each with a spoonful of salsa, a little cheese and some of the remaining
   chopped scallions. Serve immediately.

Curried Chickpea Burritos

Madras meets Mexican in this yummy cross-cultural mash-up of a burrito. The spicy chickpea-and-potato curry can easily be prepared ahead of time. When you're ready all you need to do is reheat and set it out with some warm tortillas for a last-minute roll-your-own-wrap supper. Serve with Fresh Mint & Chile Sauce or a sauce of plain yogurt mixed with minced garlic—or both if you like.

1   **tablespoon canola oil**
1   **large onion, coarsely chopped**
3   **large cloves garlic, finely chopped**
2   **tablespoons finely chopped fresh ginger**
1   **jalapeño pepper, with seeds, finely chopped**
1½   **tablespoons curry powder, preferably Madras**
1   **tablespoon ground cumin**
1   **pound potatoes (2-3 medium), preferably Yukon Gold, peeled and diced**
1½   **cups water**
⅓   **cup currants *or* raisins**
½   **teaspoon salt**
1   **15-ounce can chickpeas, rinsed**
1   **cup frozen green peas**
¼   **cup chopped fresh cilantro**
6   **8-inch whole-wheat flour tortillas, warmed (*see Note, page 219*)**

FRESH MINT & CHILE SAUCE
1   **small jalapeño pepper, seeded and chopped**
1   **tablespoon chopped fresh ginger**
1   **clove garlic, peeled**
2   **teaspoons sugar**
¼   **teaspoon salt**
2   **cups packed fresh mint leaves**
2   **tablespoons rice vinegar, or to taste**

ACTIVE TIME: 45 minutes
TOTAL: 45 minutes

TO MAKE AHEAD: Cover and refrigerate the burrito filling (Steps 1-2) for up to 1 day. Reheat just before serving.

MAKES: 6 servings

PER SERVING: 305 calories; 4 g fat (0 g sat, 2 g mono); 0 mg cholesterol; 65 g carbohydrate; 1 g added sugars; 10 g protein; 11 g fiber; 669 mg sodium; 737 mg potassium.
NUTRITION BONUS: Iron (38% daily value), Vitamin A (36% dv), Vitamin C (33% dv), Magnesium (23% dv), Potassium (21% dv).

1. Heat oil in a large nonstick skillet over medium heat. Add onion, chopped garlic, 2 tablespoons ginger and jalapeño and cook, stirring, until softened and light golden, 6 to 10 minutes. Add curry powder and cumin and cook, stirring constantly, until fragrant, about 1 minute.
2. Add potatoes, water, currants (or raisins) and ½ teaspoon salt. Bring to a simmer. Reduce heat to low, cover and simmer, stirring once or twice, until the potatoes are tender, about 10 minutes. Stir in chickpeas, green peas and cilantro. Simmer until heated through, 2 to 3 minutes. Cover to keep warm.
3. **To prepare sauce:** Process jalapeño, 1 tablespoon ginger, 1 clove garlic, sugar and ¼ teaspoon salt in a mini food processor or blender until minced. Add mint and vinegar and pulse until finely chopped, stopping to scrape down the sides as needed. Transfer to a small serving bowl.
4. **To serve:** Spread a generous ¾ cup of the potato mixture onto each warm tortilla and top with a generous 1 tablespoon sauce. Roll the tortillas up, tucking in the sides to hold the filling in. Cut in half, if desired.

Creamy Avocado & White Bean Wrap

White beans mashed with ripe avocado and blended with sharp Cheddar cheese and onion makes an incredibly rich, tasty wrap filling. The tangy, spicy slaw adds crunch to the roll-up and is worthy of being a stand-alone dish as well.

2	tablespoons cider vinegar
1	tablespoon canola oil
2	teaspoons finely chopped canned chipotle chile in adobo sauce (*see Note*)
1/4	teaspoon salt
2	cups shredded red cabbage
1	medium carrot, shredded
1/4	cup chopped fresh cilantro
1	15-ounce can white beans, rinsed
1	ripe avocado
1/2	cup shredded sharp Cheddar cheese
2	tablespoons minced red onion
4	8- to 10-inch whole-wheat wraps *or* tortillas

1. Whisk vinegar, oil, chipotle chile and salt in a medium bowl. Add cabbage, carrot and cilantro; toss to combine.
2. Mash beans and avocado in another medium bowl with a potato masher or fork. Stir in cheese and onion.
3. To assemble the wraps, spread about ½ cup of the bean-avocado mixture onto a wrap (or tortilla) and top with about ⅔ cup of the cabbage-carrot slaw. Roll up. Repeat with remaining ingredients. Cut the wraps in half to serve, if desired.

ACTIVE TIME: 25 minutes
TOTAL: 25 minutes

MAKES: 4 servings

PER SERVING: 346 calories; 17 g fat (4 g sat, 9 g mono); 15 mg cholesterol; 44 g carbohydrate; 0 g added sugars; 12 g protein; 13 g fiber; 462 mg sodium; 491 mg potassium.
NUTRITION BONUS: Vitamin A (64% daily value), Vitamin C (45% dv).

NOTE: Chipotle chiles in adobo sauce are smoked jalapeños packed in a flavorful sauce. Look for the small cans with the Mexican foods in large supermarkets. Once opened, they'll keep at least 2 weeks in the refrigerator or 6 months in the freezer.

Vietnamese Tofu-Noodle Lettuce Wraps

ACTIVE TIME: 25 minutes
TOTAL: 25 minutes

MAKES: 4 servings, 2 wraps each

H✕W   H♥H

PER SERVING: 195 calories; 6 g fat
(1 g sat, 0 g mono); 0 mg cholesterol;
24 g carbohydrate; 3 g added sugars;
14 g protein; 3 g fiber; 480 mg sodium;
299 mg potassium.
NUTRITION BONUS: Vitamin A (161%
daily value), Vitamin C (47% dv),
Iron (18% dv), Calcium (17% dv).

NOTE: Dried thin **rice noodles** (or rice
sticks) are also called "bun" or "vermi-
celli-style" rice noodles. Look for them
in the Asian section of well-stocked
supermarkets or an Asian-foods market.

*Think of it as a handheld salad: crunchy vegetables, vibrant fresh herbs, rice noodles
and seasoned tofu tossed in a sweet, tart and salty Vietnamese dressing wrapped up in
leaves of green-leaf lettuce. Seasoned tofu is available in many varieties at natural-
foods stores and well-stocked supermarkets, but you can easily make your own using
a favorite marinade or blend of dry spices.*

2	ounces thin rice noodles *or* rice sticks (*see Note*)
1/4	cup water
5	teaspoons reduced-sodium soy sauce
2	tablespoons lime juice
1	tablespoon sugar
1/2-1	teaspoon crushed red pepper
1	8-ounce package seasoned baked tofu (*see Note, page 219*), thinly sliced
1	medium carrot, cut into matchsticks
1	cup snow peas, trimmed and very thinly sliced
1/4	cup chopped fresh basil
1/4	cup chopped fresh mint
8	large leaves green-leaf lettuce

1. Bring a large saucepan of water to a boil. Add rice noodles (or rice sticks) and
cook until just tender, about 3 minutes. Drain and rinse under cold water.
Gently squeeze noodles to remove most of the water.
2. Meanwhile, combine ¼ cup water, soy sauce, lime juice, sugar and crushed
red pepper to taste in a small bowl.
3. Coarsely chop the noodles and combine in a large bowl with tofu, carrot,
snow peas, basil and mint. Pour the sauce over the salad and toss to combine.
To serve, spoon about ½ cup salad onto each lettuce leaf and roll up.

Mediterranean Tofu & Couscous Wraps

ACTIVE TIME: 40 minutes
TOTAL: 40 minutes

MAKES: 4 servings

H↑F   H♥H

PER SERVING: 518 calories; 22 g fat
(4 g sat, 11 g mono); 0 mg cholesterol;
58 g carbohydrate; 0 g added sugars;
23 g protein; 7 g fiber; 701 mg sodium;
401 mg potassium.

NUTRITION BONUS: Vitamin A (66%
daily value), Vitamin C (59% dv),
Folate (40% dv), Iron (38% dv),
Calcium (19% dv).

Baked tofu has been showing up in natural-foods stores and well-stocked super-markets for some time, but it's easy to make at home. Just marinate tofu with any seasoning you like and then bake it. The soy-lime roasted tofu on page 132 is a great example. To complete the meal, serve with a side of Provençal Summer Vegetables (page 185).

1/2	**cup water**
1/3	**cup couscous, preferably whole-wheat**
1	**cup chopped fresh parsley**
1/2	**cup chopped fresh mint**
1/4	**cup lemon juice**
3	**tablespoons extra-virgin olive oil**
2	**teaspoons minced garlic**
1/4	**teaspoon freshly ground pepper**
1	**8-ounce package seasoned baked tofu** (*see Note, page 219*), **diced**
1	**medium tomato, chopped**
1 1/2	**cups chopped cucumber**
4	**10-inch spinach *or* sun-dried tomato wraps *or* tortillas**

1. Bring water to a boil in a small saucepan. Stir in couscous and remove from the heat. Cover and let stand for 5 minutes. Fluff with a fork. Set aside.
2. Meanwhile, combine parsley, mint, lemon juice, oil, garlic and pepper in a small bowl.
3. Toss tofu in a medium bowl with 1 tablespoon of the parsley mixture. Cook the tofu in a large nonstick skillet over medium heat, turning occasionally, until heated through, 2 to 4 minutes.
4. Stir the remaining parsley mixture into the couscous along with tomato and cucumber.
5. To assemble wraps, spread about ¾ cup of the couscous mixture onto each wrap. Divide the tofu among the wraps. Roll the wraps up like a burrito, tucking in the sides to hold the ingredients in. Serve cut in half.

Chickpea Burgers

These chickpea burgers are similar to falafel, but with the added whole-grain goodness of brown rice and wheat germ. Serving them on pita breads with thick slices of tomato and a dab of plain yogurt continues the Middle Eastern theme, but if you want to take it even further, drizzle with a little sauce made with minced garlic and tahini thinned with water and lemon juice. (Photograph: page 66.)

2 tablespoons sesame seeds
1 tablespoon ground coriander
1 tablespoon ground cumin
2 teaspoons canola oil
4 scallions, chopped
3 cloves garlic, minced
1 15-ounce can chickpeas, rinsed
1 cup cooked brown rice
²⁄₃ cup wheat germ, divided
3 tablespoons lemon juice
½ teaspoon salt
¼ teaspoon freshly ground pepper
4 6-inch whole-wheat pita breads, warmed
8 slices tomato
1 cup baby spinach
4 tablespoons nonfat plain yogurt

ACTIVE TIME: 45 minutes
TOTAL: 45 minutes

MAKES: 4 servings

H↑F   H♥H

PER SERVING: 478 calories; 10 g fat (1 g sat, 3 g mono); 0 mg cholesterol; 82 g carbohydrate; 1 g added sugars; 20 g protein; 15 g fiber; 813 mg sodium; 693 mg potassium.
NUTRITION BONUS: Folate & Magnesium (45% daily value), Zinc (40% dv), Iron (38% dv), Vitamin C (30% dv), Vitamin A (23% dv), Potassium (20% dv), Calcium (17% dv).

1. Heat a small skillet over low heat. Add sesame seeds and toast, stirring, until golden brown, 2 to 4 minutes. Add coriander and cumin; cook, stirring, until fragrant, 10 to 20 seconds more. Transfer to a plate and let cool. Grind with a mortar and pestle or in a spice mill or clean coffee grinder; set aside.

2. Add oil to the pan and heat over medium heat. Add scallions and garlic; cook, stirring, until softened, about 2 minutes. Set aside.

3. Position rack in upper third of oven; preheat broiler. (*Alternatively, preheat a grill to medium-high.*)

4. Coarsely mash chickpeas in a medium bowl with a potato masher. Stir in rice, ¹⁄₃ cup wheat germ, lemon juice, salt, pepper, the reserved spice mixture and the scallion mixture; mix well. Shape the mixture into four ³⁄₄-inch-thick patties. Place the remaining ¹⁄₃ cup wheat germ in a shallow dish and dredge the patties, pressing the wheat germ onto them firmly. If broiling, place the patties on a lightly oiled rack set on a baking sheet. (If grilling, oil the grill rack; *see Note, page 219.*)

5. Broil (or grill) the patties until browned and heated through, about 3 minutes per side. Tuck the burgers into pitas with tomato slices, spinach and yogurt.

Bean Burgers with Spicy Guacamole

Plenty of pinto beans mashed together with smoked paprika- and cumin-seasoned sautéed onions and garlic make these patties as flavor-packed and satisfying as you'd expect a burger to be. We love this homemade guacamole on top but these are also great with more traditional burger fixin's.

ACTIVE TIME: 50 minutes
TOTAL: 50 minutes

MAKES: 6 servings

H✗W H↑F H♥H

PER SERVING: 393 calories; 16 g fat (2 g sat, 9 g mono); 0 mg cholesterol; 56 g carbohydrate; 4 g added sugars; 12 g protein; 13 g fiber; 543 mg sodium; 689 mg potassium.
NUTRITION BONUS: Folate (33% daily value), Magnesium (24% dv), Potassium & Vitamin A (20% dv), Iron (19% dv), Vitamin C (17% dv).

- 1/2 cup water
- 1/4 cup quinoa, rinsed (*see Notes*)
- 3 tablespoons extra-virgin olive oil, divided
- 1/2 cup chopped red onion
- 1 clove garlic, minced
- 2 1/2 cups canned pinto beans, rinsed, *or* cooked pinto beans, well drained (*see "How to Cook Beans," page 127*)
- 1 teaspoon smoked paprika
- 1/2 teaspoon ground toasted cumin seeds (*see Notes*)
- 3 tablespoons chopped fresh cilantro
- 3 tablespoons plus 1/3 cup cornmeal, divided
- 1/2 teaspoon salt
- Freshly ground pepper to taste

GUACAMOLE
- 1 ripe avocado
- 2 tablespoons finely chopped fresh cilantro
- 1 tablespoon lemon juice
- 2 teaspoons finely chopped red onion
- 1 clove garlic, minced
- 1/8 teaspoon cayenne pepper, or more to taste
- 1/8 teaspoon salt

- 6 whole-wheat hamburger buns, toasted
- 6 lettuce leaves
- 6 tomato slices

NOTES:

Quinoa is a delicately flavored, protein-rich grain. Rinsing removes any residue of saponin, quinoa's natural, bitter protective covering. Find it in natural-foods stores and the natural-foods sections of many supermarkets.

Toast **cumin seeds** in a small dry skillet over medium heat, stirring occasionally, until very fragrant, 2 to 5 minutes. Let cool. Grind into a powder in a spice mill or blender.

1. Bring water to a boil in a small saucepan. Add quinoa and return to a boil. Reduce to a low simmer, cover and cook until the water has been absorbed, about 10 minutes. Uncover and let stand.
2. Heat 1 tablespoon oil in a medium skillet over medium heat. Add 1/2 cup onion and garlic and cook, stirring occasionally, until soft and fragrant, about 3 minutes. Add beans, paprika and ground cumin and mash the beans to a smooth paste with a potato masher or fork. Transfer the mixture to a bowl and let cool slightly. Add the quinoa, 3 tablespoons cilantro, 3 tablespoons cornmeal, 1/2 teaspoon salt and pepper; stir to combine.
3. Form the bean mash into 6 patties. Coat them evenly with the remaining 1/3 cup cornmeal and transfer to a baking sheet. Refrigerate for 20 minutes.
4. **To prepare guacamole:** Mash avocado with a potato masher or fork. Stir in 2 tablespoons cilantro, lemon juice, 2 teaspoons onion, garlic, cayenne and 1/8 teaspoon salt.
5. Preheat oven to 200°F.
6. Heat 1 tablespoon oil in a large cast-iron (or similar heavy) skillet over medium-high heat. Reduce heat to medium and cook 3 burgers until heated through and brown and crisp on both sides, 2 to 4 minutes per side. Transfer to the oven to keep warm. Cook the remaining 3 burgers with the remaining 1 tablespoon oil, reducing the heat as necessary to prevent overbrowning. Serve the burgers on buns with lettuce, tomato and the guacamole.

Pecan & Mushroom Burgers

ACTIVE TIME: 1 hour
TOTAL: 1 hour

TO MAKE AHEAD: Prepare through Step 6. Wrap patties individually and refrigerate for up to 2 days or freeze for up to 3 months. Thaw in the refrigerator before cooking.

MAKES: 8 servings

H✕W   H↑F   H♥H

PER SERVING: 322 calories; 14 g fat (2 g sat, 8 g mono); 29 mg cholesterol; 42 g carbohydrate; 4 g added sugars; 10 g protein; 7 g fiber; 540 mg sodium; 395 mg potassium.
NUTRITION BONUS: Magnesium (20% daily value).

Toasted pecans have a fragrant sweetness that makes an excellent companion for the earthy flavors of fresh mushrooms and whole-grain bulgur in these savory veggie burgers. Serve on toasted whole-wheat buns with the blue cheese sauce or just a smear of whole-grain mustard.

2/3   **cup bulgur (*see Note, page 218*)**
3/4   **teaspoon salt, divided**
1   **cup boiling water**
6   **teaspoons extra-virgin olive oil, divided**
8   **ounces white *or* brown mushrooms, stemmed and chopped**
1 1/2   **cups chopped onion**
1 1/2   **tablespoons plus 1/2 teaspoon balsamic vinegar, divided**
1/3   **cup nonfat plain yogurt**
3   **tablespoons crumbled blue cheese (1 ounce)**
3/4   **cup pecan halves**
1   **large egg, lightly beaten**
1/2   **cup fine dry breadcrumbs**
   Freshly ground pepper to taste
8   **whole-wheat buns, toasted**
   Watercress for garnish

1. Place bulgur and ¼ teaspoon salt in a small bowl. Pour the boiling water over, cover and set aside until the water is absorbed, 20 to 30 minutes. Drain in a sieve, pressing out excess liquid.
2. Meanwhile, heat 2 teaspoons oil in a large nonstick skillet over medium heat. Add mushrooms, onion and remaining ½ teaspoon salt; cook, stirring, until the vegetables are softened, 8 to 10 minutes. Stir in 1½ tablespoons vinegar. Immediately transfer the mixture to a plate and let cool to room temperature, about 30 minutes.
3. Combine the remaining ½ teaspoon vinegar, yogurt and blue cheese in a small bowl and blend with a fork to make a chunky sauce. Set aside.
4. Toast pecans in a small dry skillet over medium-low heat, stirring, until fragrant, 4 to 6 minutes. Transfer to a plate to cool.
5. Combine the vegetable mixture and pecans in a food processor; pulse briefly until coarsely chopped. Add the bulgur and egg; pulse briefly, scraping down the sides if necessary, until the mixture is cohesive but roughly textured. Transfer to a bowl; stir in breadcrumbs and pepper. Mix well.
6. With dampened hands, form the mixture into eight ½-inch-thick patties, using about ½ cup for each.
7. Using 2 teaspoons oil per batch, cook 4 patties at a time in a large nonstick skillet over medium heat until evenly browned and heated through, about 4 minutes per side. Serve the burgers on toasted buns with the blue cheese sauce and watercress, if desired.

Southwestern Pumpkin Burgers

It goes without saying that canned pumpkin is both a healthy and convenient ingredient to keep on hand—but in a burger? Actually yes, it makes the perfect, fragrant binder for corn, peppers and onion in these spicy, cheesy burgers. Serve wrapped in warm tortillas with shredded lettuce, salsa and, if you like, a side of Nina's Mexican Rice (page 196).

- **6** teaspoons extra-virgin olive oil, divided
- **1** medium onion, chopped
- **1/2** cup finely chopped red *or* green bell pepper
- **1/2** cup corn, fresh *or* frozen
- **2** cloves garlic, minced
- **2** teaspoons chili powder
- **1** teaspoon ground cumin
- **1/2** cup canned unseasoned pumpkin puree
- **1/2** cup shredded Monterey Jack *or* Cheddar cheese
- **1/2** cup wheat germ
- **1/2** cup fine dry breadcrumbs
- **2** tablespoons chopped fresh parsley
- **1/2** teaspoon salt
  Freshly ground pepper to taste
- **6** 8-inch whole-wheat flour tortillas, warmed (*see Note, page 219*)
- **2** cups shredded lettuce
- **1 1/2** cups store-bought fresh salsa (*see Note*)

1. Heat 2 teaspoons oil in a large nonstick skillet over medium heat. Add onion and cook, stirring often, until softened, 5 to 7 minutes. Stir in bell pepper, corn, garlic, chili powder and cumin; cook, stirring, until fragrant, about 2 minutes more. Transfer to a large bowl; let cool to room temperature, about 10 minutes.
2. Add pumpkin, cheese, wheat germ, breadcrumbs, parsley, salt and pepper to the onion mixture; mix well. With dampened hands, form the vegetable mixture into six 1/2-inch-thick patties, using about 1/2 cup for each.
3. Using 2 teaspoons oil per batch, cook 2 to 4 patties at a time in a large non-stick skillet over medium heat until browned and heated through, about 4 minutes per side. Adjust heat as necessary for even browning. Wrap the patties in warm tortillas and serve immediately, garnished with lettuce and salsa.

ACTIVE TIME: 50 minutes
TOTAL: 50 minutes

TO MAKE AHEAD: Prepare through Step 2. Wrap patties individually and refrigerate for up to 2 days or freeze for up to 3 months. Thaw in the refrigerator before cooking.

MAKES: 6 servings

H✕W   H↑F   H♥H
PER SERVING: 271 calories; 10 g fat (3 g sat, 5 g mono); 8 mg cholesterol; 42 g carbohydrate; 0 g added sugars; 11 g protein; 7 g fiber; 719 mg sodium; 384 mg potassium.
NUTRITION BONUS: Vitamin A (106% daily value), Vitamin C (40% dv), Folate (22% dv), Magnesium (20% dv), Zinc (18% dv), Iron (16% dv).

NOTE: Store-bought **fresh salsa** (pico de gallo) is usually just a simple combination of tomatoes, onions, jalapeños and cilantro. It has a nice bright flavor and is typically lower in sodium than jarred salsas. Look for it in the refrigerated part of the produce section in well-stocked supermarkets.

89

103

108

102

PIZZA & PASTA

Think of pizza and pasta as vehicles for whatever vegetables, herbs and beans you fancy. The sky's the limit. Start with whole-grain pasta or pizza dough, which have more digestion-aiding fiber than their processed counterparts, and then go to town. This chapter includes all sorts of styles of pizza, from grilled to stuffed, with toppings from tofu to caramelized onions. Pastas need not be just the classic style, adorned with tomato sauce—try sesame noodles (*page 109*), easy lasagna rolls (*page 102*) and fettuccine with creamy mushroom sauce (*page 96*).

Cheese & Tomato Pizza

ACTIVE TIME: 40 minutes
TOTAL: 40 minutes

MAKES: 6 servings

H✕W   H♥H

PER SERVING: 258 calories; 6 g fat
(3 g sat, 1 g mono); 16 mg cholesterol;
33 g carbohydrate; 1 g added sugars;
13 g protein; 2 g fiber; 663 mg sodium;
162 mg potassium.
NUTRITION BONUS: Calcium (22% daily
value).

NOTE: Look for **whole-wheat pizza-
dough** balls at your supermarket.
Check the ingredient list to make
sure the dough doesn't contain any
hydrogenated oils.

*Sometimes pizza from your own oven can be quicker than takeout and it's usually
a whole lot healthier because you control everything that goes into it. Enjoy this pie
as is or add toppings to your heart's content.*

Cornmeal for dusting baking sheets
1 pound prepared whole-wheat pizza dough (*see Note*)
1 cup prepared tomato sauce
4 ounces fresh mozzarella cheese, thinly sliced
1/8 teaspoon salt
Freshly ground pepper to taste
1/2 cup freshly grated Parmesan cheese
Several fresh basil leaves

1. Set oven rack in lowest position; preheat to 500°F or the highest setting.
   Sprinkle 2 large baking sheets with cornmeal.
2. Divide pizza dough in half. Roll out one half of the dough on a lightly
   floured surface into a 12-inch circle. Transfer to a prepared baking sheet. Bake
   until golden, about 5 minutes. Remove the pan from the oven. Repeat with
   the second portion of dough.
3. Spread ½ cup tomato sauce on one of the crusts. Distribute half of the
   mozzarella slices on top, season with salt and pepper and sprinkle with ¼ cup
   of the Parmesan cheese.
4. Bake the pizza until the top is bubbling, about 5 minutes. Remove from
   the oven and immediately garnish with a few basil leaves. Repeat with the
   remaining crust and toppings.

Pizza with White Bean Puree & Fresh Tomatoes

A fragrant white bean puree makes a truly delightful spread on this crisp pizza with slices of fresh tomato. This pizza just has a simple topping of a bit of grated Parmesan, scallions and sliced tomatoes so it's much lower in fat than your average gourmet pie. (Photograph: page 86.)

Cornmeal for dusting baking sheets
3/4 **cup water**
1 **clove garlic, cut in half**
1 **15-ounce can cannellini *or* great northern beans, rinsed**
1 **tablespoon extra-virgin olive oil**
1 **teaspoon finely chopped fresh sage *or* 1/4 teaspoon dried rubbed**
1/8 **teaspoon salt**
Freshly ground pepper to taste
1 **pound prepared whole-wheat pizza dough (*see Note, page 219*)**
4 **tablespoons freshly grated Parmesan cheese**
6 **plum tomatoes, sliced**
2 **scallions, thinly sliced**
1/2 **teaspoon crushed red pepper**
Olive oil cooking spray

1. Set oven rack in lowest position; preheat to 500°F or the highest setting. Sprinkle 2 large baking sheets with cornmeal.
2. Combine water and garlic in a saucepan and bring to a boil over high heat. Add beans and return to a boil. Drain, reserving 1/4 cup of the cooking liquid.
3. Transfer the beans and garlic to a food processor. Add oil and process, adding just enough of the reserved cooking liquid to make a thick, smooth paste. Stir in sage and season with salt and pepper.
4. Divide pizza dough in half. Roll out one half of the dough on a lightly floured surface into a 12-inch circle. Transfer the dough to a prepared pan. Pierce the dough several times with a fork to prevent air bubbles from forming. Prebake the crust until lightly browned, 5 to 6 minutes. Repeat with the remaining half of dough.
5. Spread the first crust with half of the white bean puree. Sprinkle 1 tablespoon Parmesan over the puree. Arrange half of the tomato slices evenly over the pizza; sprinkle with half of the scallions, another 1 tablespoon Parmesan and 1/4 teaspoon crushed red pepper. Lightly mist with olive oil cooking spray.
6. Bake the pizza until the bottom and edges of crust are browned, 5 to 7 minutes. Repeat with the remaining toppings on the second crust. Slice and serve.

ACTIVE TIME: 45 minutes
TOTAL: 45 minutes

MAKES: 4 servings

H⬆F   H♥H
PER SERVING: 373 calories; 11 g fat (1 g sat, 3 g mono); 4 mg cholesterol; 62 g carbohydrate; 1 g added sugars; 15 g protein; 9 g fiber; 648 mg sodium; 257 mg potassium.
NUTRITION BONUS: Vitamin C (23% daily value), Vitamin A (20% dv).

Individual Grilled Pizzas with Pesto, Tomatoes & Feta

ACTIVE TIME: 30 minutes
TOTAL: 30 minutes

MAKES: 4 servings

H↑F

PER SERVING: 455 calories; 18 g fat (7 g sat, 10 g mono); 27 mg cholesterol; 49 g carbohydrate; 1 g added sugars; 17 g protein; 4 g fiber; 749 mg sodium; 259 mg potassium.
NUTRITION BONUS: Calcium (32% daily value), Vitamin A (21% dv), Vitamin C (18% dv).

Once you've learned the technique of making pizza on the grill, you may never want to make it in the oven again. There's no need to heat up the kitchen from turning on the oven, and the unmistakable char-grilled flavor is irresistible. Here, store-bought dough and prepared pesto from the market makes it a 30-minute affair, but you can customize your grilled pies to make them as simple or sophisticated as you like.

1	**pound prepared whole-wheat pizza dough (*see Note, page 219*)**
½	**cup prepared pesto**
4	**plum tomatoes, thinly sliced**
½	**cup crumbled feta cheese**
	Freshly ground pepper to taste
¼	**cup lightly packed fresh basil leaves, torn**

1. Heat grill to medium-high.
2. Meanwhile, place dough on a lightly floured surface. Divide into 4 pieces. Roll each piece into an 8-inch round crust, about ¼ inch thick. Place crusts on a floured baking sheet. Carry crusts and toppings out to the grill.
3. Lay the crusts on the grill (they won't stay perfectly round). Close the lid and cook until the crusts are lightly puffed and the undersides are lightly browned, about 3 minutes.
4. Using tongs, flip the crusts. Immediately spread pesto over the crusts. Top with tomatoes. Sprinkle with feta and pepper. Close the lid and cook until the undersides are lightly browned, about 3 minutes more. Sprinkle with basil and serve immediately.

French Onion Pizza

Flecks of rosemary, cured olives and sweet sautéed onions give this pizza the feel of a Provençal pissaladière. If you enjoy anchovies, try scattering a few on top of this pizza.

1	pound prepared whole-wheat pizza dough (*see Note, page 219*)
1/3	cup chopped Kalamata olives
2 1/2	teaspoons chopped fresh rosemary *or* 1/2 teaspoon crumbled dried
	Cornmeal for dusting baking sheets
1	tablespoon extra-virgin olive oil
4	cups sliced onions
1	cup shredded part-skim mozzarella cheese, divided
1/2	cup grated Parmesan cheese, divided
	Freshly ground pepper to taste
	Olive oil cooking spray

1. Place dough on a lightly floured surface and knead olives and rosemary into it until thoroughly combined. Cover with plastic wrap and let rest for 10 to 15 minutes.
2. Set oven rack in lowest position; preheat to 500°F or the highest setting. Sprinkle 2 large baking sheets with cornmeal.
3. Heat oil in a large nonstick skillet over medium heat. Add onions and cook, stirring occasionally, until golden brown and very tender, about 10 minutes. Set aside to cool.
4. Divide the pizza dough in half. Roll out one half of the dough on a lightly floured surface into a 12-inch circle. Transfer to a prepared baking sheet, and pierce the dough several times with a fork to prevent large air bubbles from forming. Bake until golden, about 5 minutes. Remove the pan from the oven and roll and bake the second portion of dough.
5. Sprinkle 1/2 cup mozzarella and 1/4 cup Parmesan on one of the crusts. Arrange half the onions over the cheese and top with a generous grinding of pepper. Mist lightly with olive oil cooking spray.
6. Bake the pizza until the cheese is melted and the onions are heated through, about 5 minutes. Remove from the oven. Repeat with the remaining crust and toppings. Slice and serve.

ACTIVE TIME: 45 minutes
TOTAL: 45 minutes

TO MAKE AHEAD: The olive-and-herb dough (Step 1) can be stored in a plastic bag in the refrigerator overnight. Bring to room temperature before using.

MAKES: 6 servings

H✖W
PER SERVING: 318 calories; 10 g fat (4 g sat, 4 g mono); 16 mg cholesterol; 39 g carbohydrate; 1 g added sugars; 14 g protein; 3 g fiber; 505 mg sodium; 141 mg potassium.
NUTRITION BONUS: Calcium (23% daily value).

Pear & Blue Cheese Flatbread

Sweet ripe pears, assertive blue cheese and rich, crunchy walnuts are a brilliant culinary ménage à trois in any dish, but are particularly well suited to this gourmet flatbread. Stilton, the King of Cheeses, is an obvious choice, but any blue that suits your tastes will do. Round out the full flavors of the meal with an arugula salad tossed with walnut oil and sherry vinegar dressing.

ACTIVE TIME: 30 minutes
TOTAL: 45 minutes

MAKES: 6 servings

H↑F   H♥H

PER SERVING: 361 calories; 9 g fat
(3 g sat, 3 g mono); 8 mg cholesterol;
54 g carbohydrate; 1 g added sugars;
12 g protein; 5 g fiber; 410 mg sodium;
251 mg potassium.

2 teaspoons extra-virgin olive oil
3 cups thinly sliced onions
20 ounces prepared whole-wheat pizza dough (*see Note, page 219*)
⅓ cup chopped walnuts
2 teaspoons balsamic vinegar
2 teaspoons chopped fresh sage
Freshly ground pepper to taste
2 ripe but firm pears, sliced
½ cup finely crumbled blue cheese

1. Set oven rack in lowest position; preheat to 450°F. Coat a large baking sheet with cooking spray.

2. Heat oil in a large skillet over medium-high heat. Add onions and cook, stirring occasionally, until starting to brown, about 6 minutes. Reduce heat to low, cover and cook, stirring occasionally, until very soft and golden, 5 to 8 minutes more.

3. Meanwhile, roll out dough on a lightly floured surface to the size of the baking sheet. Transfer to the baking sheet. Bake on the bottom rack until puffed and lightly crisped on the bottom, 8 to 10 minutes. Toast walnuts in a small dry skillet over medium-low heat, stirring, until lightly browned and fragrant, 2 to 3 minutes.

4. Stir vinegar, sage and pepper into the onions. Spread on the crust and top with pears, walnuts and cheese. Bake on the bottom rack until the crust is crispy and golden and the cheese is melted, 11 to 13 minutes. Slice and serve.

Spinach & Sun-Dried Tomato Stuffed Pizza

ACTIVE TIME: 20 minutes
TOTAL: 40 minutes

MAKES: 6 servings

H✂W   H♥H

PER SERVING: 291 calories; 7 g fat
(3 g sat, 2 g mono); 10 mg cholesterol;
36 g carbohydrate; 1 g added sugars;
18 g protein; 4 g fiber; 607 mg sodium;
419 mg potassium.
NUTRITION BONUS: Vitamin A (119% daily
value), Calcium (37% dv), Magnesium
(20% dv), Folate (19% dv).

NOTE: For this recipe, look for **soft
sun-dried tomatoes** (*not* packed in oil).
If you can only find tomatoes that are
very dry (and hard), soak in boiling
water for about 20 minutes, drain,
chop and then add to the pizza filling.

*A satisfying filling made with crumbled tofu, spinach, sun-dried tomatoes, cheese and
fresh basil fills this large, calzone-like stuffed pizza. Using convenient frozen spinach
and store-bought whole-wheat dough, you can have this double-crusted pie on the
table in less time than you'd need to get takeout or delivery. Serve with your favorite
jarred marinara sauce for dipping.*

	Cooking spray, preferably canola *or* olive oil
1	**14-ounce package firm water-packed tofu, drained**
1	**10-ounce package frozen chopped spinach, thawed and squeezed dry**
½	**cup chopped soft *or* reconstituted sun-dried tomatoes (*see Note*)**
½	**cup finely shredded Parmesan cheese**
½	**cup shredded part-skim mozzarella cheese**
¼	**cup chopped fresh basil**
½	**teaspoon onion powder**
¼	**teaspoon salt**
¼	**teaspoon freshly ground pepper**
1	**pound prepared whole-wheat pizza dough (*see Note, page 219*)**

1. Position rack in lower third of oven; preheat to 475°F. Coat a large baking
   sheet with cooking spray.
2. Finely crumble tofu; pat dry. Place in a large bowl and use your hands to
   combine with spinach, tomatoes, Parmesan, mozzarella, basil, onion powder,
   salt and pepper.
3. Roll out dough on a lightly floured surface to about the length of the prepared
   baking sheet and twice as wide (approximately 16 by 18 inches). Transfer the
   dough to the baking sheet, allowing the extra width to hang over on one side
   onto a clean surface. Spread the filling on the dough in the pan, leaving
   a 1-inch border. Fold the overhanging dough over the filling. Fold the edges
   closed and crimp with a fork to seal. Make several small slits in the top to vent
   steam; lightly coat the top with cooking spray.
4. Bake the stuffed pizza until well browned on top, 18 to 20 minutes. Let cool
   slightly before cutting.

Orecchiette alla Carrettiera ("Wagon-Driver Style")

In this extremely simple take on pasta with tomato sauce, the sauce is raw. This is best in summer when tomatoes are at their peak. Add some drained, rinsed canned white cannellini beans if you want to give it a little more heft.

- 6 ounces whole-wheat orecchiette (*see Note*) *or* spaghetti
- 2 cloves garlic, peeled
- 4 very ripe plum tomatoes, coarsely chopped
- 1/4 cup fresh basil leaves, torn
- 1/2 teaspoon dried oregano
- 1/2 teaspoon salt
- Freshly ground pepper to taste
- 1 1/2 tablespoons extra-virgin olive oil

1. Bring a pot of water to a boil. Cook pasta until just tender, 10 to 12 minutes or according to package directions.
2. Rub a serving bowl with one half of a garlic clove. Coarsely chop the remaining garlic. Transfer to the bowl along with tomatoes, basil, oregano, salt and pepper. Drizzle with oil. Toss well.
3. Drain the pasta and add to the bowl. Toss well. Serve immediately.

ACTIVE TIME: 25 minutes
TOTAL: 25 minutes

MAKES: 2 servings, about 2 cups each

PER SERVING: 428 calories; 12 g fat (2 g sat, 8 g mono); 0 mg cholesterol; 72 g carbohydrate; 0 g added sugars; 14 g protein; 13 g fiber; 598 mg sodium; 619 mg potassium.
NUTRITION BONUS: Vitamin C (40% daily value), Magnesium (36% dv), Vitamin A (34% dv), Iron (22% dv), Folate (20% dv), Potassium (18% dv), Zinc (16% dv).

NOTE: Orecchiette is a traditional ear-shaped pasta. Look for whole-wheat orecchiette in natural-foods stores.

Spaghetti with Melted Tomato Sauce

This easy sauce starts with the same basic lineup of ingredients as the raw sauce above, but instead it's cooked. Cooking sweetens up the tomatoes a bit.

- 2 tablespoons extra-virgin olive oil
- 6 cloves garlic, thinly sliced
- 2 1/2 pounds ripe tomatoes (about 6), peeled, seeded (*see Note*) and chopped
- 1/4 teaspoon salt
- Freshly ground pepper to taste
- 1/2 cup fresh basil leaves, slivered
- 1 pound whole-wheat spaghetti *or* linguine
- 1/2 cup freshly grated Parmesan cheese

1. Put a large pot of water on to boil for cooking pasta.
2. Heat oil in a large skillet over medium heat; add garlic and cook, stirring, until tender, 1 to 2 minutes. Add tomatoes, salt and pepper. Mash the tomatoes with a potato masher or wooden spoon and simmer until the sauce has thickened, 15 to 20 minutes. Stir in basil. Taste and adjust seasonings.
3. Cook pasta until just tender, 8 to 10 minutes or according to package directions. Drain and transfer to a large serving bowl. Toss with the sauce and serve immediately, passing the cheese at the table.

ACTIVE TIME: 20 minutes
TOTAL: 35 minutes

MAKES: 4 servings

PER SERVING: 373 calories; 8 g fat (2 g sat, 4 g mono); 6 mg cholesterol; 66 g carbohydrate; 0 g added sugars; 16 g protein; 11 g fiber; 215 mg sodium; 642 mg potassium.
NUTRITION BONUS: Vitamin C (43% daily value), Vitamin A (36% dv), Magnesium (34% dv), Folate & Iron (19% dv), Potassium (18% dv), Zinc (16% dv).

NOTE: To quickly seed a tomato, cut it in half crosswise and scoop out the seeds with your finger while gently squeezing each half.

Fettuccine with Creamy Mushroom Sauce

ACTIVE TIME: 40 minutes
TOTAL: 40 minutes

MAKES: 6 servings, about 1½ cups each

H✂W   H↑F   H♥H

PER SERVING: 341 calories; 8 g fat
(3 g sat, 3 g mono); 15 mg cholesterol;
54 g carbohydrate; 0 g added sugars;
15 g protein; 9 g fiber; 489 mg sodium;
556 mg potassium.
NUTRITION BONUS: Zinc (18% daily value),
Magnesium (17% dv), Potassium
(16% dv), Iron (15% dv).

Shiitake, oyster and cremini mushrooms give this creamy pasta sauce a rich, earthy flavor, but really, any type of mushroom will work. If you want to take the dish to where the wild things are, add a few foraged varieties, such as chanterelle or lobster mushrooms.

12	ounces whole-wheat fettuccine
1	tablespoon extra-virgin olive oil
½	cup chopped shallot
2	tablespoons chopped garlic
1½	teaspoons chopped fresh thyme *or* ½ teaspoon dried
¾	teaspoon salt
½	teaspoon freshly ground pepper
1½	pounds mixed mushrooms, sliced
2	tablespoons brandy *or* dry sherry
3	tablespoons all-purpose flour
1	cup vegetable broth *or* "no-chicken" broth (*see Note, page 218*)
⅓	cup light cream
½	cup grated Parmesan cheese, divided

1. Bring a large pot of water to a boil. Cook pasta until just tender, 8 to 10 minutes or according to package directions. Drain, reserving ½ cup of the cooking liquid, and return the pasta to the pot.
2. Meanwhile, heat oil in a large skillet over medium-high heat. Add shallot, garlic, thyme, salt and pepper and cook, stirring, until the shallot and garlic start to soften and brown slightly, 1 to 3 minutes. Add mushrooms and cook, stirring occasionally, until the mushrooms have cooked down and their juices have evaporated, 7 to 10 minutes.
3. Stir in brandy (or sherry) and cook until the liquid has evaporated, about 1 minute. Sprinkle flour over the mushroom mixture and stir to coat. Pour in broth and bring to a boil, stirring constantly. Simmer, stirring, until thickened, about 1 minute. Remove from the heat. Stir in cream and ¼ cup Parmesan.
4. Stir the mushroom sauce into the drained pasta. If the sauce seems too thick, stir in some of the reserved pasta-cooking liquid to thin to desired consistency. Serve topped with the remaining ¼ cup Parmesan.

Roasted Vegetable & Linguine Salad

ACTIVE TIME: 20 minutes
TOTAL: 40 minutes

TO MAKE AHEAD: Cover and refrigerate for up to 1 day. Bring to room temperature before serving.

MAKES: 6 servings, about 1 1/3 cups each

H✂W H↑F H♥H

PER SERVING: 329 calories; 9 g fat (2 g sat, 5 g mono); 6 mg cholesterol; 54 g carbohydrate; 0 g added sugars; 14 g protein; 10 g fiber; 514 mg sodium; 511 mg potassium.
NUTRITION BONUS: Vitamin C (138% daily value), Vitamin A (56% dv), Folate (43% dv), Magnesium (27% dv), Iron (21% dv), Calcium, Potassium & Zinc (15% dv).

The high heat of roasting transforms vegetables by caramelizing their natural sugars. Here, they bring their mellow sweetness to a summery linguine salad that's perfect for make-ahead suppers or even potlucks. Asparagus, red bell peppers and scallions are used here, but try roasting whatever you have in your garden or can pick up at your local farmstand or market.

- **12 ounces whole-wheat linguine**
- **1 teaspoon plus 2 tablespoons extra-virgin olive oil, divided**
- **1 1/2 pounds asparagus, trimmed and cut into 3-inch pieces**
- **3 bunches scallions, trimmed and cut into 3-inch pieces**
- **2 large red bell peppers, cut into thin strips**
- **1 teaspoon salt**
- **1 teaspoon freshly ground pepper**
- **1/2 cup freshly grated Parmesan cheese**
- **1/4 cup balsamic vinegar**

1. Position racks in lower third and middle of oven; preheat to 450°F. Put a large pot of water on to boil for cooking pasta.
2. Break linguine into pieces about 3 inches long. Cook the broken linguine until just tender, 8 to 10 minutes or according to package directions. Drain and rinse under cold water until cool. Press to remove excess water. Transfer to a large bowl, toss with 1 teaspoon oil and set aside.
3. Meanwhile, toss asparagus, scallions and bell peppers in a large bowl with the remaining 2 tablespoons oil, salt and pepper. Divide the vegetables between 2 large baking sheets, spreading them in an even layer.
4. Roast for about 10 minutes, stir the vegetables and switch the positions of the baking sheets. Continue roasting, stirring occasionally, until the vegetables are tender and well-browned, 10 to 15 minutes more.
5. Add the vegetables to the linguine and toss to combine. Add Parmesan and vinegar and toss again.

Mediterranean Baked Penne

Lots of plum tomatoes, zucchini, eggplant and red bell peppers make this baked casserole perfect for a late summer or early fall supper. The leftovers are great for lunch the following day.

- 1/2 cup fine dry breadcrumbs, divided
- 1 tablespoon extra-virgin olive oil
- 2 small zucchini, chopped
- 1 medium eggplant (about 1 pound), chopped
- 1 green *or* red bell pepper, chopped
- 1 medium onion, chopped
- 1 stalk celery, sliced
- 1 clove garlic, minced
- 1/4 cup dry white wine
- 1 28-ounce can plum tomatoes, drained and coarsely chopped, juice reserved
- 1/2 teaspoon salt
  Freshly ground pepper to taste
- 1 pound whole-wheat penne *or* rigatoni
- 1 1/2 cups shredded part-skim mozzarella cheese
- 2 large eggs, lightly beaten
- 2 tablespoons freshly grated Parmesan cheese

1. Preheat oven to 375°F. Coat a 3-quart baking dish with cooking spray. Coat the dish with 1/4 cup breadcrumbs, tapping out the excess. Put a large pot of water on to boil for cooking pasta.
2. Heat oil in a large nonstick skillet over medium-high heat. Add zucchini, eggplant, bell pepper, onion and celery; cook, stirring occasionally, until tender, about 10 minutes. Add garlic and cook, stirring, for 1 minute more. Add wine and stir until almost evaporated, about 2 minutes. Add tomatoes and juice. Bring to a simmer and cook until thickened, 10 to 15 minutes. Season with salt and pepper. Transfer to a large bowl; let cool to room temperature.
3. Meanwhile, cook pasta until just tender, 8 to 10 minutes or according to package directions. Drain and rinse well. Toss the pasta with the vegetable mixture; stir in mozzarella.
4. Spoon the pasta mixture into the prepared baking dish and drizzle eggs evenly over the top. Combine the remaining 1/4 cup breadcrumbs and Parmesan in a small bowl. Sprinkle evenly over the top.
5. Bake the pasta until golden and bubbly, 40 to 50 minutes. Let stand for 10 minutes before serving.

ACTIVE TIME: 35 minutes
TOTAL: 1 hour 45 minutes

TO MAKE AHEAD: Prepare through Step 3, cover and refrigerate for up to 2 days.

MAKES: 8 servings

H✕W   H↑F   H♥H
PER SERVING: 372 calories; 9 g fat (3 g sat, 3 g mono); 65 mg cholesterol; 57 g carbohydrate; 0 g added sugars; 19 g protein; 8 g fiber; 358 mg sodium, 394 mg potassium.
NUTRITION BONUS: Vitamin C (33% daily value), Calcium (23% dv), Magnesium (19% dv), Zinc (16% dv), Iron (15% dv).

Braised Winter Vegetable Pasta

Braising the pasta and vegetables in white wine and broth ensures that the aromatic flavors are infused throughout this hearty vegan dish. Although already quick to prepare, look for super-convenient prepeeled and diced squash at your grocer's to really get dinner on the table in a flash. Serve with a mixed green salad with a Dijon vinaigrette.

2	tablespoons extra-virgin olive oil
1	small onion, diced
4	cloves garlic, minced
1	tablespoon finely chopped fresh sage *or* 1 teaspoon dried rubbed
4	cups vegetable broth
1	cup dry white wine
8	ounces whole-wheat medium pasta shells *or* other small pasta
2	cups bite-size cauliflower florets
2	cups bite-size butternut squash cubes
¼	teaspoon salt
	Freshly ground pepper to taste
1	10-ounce bag frozen lima beans, thawed

1. Heat oil in a Dutch oven over medium heat. Add onion, garlic and sage and cook, stirring, until softened, 3 to 4 minutes.
2. Add broth and wine; bring to a boil over medium-high heat. Add pasta, cauliflower, squash, salt and pepper and cook, stirring occasionally, until the pasta is not quite tender, about 10 minutes. Stir in lima beans and cook, stirring occasionally, until the lima beans and pasta are tender and most of the liquid is absorbed, about 5 minutes more.

ACTIVE TIME: 25 minutes
TOTAL: 40 minutes

MAKES: 4 servings, about 2 cups each

PER SERVING: 468 calories; 9 g fat (1 g sat, 6 g mono); 0 mg cholesterol; 76 g carbohydrate; 0 g added sugars; 16 g protein; 13 g fiber; 655 mg sodium; 863 mg potassium.
NUTRITION BONUS: Vitamin A (172% daily value), Vitamin C (78% dv), Magnesium (32% dv), Iron & Potassium (25% dv), Folate (18% dv).

Lasagna Rolls

ACTIVE TIME: 45 minutes
TOTAL: 45 minutes

TO MAKE AHEAD: Freeze the cooked rolls and sauce for up to 1 month.

MAKES: 6 servings, 2 rolls each

H✂W H⬆F H❤H

PER SERVING: 338 calories; 11 g fat (3 g sat, 4 g mono); 11 mg cholesterol; 45 g carbohydrate; 0 g added sugars; 19 g protein; 6 g fiber; 444 mg sodium; 233 mg potassium.
NUTRITION BONUS: Calcium (35% daily value), Vitamin A (31% dv), Iron (24% dv), Magnesium (20% dv), Zinc (15% dv).

Crumbled tofu stands in for the traditional ricotta in our spinach-and-olive-filled lasagna rolls. For a full-flavored variation on the veggies, consider using sautéed and chopped broccoli rabe or kale instead of the spinach. Serve with a mixed green salad tossed with Mustard-Balsamic Vinaigrette (page 38). (Photograph: page 86.)

12 whole-wheat lasagna noodles
 1 tablespoon extra-virgin olive oil
 3 cloves garlic, minced
 1 14-ounce package extra-firm water-packed tofu, drained and crumbled
 3 cups chopped spinach
1/2 cup shredded Parmesan cheese
 2 tablespoons finely chopped Kalamata olives
1/4 teaspoon crushed red pepper
1/4 teaspoon salt
 1 25-ounce jar marinara sauce, preferably lower-sodium, divided
1/2 cup shredded part-skim mozzarella cheese

1. Bring a large pot of water to a boil. Cook noodles according to package directions. Drain, rinse, return to the pot and cover with cold water until ready to use.
2. Meanwhile, heat oil in a large nonstick skillet over medium heat. Add garlic and cook, stirring, until fragrant, about 20 seconds. Add tofu and spinach and cook, stirring often, until the spinach is wilted and the mixture is heated through, 3 to 4 minutes. Transfer to a bowl; stir in Parmesan, olives, crushed red pepper, salt and ⅔ cup marinara sauce.
3. Wipe out the pan and spread 1 cup of the remaining marinara sauce in the bottom. To make lasagna rolls, place a noodle on a clean work surface and spread ¼ cup of the tofu filling evenly over the noodle. Roll up and place the roll, seam-side down, in the pan. Repeat with the remaining noodles and filling. (The tofu rolls will be tightly packed in the pan.) Spoon the remaining marinara sauce over the rolls.
4. Place the pan over medium-high heat, cover and bring to a simmer. Reduce heat to medium; let simmer for 3 minutes. Sprinkle the rolls with mozzarella and cook, covered, until the cheese is melted and the rolls are heated through, 1 to 2 minutes more. Serve hot.

Greek Orzo Stuffed Peppers

We've given a Greek treatment to this twist on traditional rice-stuffed peppers. Orzo pasta, spinach, feta and a sprinkling of fresh oregano set the tone, while the addition of convenient canned chickpeas makes the dish a completely satisfying main dish. Once you've made these once, try customizing the recipe by substituting different types of cheese, herbs or beans. (Photograph: page 86.)

4	yellow, orange and/or red bell peppers
½	cup whole-wheat orzo
1	15-ounce can chickpeas, rinsed
1	tablespoon extra-virgin olive oil
1	medium onion, chopped
6	ounces baby spinach, coarsely chopped
1	tablespoon chopped fresh oregano *or* 1 teaspoon dried
¾	cup crumbled feta cheese, divided
¼	cup soft sun-dried tomatoes (*not* oil-packed; *see Note, page 94*), chopped
1	tablespoon sherry vinegar *or* red-wine vinegar
¼	teaspoon salt

1. Halve peppers lengthwise through the stems, leaving the stems attached. Remove the seeds and white membrane. Place the peppers cut-side down in a large microwave-safe dish. Add ½ inch water, cover and microwave on High until the peppers are just softened, 7 to 9 minutes. Let cool slightly, drain and set aside.
2. Meanwhile, bring a large saucepan of water to a boil. Add orzo and cook until just tender, 8 to 10 minutes or according to package directions. Drain and rinse with cold water.
3. Mash chickpeas into a chunky paste with a fork, leaving some whole.
4. Heat oil in a large nonstick skillet over medium heat. Add onion and cook, stirring, until soft, about 4 minutes. Add spinach and oregano and cook, stirring, until the spinach is wilted, about 1 minute. Stir in the orzo, chickpeas, ½ cup feta, tomatoes, vinegar and salt; cook until heated though, about 1 minute. Divide the filling among the pepper halves and sprinkle each pepper with some of the remaining ¼ cup feta.

ACTIVE TIME: 40 minutes
TOTAL: 40 minutes

MAKES: 4 servings

H✖W   H⬆F
PER SERVING: 344 calories; 11 g fat (5 g sat, 4 g mono); 25 mg cholesterol; 48 g carbohydrate; 0 added sugars; 14 g protein; 11 g fiber; 656 mg sodium; 689 mg potassium.
NUTRITION BONUS: Vitamin C (338% daily value), Vitamin A (125% dv), Folate (48% dv), Calcium (24% dv), Magnesium & Potassium (20% dv), Iron (19% dv), Zinc (15% dv).

Baked Tortellini

Here's a triple play: delicious, easy-to-prepare and freezes well. Nutty-flavored fontina cheese gives this homey casserole a real taste twist and the cheesy breadcrumb topping makes it all but irresistible. You can easily double this recipe and make one for today and an extra to pop in the freezer for a heat-and-eat meal some day in the future.

- 1 tablespoon extra-virgin olive oil
- 2 tablespoons all-purpose flour
- 2½ cups low-fat milk, heated
- ½ cup shredded fontina cheese, divided
- ½ teaspoon ground nutmeg
- ¼ teaspoon salt
  Freshly ground pepper to taste
- 1 pound fresh *or* frozen cheese tortellini, preferably whole-wheat
- ¼ cup fine dry breadcrumbs
- 2 tablespoons freshly grated Parmesan cheese

1. Preheat oven to 350°F. Coat 6 individual gratin dishes or a 1½-quart shallow baking dish with cooking spray. Put a large pot of water on to boil for cooking pasta.
2. Heat oil in a large saucepan over medium heat. Add flour and cook, whisking constantly, for 1 to 2 minutes. Add hot milk and bring to a simmer, whisking, until smooth and slightly thickened, 3 to 4 minutes. Remove from heat and add ¼ cup fontina and nutmeg, stirring to melt the cheese. Season with salt and pepper.
3. Meanwhile, cook tortellini until just tender, 6 to 8 minutes or according to package directions. Drain and rinse well.
4. Combine the tortellini with the cheese sauce and toss. Transfer to the prepared dishes or baking dish. Top with the remaining ¼ cup fontina. Combine breadcrumbs and Parmesan and sprinkle evenly over the tortellini.
5. Bake the tortellini until golden and bubbly, 15 to 25 minutes. Serve immediately.

ACTIVE TIME: 25 minutes
TOTAL: 45 minutes

TO MAKE AHEAD: Prepare through Step 4; cover and refrigerate for up to 2 days or freeze for up to 6 months. Thaw in the refrigerator before baking.

EQUIPMENT: 6 individual gratin dishes or a 1½-quart shallow baking dish

MAKES: 6 servings

H✖W

PER SERVING: 366 calories; 12 g fat (6 g sat, 5 g mono); 49 mg cholesterol; 46 g carbohydrate; 0 g added sugars; 17 g protein; 2 g fiber; 738 mg sodium; 241 mg potassium.
NUTRITION BONUS: Calcium (32% daily value), Folate (27% dv).

Ravioli with Arugula & Pecorino

ACTIVE TIME: 20 minutes
TOTAL: 20 minutes

MAKES: 4 servings, 1 1/4 cups each

PER SERVING: 413 calories; 24 g fat
(8 g sat, 11 g mono); 57 mg cholesterol;
34 g carbohydrate; 0 g added sugars;
16 g protein; 2 g fiber; 585 mg sodium;
156 mg potassium.
NUTRITION BONUS: Calcium (25% daily
value), Vitamin A (19% dv).

NOTE: Use a vegetable peeler to **shave
curls** off a block of hard cheese.

*Frozen cheese ravioli is quite convenient for creating quick suppers, but on its own or
with just tomato sauce it's a bit ho-hum. Here, ravioli gets a full-flavor makeover
with sizzled garlic and shallots, shaved Pecorino and fresh arugula. Make it a meal
with warm slices of whole-grain baguette, steamed asparagus and a light-bodied red
wine, such as pinot noir.*

1	**pound fresh *or* frozen cheese ravioli, preferably whole-wheat**
1	**large clove garlic, minced**
1/2	**teaspoon kosher salt**
1/4	**cup extra-virgin olive oil**
2	**large shallots, sliced**
3	**tablespoons red-wine vinegar**
1	**teaspoon Dijon mustard**
	Freshly ground pepper to taste
6	**cups arugula**
1/2	**cup shaved Pecorino Romano *or* Parmesan cheese (*see Note*)**

1. Bring a large pot of water to a boil. Cook ravioli until tender, 7 to 9 minutes
   or according to package directions.
2. Meanwhile, mash garlic and salt into a paste with the side of a chef's knife or
   back of a spoon. Heat oil in a small skillet over medium heat. Add the garlic
   paste and shallots and cook, stirring often, until just starting to brown, 2 to 3
   minutes. Stir in vinegar, mustard and pepper; remove from the heat.
3. Drain the ravioli well. Place in a large bowl and toss with arugula and the
   dressing. Serve sprinkled with cheese.

Edamame Lo Mein

ACTIVE TIME: 30 minutes
TOTAL: 40 minutes

MAKES: 4 servings, 2 cups each

H↑F   H♥H

PER SERVING: 448 calories; 14 g fat
(1 g sat, 5 g mono); 0 mg cholesterol;
61 g carbohydrate; 2 g added sugars;
18 g protein; 13 g fiber; 960 mg
sodium; 647 mg potassium.
NUTRITION BONUS: Vitamin A (138%
daily value), Vitamin C (95% dv),
Folate (62% dv), Magnesium (33% dv),
Iron (25% dv), Potassium (18% dv),
Zinc (16% dv).

The problem with most Chinese takeout is that it's greasy and it's hard to know exactly what's in it. With this 40-minute lo mein you have a healthy noodle stir-fry, plus you get plenty of nutrients from the edamame (soybeans), which are also a great source of plant protein. Want more veggies? Serve with a simple side of steamed baby bok choy drizzled with soy sauce and sprinkled with sesame seeds. (Photograph: page 86.)

8   **ounces whole-wheat spaghetti**
2   **cups frozen shelled edamame**
4   **scallions, thinly sliced**
¼   **cup vegetarian "oyster" sauce (*see Note, page 219*)**
¼   **cup rice-wine vinegar**
3   **tablespoons reduced-sodium soy sauce**
2   **teaspoons sugar**
2   **teaspoons toasted sesame oil**
⅛   **teaspoon crushed red pepper**
2   **tablespoons canola oil**
2   **medium carrots, cut into matchsticks**
2   **small red bell peppers, cut into matchsticks**

1. Bring a large pot of water to a boil. Add spaghetti and edamame and cook, stirring occasionally, until the pasta is just tender, 8 to 10 minutes or according to package directions. Drain.
2. Meanwhile, whisk scallions, "oyster" sauce, vinegar, soy sauce, sugar, sesame oil and crushed red pepper in a small bowl until the sugar is dissolved.
3. Heat canola oil in a large nonstick skillet over medium-high heat. Add carrots and bell peppers and cook, stirring often, until slightly softened, 3 to 5 minutes. Add the pasta and edamame. Cook, stirring occasionally, until the pasta is crispy in spots, 2 to 3 minutes. Add the sauce and stir to combine.

Elise's Sesame Noodles

Whole-wheat pasta and colorful fresh veggies bolster fiber and nutrients in this popular Asian noodle salad.

1	**pound whole-wheat spaghetti**
½	**cup reduced-sodium soy sauce**
2	**tablespoons toasted sesame oil**
2	**tablespoons canola oil**
2	**tablespoons rice-wine vinegar *or* lime juice**
1½	**teaspoons crushed red pepper**
1	**bunch scallions, sliced, divided**
¼	**cup chopped fresh cilantro, divided (optional)**
4	**cups snow peas, trimmed and sliced on the bias**
1	**medium red bell pepper, thinly sliced**
½	**cup toasted sesame seeds**

1. Bring a large pot of water to a boil. Cook spaghetti until just tender, 9 to 11 minutes or according to package directions. Drain; rinse under cold water.
2. Meanwhile, whisk soy sauce, sesame oil, canola oil, vinegar (or lime juice), crushed red pepper, ¼ cup scallions and 2 tablespoons cilantro (if using) Add the noodles, snow peas and bell pepper; toss to coat.
3. To serve, mix in sesame seeds and garnish with the remaining scallions and cilantro.

ACTIVE TIME: 20 minutes
TOTAL: 20 minutes

TO MAKE AHEAD: Prepare through Step 2 up to 2 hours in advance.

MAKES: 8 servings, about 1 ½ cups each

PER SERVING: 343 calories; 12 g fat (2 g sat, 6 g mono); 0 mg cholesterol; 51 g carbohydrate; 0 g added sugars; 12 g protein; 10 g fiber; 542 mg sodium; 336 mg potassium.
NUTRITION BONUS: Vitamin C (104% daily value), Vitamin A (40% dv), Magnesium (33% dv), Iron (26% dv), Folate (16% dv), Zinc (15% dv).

112

124

119

125

GRAINS & BEANS

Beans and grains, building blocks of a balanced vegetarian diet, are incredibly versatile. Beans and rice, like the version on page 120, might come to mind first, but we also like to mix it up with new approaches, such as Baked Curried Brown Rice & Lentil Pilaf (*page 121*) or Acorn Squash Stuffed with Chard & White Beans (*page 125*). To keep recipes quick we usually call for canned beans. (Rinse them before you use them to reduce the sodium by about 35 percent.) If you have time on a weekend, make a big pot of beans from scratch (*see page 127*), then package them up and freeze them for when you need them.

Mediterranean Couscous Cabbage Rolls

ACTIVE TIME: 40 minutes
TOTAL: 40 minutes

TO MAKE AHEAD: Prepare through Step 4; refrigerate sauce and cabbage rolls separately for up to 8 hours. Reheat the sauce before finishing with Step 5.

MAKES: 4 servings, 2 rolls & ⅓ cup sauce each

H✖W   H▲F   H♥H

PER SERVING: 334 calories; 12 g fat (3 g sat, 7 g mono); 11 mg cholesterol; 49 g carbohydrate; 1 g added sugars; 11 g protein; 9 g fiber; 710 mg sodium; 498 mg potassium.
NUTRITION BONUS: Vitamin C (52% daily value), Vitamin A (37% dv).

For this vegetarian take on the classic dish, cabbage leaves are rolled around a filling of whole-wheat couscous studded with chopped Kalamata olives and crumbles of salty feta cheese. The rolls are then simmered in a tomato sauce, infused with a touch of cinnamon. Serve with roasted carrots or squash. (Photograph: page 110.)

4¼	cups water, divided
¾	teaspoon salt, divided
1	cup whole-wheat couscous
8	large Savoy *or* other green cabbage leaves
2	tablespoons extra-virgin olive oil
4	cloves garlic, minced
4	cups chopped plum tomatoes
2	teaspoons red-wine vinegar
1	teaspoon sugar
¼	teaspoon ground cinnamon
⅓	cup crumbled feta cheese
3	tablespoons chopped Kalamata olives
2	tablespoons chopped fresh mint, plus more for garnish

1. Bring 1½ cups water and ¼ teaspoon salt to a boil in a small saucepan. Stir in couscous, cover and remove from the heat. Let stand while you prepare the cabbage and sauce.
2. Bring 2½ cups water to a boil in a large skillet. Add cabbage leaves, cover, reduce heat to medium-high and simmer until softened, about 5 minutes. Transfer the cabbage leaves to a clean work surface to cool. Discard the water and dry the pan.
3. Heat oil in the skillet over medium heat. Add garlic and cook, stirring often, until fragrant, about 30 seconds. Add tomatoes, vinegar, sugar, cinnamon, the remaining ½ teaspoon salt and the remaining ¼ cup water. Cover and cook, stirring occasionally, until the tomatoes are mostly broken down, 8 to 10 minutes.
4. Meanwhile, stir feta, olives and 2 tablespoons mint into the couscous. Mound about ½ cup of the couscous mixture at the stem end of each cabbage leaf. Roll into a bundle, tucking in the sides.
5. When the tomato sauce is ready, add the cabbage rolls seam-side down. Cover and cook until the rolls are hot all the way through and the cabbage is very tender, 5 to 8 minutes. Serve the cabbage rolls topped with the sauce. Garnish with mint, if desired.

Barley "Risotto" with Asparagus & Shiitakes

Convenient, quick-cooking barley, which is available in most supermarkets, makes for speedy preparation of this nutty-flavored risotto-style dish. Try it with other types of mushrooms if you can't find shiitakes.

ACTIVE TIME: 35 minutes
TOTAL: 35 minutes

MAKES: 4 servings

H✂W   H⬆F   H♥H

PER SERVING: 273 calories; 8 g fat (2 g sat, 4 g mono); 9 mg cholesterol; 38 g carbohydrate; 0 g added sugars; 11 g protein; 7 g fiber; 604 mg sodium; 445 mg potassium.
NUTRITION BONUS: Folate (33% daily value), Vitamin A (29% dv), Calcium & Vitamin C (16% dv)

12	ounces asparagus, trimmed and cut into 1 1/2-inch pieces
2 1/2	cups "no-chicken" broth (*see Note, page 218*) *or* vegetable broth
1	tablespoon extra-virgin olive oil
1	bunch scallions (white and light green parts), chopped
4	ounces shiitake mushrooms, stems removed, caps thinly sliced
1	cup quick-cooking barley
1/2	cup dry white wine
1/2	cup freshly grated Parmesan cheese
1/4	teaspoon salt
	Freshly ground pepper to taste

1. Place a steamer basket in a large saucepan, add 1 inch of water and bring to a boil. Add asparagus; cover and steam for 3 minutes. Uncover, remove from the heat and set aside.

2. Bring broth to a simmer in a saucepan or in the microwave; keep warm. Heat oil in a Dutch oven or other heavy, wide pan over medium heat. Add scallions and shiitakes; cook, stirring occasionally, until tender, 3 to 4 minutes. Add barley and stir for 1 minute. Add wine; stir until evaporated, about 1 minute.

3. Add about 1/2 cup of the hot broth and cook, stirring frequently, until most of the liquid has been absorbed. Continue cooking, adding broth, 1/2 cup at a time, and stirring frequently, until the barley is just tender and the mixture has a slightly saucy consistency, about 10 minutes. Remove from the heat and stir in the cheese and the reserved asparagus. Season with salt and pepper and serve.

Butternut Squash Pilaf

ACTIVE TIME: 35 minutes
TOTAL: 1 hour

MAKES: 6 servings, about 1 cup each

H✕W   H↑F   H♥H

PER SERVING: 202 calories; 8 g fat
(1 g sat, 5 g mono); 0 mg cholesterol;
29 g carbohydrate; 0 g added sugars;
3 g protein; 5 g fiber; 422 mg sodium;
472 mg potassium.
NUTRITION BONUS: Vitamin A (289% daily
value), Vitamin C (38% dv), Magnesium
(16% dv).

NOTE: Fennel "fronds" are the feathery
tops on fennel bulbs. Look for fresh
fennel bulbs—with their fronds still
attached—in the produce section.
The fronds look similar to fresh dill and
have a mild licorice flavor. You'll need
to buy one large or two smaller bulbs of
fennel to have enough fronds to make
1/2 cup chopped.

*This colorful vegan pilaf makes a delightfully warming entree in the fall and winter
when butternut squash are in season. Here the Greek-inspired dish is prepared with
butternut squash but if you like, you can use sugar or pie pumpkin, which is different
than the standard jack-o'-lantern variety. To continue the Greek theme and add a
bit more protein, serve the pilaf topped with either grated kasseri or crumbled feta cheese.*

2	**pounds butternut squash, peeled, halved and seeded**
3	**tablespoons extra-virgin olive oil**
1	**large red onion, finely chopped**
1	**clove garlic, minced**
2	**tablespoons water**
1	**tablespoon tomato paste**
1	**cup instant *or* parboiled brown rice**
1 3/4	**cups water *or* one 14-ounce can vegetable broth**
1/2	**cup dry white wine**
1/2	**cup chopped fennel fronds (*see Note*)**
2	**tablespoons chopped fresh oregano**
1	**teaspoon salt**
	Pinch of ground cinnamon
	Freshly ground pepper to taste

1. Grate the squash through the large holes of a box grater.
2. Heat oil in a large cast-iron or nonstick skillet over medium-low heat. Add onion and garlic and cook, stirring, until soft and lightly colored, 10 to 12 minutes. Combine 2 tablespoons water and tomato paste in a small bowl and stir it into the pan. Add rice and stir to coat. Add the squash, in batches if necessary, and stir until it has reduced in volume enough so that you can cover the pan.
3. Increase the heat to medium-high, pour in 1 3/4 cups water (or broth) and wine, cover and bring to a boil. Reduce the heat to medium-low and cook, covered, stirring once or twice, until the rice has absorbed most of the liquid and the squash is tender, 25 to 30 minutes.
4. Add fennel fronds, oregano, salt, cinnamon and pepper; gently stir to combine. Remove from the heat and let stand, covered, for 5 minutes. Serve hot or at room temperature.

Mexican Polenta Scramble

Store-bought prepared polenta makes this Mexican-style scramble satisfying and quick to prepare. To adjust the level of heat in this dish, vary the type of peppers you use. Choose poblanos for a medium level of spiciness or, if you prefer, mild green bell peppers. Diced avocado makes a creamy and nutrient-rich topping, but you can lighten up the dish by substituting your favorite salsa instead. To round out the meal, serve with a side of black beans or lay a fried egg on top.

1 tablespoon extra-virgin olive oil
4 poblano peppers *or* 2 green bell peppers, diced
1 pint cherry tomatoes, halved
2 teaspoons ground cumin
1/4 teaspoon salt
1 16-ounce tube prepared plain polenta (*see Notes*), cut into 1/2-inch slices
1 bunch scallions, trimmed and sliced
1 cup shredded reduced-fat Cheddar cheese, preferably sharp
1/4 cup chopped fresh cilantro
1 tablespoon lime juice
1 ripe avocado, diced
2 tablespoons pepitas, toasted (*see Notes*)

Heat oil in a large nonstick skillet over medium-high heat. Add peppers and cook, stirring occasionally, until just starting to soften, about 3 minutes. Stir in tomatoes, cumin and salt; cook, stirring often, until the tomatoes start to break down, 2 to 3 minutes. Crumble polenta slices into the pan and cook, stirring occasionally, until heated through, 1 to 2 minutes. Stir in scallions, cheese, cilantro and lime juice. Serve the scramble topped with diced avocado and toasted pepitas.

ACTIVE TIME: 30 minutes
TOTAL: 30 minutes

MAKES: 4 servings, 1 1/2 cups each

H↑F
PER SERVING: 347 calories; 20 g fat (6 g sat, 8 g mono); 20 mg cholesterol; 33 g carbohydrate; 0 g added sugars; 14 g protein; 7 g fiber; 744 mg sodium; 645 mg potassium.
NUTRITION BONUS: Vitamin C (215% daily value), Calcium (45% dv), Vitamin A (36% dv), Folate (20% dv), Potassium (18% dv).

NOTES:
Although you might have to search for tubes of **prepared polenta** at your supermarket (we've found it refrigerated near both the tofu and the deli, on the shelf by other grains or in the pasta aisle), it's worth seeking out this versatile timesaver. Buy a few tubes to have on hand when you find it.

Toast pepitas in a small dry skillet over medium-low heat, stirring constantly, until fragrant and lightly browned, 2 to 4 minutes.

Creamy Gorgonzola Polenta with Summer Squash Sauté

ACTIVE TIME: 40 minutes
TOTAL: 40 minutes

MAKES: 4 servings, ¾ cup polenta & 1 cup vegetables each

PER SERVING: 274 calories; 14 g fat (5 g sat, 5 g mono); 17 mg cholesterol; 30 g carbohydrate; 0 g added sugars; 9 g protein; 5 g fiber; 643 mg sodium; 350 mg potassium.
NUTRITION BONUS: Vitamin C (38% daily value), Vitamin A (28% dv), Calcium (16% dv).

This creamy polenta calls for just enough Gorgonzola to make it luxurious without being overly rich. You can modify the dish seasonally by substituting mushrooms or squash in the fall or winter and peas with asparagus in the spring. Serve with crusty garlic bread and a salad of baby lettuce or mesclun greens. (Photograph: page 214.)

> 2 **14-ounce cans vegetable broth, divided**
> 1 **cup water**
> ¾ **cup cornmeal**
> ½ **teaspoon freshly ground pepper**
> ⅔ **cup crumbled Gorgonzola cheese**
> 2 **tablespoons extra-virgin olive oil**
> 3 **tablespoons minced garlic**
> 2 **small zucchini, halved lengthwise and sliced**
> 2 **small summer squash, halved lengthwise and sliced**
> 2 **tablespoons flour**
> ¼ **cup chopped fresh basil**

1. Combine 2½ cups broth and water in a small saucepan. Bring to a boil. Slowly whisk in cornmeal and pepper until smooth. Reduce heat to low, cover and cook, stirring occasionally, until very thick and no longer grainy, 10 to 15 minutes. Stir in Gorgonzola; remove the polenta from the heat and cover to keep warm.

2. Meanwhile, heat oil in a large nonstick skillet over medium-high heat. Add garlic and cook, stirring constantly, until fragrant, 30 seconds to 1 minute. Stir in zucchini and squash and cook, stirring occasionally, until starting to soften and brown in places, about 5 minutes. Sprinkle flour over the vegetables; stir to coat. Stir in the remaining 1 cup broth and bring to a boil, stirring often. Reduce heat to medium-low and simmer, stirring occasionally, until thickened and the vegetables are tender, 1 to 3 minutes. Stir in basil; serve the sauté over the polenta.

Polenta with Creamy Mushroom Sauce

Slices of store-bought, prepared polenta make a great foundation for plenty of quick and tasty vegetarian entrees. Here, they are baked crisp and topped with a rich-tasting blend of full-flavored cremini and shiitake mushrooms nestled in a creamy sauce of sour cream and fontina cheese. If you like, mix it up by substituting another melting cheese, such as Gruyère or Cheddar. Serve this dish with a side of roasted asparagus or sautéed greens drizzled with olive oil and a squeeze of fresh lemon juice. (Photograph: page 110.)

- 1 **16-ounce tube prepared plain polenta (*see Note, page 219*), sliced into 8 rounds**
- 1 **tablespoon extra-virgin olive oil**
- 1/2 **cup minced onion**
- 1 **pound mushrooms, such as white or cremini, sliced**
- 2 **cups stemmed and sliced shiitake mushrooms (4 1/2 ounces with stems)**
- 1/4 **teaspoon salt**
- 1/4 **teaspoon freshly ground pepper**
- 1/2 **cup dry white wine**
- 1/2 **cup reduced-fat sour cream**
- 2/3 **cup shredded fontina, Gruyère *or* Swiss cheese**
- 2 **teaspoons minced fresh tarragon**

1. Preheat oven to 400°F. Coat a baking sheet with cooking spray.
2. Arrange the polenta on the prepared baking sheet and bake until crispy on the bottom and heated through, about 20 minutes.
3. Meanwhile, heat oil in a large skillet over medium-high heat. Add onion and cook, stirring often, until lightly browned, 2 to 3 minutes. Stir in mushrooms, salt and pepper, and cook, stirring often, until the mushrooms are softened and most of the liquid has evaporated, 8 to 10 minutes.
4. Pour in wine; bring to a boil and scrape up any browned bits from the bottom of the pan. Cook until the wine has almost evaporated, 2 to 3 minutes. Stir in sour cream and bring to a simmer. Remove from the heat, stir in cheese and tarragon. Serve the sauce over the polenta.

ACTIVE TIME: 25 minutes
TOTAL: 30 minutes

MAKES: 4 servings, 2 slices polenta & 3/4 cup sauce each

PER SERVING: 290 calories; 13 g fat (6 g sat, 5 g mono); 33 mg cholesterol; 27 g carbohydrate; 0 g added sugars; 12 g protein; 3 g fiber; 664 mg sodium; 564 mg potassium.
NUTRITION BONUS: Potassium (16% daily value).

Black Beans & Rice

ACTIVE TIME: 20 minutes

TOTAL: 2½ hours (plus soaking time)

TO MAKE AHEAD: Prepare through Step 3. Cover and refrigerate for up to 3 days. Reheat before serving.

MAKES: 8 servings, 1½ cups each

H✖W   H⬆F   H❤H

PER SERVING: 399 calories; 3 g fat (0 g sat, 1 g mono); 0 mg cholesterol; 76 g carbohydrate; 0 g added sugars; 16 g protein; 9 g fiber; 384 mg sodium; 167 mg potassium.

NUTRITION BONUS: Vitamin C (41% daily value), Iron (25% dv), Magnesium (20% dv).

Rice-and-bean combos appear in almost every cuisine in the world for three reasons: they're delicious, nutritionally balanced and economical. This recipe calls for dried beans rather than canned, because although we love the convenience of canned beans, cooking them from scratch gives you fabulous flavor and texture with very little effort. All you need to do is pick a time when you're around the house (even after dinner in the evening works well) and put on the pot of beans to slowly simmer unattended. Then you'll have dinner almost done for the next night, as well as leftovers that you can eat later in the week or throw in the freezer.

1   **pound dried black beans (3 cups), picked over and rinsed**
9   **cups water, divided**
6   **cloves garlic, crushed**
2   **tablespoons dried oregano**
1   **bay leaf**
2   **teaspoons extra-virgin olive oil**
1   **large onion, chopped**
1   **red bell pepper, chopped**
1   **tablespoon ground cumin**
1   **jalapeño pepper, seeded and chopped**
2   **tablespoons balsamic vinegar**
1¼ **teaspoons salt, divided**
    Freshly ground pepper to taste
2   **cups long-grain brown rice**
1   **lime, cut into 8 wedges**

1. Soak beans in cold water overnight. (*Alternatively, use the quick-soak method; see page 127.*)
2. Drain and rinse beans. Place in a soup pot or Dutch oven. Add 4 cups water, garlic, oregano and bay leaf. Bring to a boil. Reduce heat to low, cover and simmer until beans are tender, about 2 hours. Drain and return to the pot.
3. Heat oil in a large skillet over medium heat. Add onion and bell pepper; cook, stirring, until softened, about 5 minutes. Add cumin and jalapeño; cook, stirring, for 1 minute more. Stir the onion mixture and vinegar into beans. Season with ¼ teaspoon salt and pepper.
4. Meanwhile, bring the remaining 5 cups water and 1 teaspoon salt to a boil in a medium saucepan. Add rice, cover and reduce heat to low. Simmer until the rice is tender and the liquid is absorbed, 40 to 50 minutes. Let stand for 5 minutes, then fluff with a fork.
5. Serve the beans over the rice, with lime wedges on the side.

Baked Curried Brown Rice & Lentil Pilaf

In this recipe, satisfying lentils and brown jasmine rice get multiple layers of flavor from a single ingredient—red curry paste. The fragrant dish takes only 10 minutes to get in the oven, so it's weeknight fast. With the addition of a green side, such as Sesame-Seasoned Spinach (page 191), which you can prepare while the pilaf is in the oven, you have a complete supper in an hour.

1	tablespoon butter
1	cup brown basmati rice *or* brown jasmine rice
4¼	cups water
1	cup dried brown lentils
4	cloves garlic, peeled
1	cinnamon stick
4	⅛-inch-thick slices peeled fresh ginger
1-2	teaspoons red curry paste (*see Note*) *or* 1 tablespoon curry powder
½	teaspoon salt
4	scallions, sliced

1. Place rack in lower third of oven; preheat to 350°F.
2. Melt butter in an ovenproof Dutch oven over medium-high heat; add rice and cook, stirring, until lightly toasted, 1 to 2 minutes. (If using curry powder, add it now and cook, stirring, until fragrant, about 15 seconds.) Add water. Stir in lentils, garlic, cinnamon stick, ginger, curry paste, if using, and salt; bring to a boil, stirring to dissolve the curry paste.
3. Cover the pot tightly with a lid or foil. Transfer to the oven and bake until the rice and lentils are tender and all the water is absorbed, 50 to 55 minutes. Fluff with a fork, removing the cinnamon stick and ginger slices. Serve garnished with scallions.

ACTIVE TIME: 10 minutes
TOTAL: 1 hour

MAKES: 4 servings, 1¼ cups each

H✳W   H⬆F   H♥H
PER SERVING: 338 calories; 5 g fat (2 g sat, 1 g mono); 8 mg cholesterol; 62 g carbohydrate; 0 g added sugars; 16 g protein, 13 g fiber; 327 mg sodium; 578 mg potassium.
NUTRITION BONUS: Folate (65% daily value), Iron (31% dv), Potassium (17% dv).

NOTE: Red curry paste is a blend of chile peppers, garlic, lemongrass and galangal (a root with a flavor similar to ginger). The heat and salt level can vary widely depending on brand. Be sure to taste as you go. Look for it in the Asian section of the supermarket or specialty stores. Once opened, it will keep in the refrigerator for up to 1 year.

Barley Hoppin' John

Quick-cooking barley stands in for rice in this toothsome take on the classic Southern dish. The black-eyed peas make this Hoppin' John plenty satisfying and filling, but for an additional riff on the original, consider adding a cup of finely diced smoked tofu.

1   tablespoon extra-virgin olive oil
1   medium onion, chopped
1   small red bell pepper, chopped
2   stalks celery, chopped
2   cloves garlic, minced
1   14-ounce can vegetable broth
1   cup quick-cooking barley
1   tablespoon chopped fresh thyme *or* 1 teaspoon dried
2   teaspoons lemon juice
¼   teaspoon crushed red pepper
¼   teaspoon salt
2   15-ounce cans black-eyed peas, rinsed

Heat oil in a large nonstick skillet over medium heat. Add onion, bell pepper and celery. Cook until the vegetables soften, 3 to 4 minutes. Add garlic and cook 1 minute. Add broth, barley, thyme, lemon juice, crushed red pepper and salt; bring to a boil. Reduce heat, cover and simmer until the barley is tender, 15 to 20 minutes. Remove from the heat and stir in black-eyed peas. Cover and let stand for 5 minutes. Serve hot.

ACTIVE TIME: 20 minutes
TOTAL: 40 minutes

MAKES: 4 servings, 1½ cups each

H✖W   H⬆F   H♥H
PER SERVING: 320 calories; 5 g fat (1 g sat, 3 g mono); 0 mg cholesterol; 58 g carbohydrate; 0 g added sugars; 12 g protein; 11 g fiber; 677 mg sodium; 529 mg potassium.
NUTRITION BONUS: Vitamin C (58% daily value), Folate & Vitamin A (24% dv), Potassium (15% dv).

Wholesome Grains

On average, we get about half of our calories from grains. Americans tend to opt for less-nutritious refined grains (their nutrient-rich bran and germ have been removed) and products that contain processed flours, despite research that shows whole grains are healthier. Studies show that whole grains are protective against cancer, cardiovascular disease, diabetes and obesity. Here are some we like to keep on hand for simple side dishes instead of potatoes or pasta. Just cook them up and season with fresh herbs, sliced scallions, a squeeze of lemon or olive oil.

Barley is available "pearled" (the bran has been removed) or "quick cooking" (parboiled). Technically neither are whole grains but nutritionally speaking they count toward your whole-grain servings because of their high fiber content. (*Other recipes on pages 59, 113.*)

Bulgur is available in fine, medium and coarse textures. (If it's not labeled, it's usually fine or medium.) It is made by parboiling, drying and coarsely grinding or cracking wheat berries. Don't confuse bulgur with cracked wheat, which is simply that—cracked wheat. Since the parboiling step is skipped, cracked wheat must be cooked for up to an hour, whereas bulgur simply needs a quick soak in hot water for most uses. (*Recipes on pages 65, 84, 193, 195.*)

Quinoa is a delicately flavored, protein-rich grain. Rinsing removes any residue of saponin, quinoa's natural, bitter protective covering. Toast quinoa in a little oil before cooking to enhance its nutty flavor. (*Recipes on pages 83, 144.*)

Wheat Berries of any variety (hard, soft, spring or winter) can be used interchangeably. Labeling is inconsistent—you may find them labeled "hard red winter wheat" without the words "wheat berries." Some recipes instruct soaking overnight, but we found it unnecessary. (*Recipe on page 193.*)

Sweet Potato Fritters with Smoky Pinto Beans

ACTIVE TIME: 35 minutes
TOTAL: 45 minutes

MAKES: 4 servings, 2 fritters & ½ cup beans each

H↑F   H♥H

PER SERVING: 380 calories; 14 g fat (1 g sat, 7 g mono); 53 mg cholesterol; 57 g carbohydrate; 0 g added sugars; 10 g protein; 10 g fiber; 664 mg sodium; 780 mg potassium.
NUTRITION BONUS: Vitamin A (279% daily value), Vitamin C (110% dv), Folate (23% dv), Potassium (22% dv), Iron & Magnesium (20% dv).

NOTE: Smoked paprika is a spice made from ground smoke-dried red peppers. It's available in some large supermarkets with other spices and at *tienda.com*.

Just say the word fritters and chances are dinner will be a hit before it reaches the table. Here, crispy, golden sweet potato fritters are paired with a pinto bean and chile pepper topping that's scented with smoked sweet paprika, a signature Spanish seasoning. Best of all, you can have this crowd-pleaser on the table in about 45 minutes from start to finish. For added tang, serve with a dollop of reduced-fat sour cream or plain Greek-style yogurt. (Photograph: page 110.)

1	large sweet potato (about 1 pound)
3	tablespoons canola oil, divided
1	medium onion, chopped
2	large poblano peppers *or* small green bell peppers, chopped
1	15-ounce can pinto beans, rinsed
1¼	teaspoons smoked paprika (*see Note*), divided
¾	teaspoon salt, divided
¾	cup fine yellow cornmeal
¼	cup all-purpose flour
¾	teaspoon baking powder
1	large egg, lightly beaten
¼	cup water
4	lime wedges for garnish

1. Preheat oven to 425°F. Coat a baking sheet with cooking spray.
2. Prick sweet potato in several places with a fork. Microwave on High until just cooked through, 7 to 10 minutes. (*Alternatively, place in a baking dish and bake at 425°F until tender all the way to the center, about 1 hour.*) Set aside to cool.
3. Meanwhile, heat 1 tablespoon oil in a large saucepan over medium heat. Add onion and peppers and cook, stirring occasionally, until softened, 4 to 6 minutes. Set aside ½ cup of the mixture. Add beans, ½ teaspoon paprika and ¼ teaspoon salt to the pan. Cook, stirring occasionally, until heated through, about 2 minutes. Cover and set aside.
4. Whisk cornmeal, flour, baking powder, the remaining ¾ teaspoon paprika and ½ teaspoon salt in a medium bowl. Peel the sweet potato and mash in a large bowl with a fork. Stir in the reserved onion-pepper mixture, egg and water. Add the cornmeal mixture and stir until just combined.
5. Form the sweet potato mixture into eight 3-inch oval fritters, using a generous ¼ cup for each. Heat 1 tablespoon oil in a large nonstick skillet over medium heat. Cook 4 fritters until golden brown, 1 to 2 minutes per side. Transfer to the prepared baking sheet. Repeat with the remaining fritters and oil.
6. Bake the fritters until puffed and firm to the touch, 8 to 10 minutes. Serve the fritters with the reserved bean mixture and lime wedges, if desired.

Acorn Squash Stuffed with Chard & White Beans

Convenient canned white beans star in the savory, Italian-themed filling for sweet and tender acorn squash. Using the microwave cuts at least 30 minutes off the cooking time for the squash, but a few minutes under the broiler after stuffing gives the whole dish a lovely, golden-brown finish. Add a salad peppered with feisty-flavored greens, such as radicchio or arugula, and a glass of dry white wine to complete the meal. (Photograph: page 110.)

2 medium acorn squash, halved and seeded (*see Note*)
1 teaspoon plus 2 tablespoons extra-virgin olive oil, divided
1/2 teaspoon salt, divided
1/2 teaspoon freshly ground pepper, divided
1/2 cup chopped onion
2 cloves garlic, minced
2 tablespoons water
1 tablespoon tomato paste
8 cups chopped chard leaves (about 1 large bunch chard)
1 15-ounce can white beans, rinsed
1/4 cup chopped Kalamata olives
1/3 cup coarse dry whole-wheat breadcrumbs (*see Note, page 218*)
1/3 cup grated Parmesan cheese

1. Cut a small slice off the bottom of each squash half so it rests flat. Brush the insides with 1 teaspoon oil; sprinkle with ¼ teaspoon each salt and pepper. Place in a 9-by-13-inch (or similar-size) microwave-safe dish. Cover with microwave-safe plastic wrap and microwave on High until the squash is fork-tender, about 12 minutes.

2. Meanwhile, heat 1 tablespoon oil in a large skillet over medium heat. Add onion; cook, stirring, until starting to brown, 2 to 3 minutes. Add garlic; cook, stirring, for 1 minute. Stir in water, tomato paste and the remaining ¼ teaspoon each salt and pepper. Stir in chard, cover and cook until tender, 3 to 5 minutes. Stir in white beans and olives; cook until heated through, 1 to 2 minutes more. Remove from the heat.

3. Position rack in center of oven; preheat broiler.

4. Combine breadcrumbs, Parmesan and the remaining 1 tablespoon oil in a bowl. Fill each squash half with about 1 cup of the chard mixture. Place in a baking pan or on a baking sheet. Sprinkle with the breadcrumb mixture. Broil in the center of the oven until the breadcrumbs are browned, 1 to 2 minutes.

ACTIVE TIME: 40 minutes
TOTAL: 40 minutes

MAKES: 4 servings

PER SERVING: 342 calories; 13 g fat (3 g sat, 8 g mono); 6 mg cholesterol; 49 g carbohydrate; 0 g added sugars; 11 g protein; 12 g fiber; 665 mg sodium; 1,154 mg potassium.
NUTRITION BONUS: Vitamin A (99% daily value), Vitamin C (63% dv), Magnesium & Potassium (33% dv), Iron (20% dv), Calcium (19%).

NOTE: Remove the seeds and stringy fibers from **acorn squash** with a spoon.

Black Bean Quesadillas

Quick, delicious and satisfying—these spicy cheese-and-bean quesadillas win the weeknight supper triple crown, hands down. Turn the avocado and salsa into guacamole if you prefer: just mash together with a squeeze of lime juice and a pinch of salt.

1   15-ounce can black beans, rinsed
½   cup shredded Monterey Jack cheese, preferably pepper Jack
½   cup prepared fresh salsa (*see Note, page 219*), divided
4   8-inch whole-wheat tortillas
2   teaspoons canola oil, divided
1   ripe avocado, diced

1. Combine beans, cheese and ¼ cup salsa in a medium bowl. Place tortillas on a work surface. Spread ½ cup filling on half of each tortilla. Fold tortillas in half, pressing gently to flatten.
2. Heat 1 teaspoon oil in a large nonstick skillet over medium heat. Add 2 quesadillas and cook, turning once, until golden on both sides, 2 to 4 minutes total. Transfer to a cutting board and tent with foil to keep warm. Repeat with the remaining 1 teaspoon oil and quesadillas. Serve the quesadillas with avocado and the remaining salsa.

ACTIVE TIME: 15 minutes
TOTAL: 15 minutes

MAKES: 4 servings

H↑F

PER SERVING: 375 calories; 16 g fat (4 g sat, 8 g mono); 13 mg cholesterol; 45 g carbohydrate; 0 g added sugars; 13 g protein; 10 g fiber; 599 mg sodium; 486 mg potassium.
NUTRITION BONUS: Calcium (24% daily value), Folate (22% dv), Iron (18% dv).

How to Cook Beans

By cooking your own dried beans, you save money, reduce sodium and get better flavor. Freeze any extra cooked beans to use in soups, salads and dips. The range of time for cooking beans varies *widely* with the age and type of beans selected.

SOAKING

To soak or not to soak? Soaking beans before cooking helps them to cook more evenly and cuts down on the total cooking time. So if you've planned ahead, soak them. If you don't have time, skip the soaking, but plan to cook the beans longer. Fresher beans, which are less dry, need less soaking time than beans that were harvested more than a year ago.

Overnight Soak: Rinse and pick over the beans, then place in a large bowl with enough cold water to cover them by 2 inches. Let the beans soak for at least 8 hours or overnight. Drain.

Quick Soak: Rinse and pick over the beans, then place them in a large pot with enough cold water to cover them by 2 inches. Bring to a boil. Boil for 2 minutes. Remove from the heat and let stand, covered, for 1 hour; drain.

EQUIVALENTS

1 pound dried beans (about 2 cups) = 5-6 cups cooked
19-ounce can = about 2 cups beans
15-ounce can = about 1½ cups beans

COOKING

Conventional Method: Place (drained) soaked beans in a large pot. Add enough cold water to cover them by 2 inches (about 2 quarts of water for 1 pound of beans). Bring to a boil, skimming off any foam that rises to the surface. Reduce the heat to low and simmer gently, stirring occasionally, until the beans are tender, 20 minutes to 3 hours (cooking time will vary with the type and age of bean). Add salt to taste.

Pressure Cooker: Place (drained) soaked beans in a 4-quart or larger pressure cooker. Add 3 cups water and 1 tablespoon oil for each cup of beans. Secure the lid and bring to high pressure over high heat. Reduce heat to lowest setting that maintains high pressure and cook until tender. *Suggested timing: black beans: 12 minutes; cannellini: 16 minutes; chickpeas: 12 minutes; pinto: 10 minutes.* Let pressure release naturally before removing the lid.

Slow Cooker: Place (drained) soaked beans in a slow cooker. Add 5 cups boiling water. Cover and cook on High until tender, 1 to 3½ hours. Add salt to taste; cook 15 minutes more.

Spicy Kidney Bean & Bell Pepper Ragout

ACTIVE TIME: 20 minutes
TOTAL: 45 minutes

MAKES: 4 servings

H✖W H⬆F H♥H
PER SERVING: 241 calories; 6 g fat
(1 g sat, 2 g mono); 0 mg cholesterol;
42 g carbohydrate; 0 g added sugars;
10 g protein; 14 g fiber; 751 mg
sodium; 1,160 mg potassium.
NUTRITION BONUS: Vitamin C (207%
daily value), Vitamin A (59% dv),
Potassium (33% dv), Folate (32% dv),
Iron (28% dv), Magnesium (22% dv),
Calcium (15% dv).

Smoky chipotle peppers are simmered with two kinds of bell peppers and canned tomatoes to make the base for this full-flavored ragout. Kidney beans add earthy flavor and texture along with protein to make this quick-to-prepare sauce a filling meal. Serve over long-grain brown rice.

1   tablespoon canola oil
2   large onions, chopped
3   cloves garlic, finely chopped
2   tablespoons chili powder
1   tablespoon chopped chipotle pepper in adobo sauce, or to taste
2   teaspoons ground cumin
1   teaspoon dried oregano
1   28-ounce can plum tomatoes (with juices), chopped
1   large green bell pepper, chopped
1   large red bell pepper, chopped
2   small zucchini, chopped
¼   teaspoon salt
    Freshly ground pepper to taste
1   19-ounce can red kidney beans, rinsed
6   tablespoons reduced-fat sour cream *or* nonfat plain yogurt for garnish
    Fresh cilantro leaves for garnish

1. Heat oil in a large cast-iron or nonstick skillet over medium heat. Add onions and cook, stirring, until soft and lightly browned, 5 to 10 minutes. Add garlic, chili powder, chipotle, cumin and oregano; cook, stirring, for 1 minute. Add tomatoes, green and red bell peppers, zucchini, salt and pepper. Bring to a boil over medium-high heat. Reduce heat to low and simmer, partially covered, stirring often, until the juices have thickened and the vegetables are tender, about 20 minutes.
2. Add beans and simmer, covered, stirring often, for 10 minutes; add a little water to thin, if necessary. Taste and adjust seasonings. Serve garnished with a dollop of sour cream (or yogurt) and a sprinkling of cilantro.

Portobello Paillards with Spinach, White Beans & Caramelized Onions

Here's a meatless meal that will even please a carnivore. Toothsome portobello mushrooms are dredged in breadcrumbs and pan-griddled until golden and crisp. A hearty topping of white beans and garlicky spinach plus layers of sweet, caramelized red onions balanced with salty Manchego cheese make this entree a satisfying meal. To make this dish vegan, use soymilk instead of milk and omit the cheese. Try garnishing with chopped fresh herbs instead. Serve with slabs of grilled whole-grain bread.

ACTIVE TIME: 1 hour

TOTAL: 1 hour

MAKES: 4 servings

PER SERVING: 359 calories; 17 g fat (3 g sat, 11 g mono); 5 mg cholesterol; 43 g carbohydrate; 0 g added sugars; 15 g protein; 11 g fiber; 721 mg sodium; 1,506 mg potassium.

NUTRITION BONUS: Vitamin A (217% daily value), Folate (88% dv), Vitamin C (70% dv), Potassium (43% dv), Iron (31% dv), Magnesium (27% dv), Calcium (26% dv), Zinc (18% dv).

4	tablespoons extra-virgin olive oil, divided
1	large red onion, halved and thinly sliced
1/2	teaspoon freshly ground pepper, divided
1/4	teaspoon salt, divided
1/3	cup low-fat milk *or* soymilk
1/2	cup plain dry breadcrumbs
4	portobello mushroom caps, 3-4 inches in diameter
3	cloves garlic, minced
1	pound spinach, tough stems removed
1	15-ounce can white beans, rinsed
3/4	cup vegetable broth
1/2	cup shredded Manchego, Gruyère *or* Parmesan cheese (optional)

1. Heat 1 tablespoon oil in a medium nonstick skillet over medium heat. Add onion and cook, stirring occasionally, until brown, 8 to 10 minutes. Reduce heat to very low, season with 1/4 teaspoon pepper and 1/8 teaspoon salt. Continue cooking, stirring occasionally, until caramelized, about 15 minutes. Transfer to a bowl and keep warm.

2. Meanwhile, place milk (or soymilk) in a small shallow bowl and place breadcrumbs on a large plate. Dip each mushroom cap in the milk, then dredge in the breadcrumbs.

3. Heat 1 tablespoon oil in a large nonstick skillet over medium heat. Add mushrooms, gill-side down. Place a heavy, heatproof plate or pie pan on top of the mushrooms and cook until golden brown, pressing down on the plate periodically to flatten them, about 6 minutes. Carefully remove the plate using an oven mitt or tongs, add 1 tablespoon oil to the pan and turn the mushrooms over. Replace the plate and cook, pressing the plate once or twice, until the mushrooms are golden brown and cooked through, 5 to 6 minutes more. Remove from heat; cover to keep warm.

4. Heat the remaining 1 tablespoon oil in a Dutch oven over medium-high heat. Add garlic and cook until fragrant, 20 to 30 seconds. Add spinach and cook, stirring, until just wilted, about 2 minutes. Stir in beans, broth and the remaining 1/4 teaspoon pepper and 1/8 teaspoon salt. Cook, stirring occasionally, until heated through, 1 to 2 minutes.

5. Cut each mushroom into thin slices and serve over the spinach, topped with the reserved onions and cheese (if using).

147

146

137

143

TOFU, TEMPEH & SEITAN

Because they are good sources of protein, tofu, tempeh and seitan are often thought of as meat substitutes in vegetarian meals. But don't just treat them like meat: each ingredient has its own unique qualities to consider. Tofu is an amazing sponge for flavor, so it takes well to marinating. Seitan, which is made from wheat gluten, has a wonderful chewy texture that is closest to that of meat. And tempeh, made from fermented soy, has an assertive nutty flavor. We like it paired with other bold flavors, as in the Smothered Tempeh Sandwich (*page 143*), made with provolone cheese and a red-wine sauce.

Soy-Lime Roasted Tofu

ACTIVE TIME: 10 minutes

TOTAL: 1½ hours (including 1 hour marinating time)

TO MAKE AHEAD: Marinate for up to 4 hours. Refrigerate roasted tofu for up to 3 days.

MAKES: 2 servings, about 1 cup each

H✖W   H♥H

PER SERVING: 155 calories; 10 g fat (2 g sat, 3 g mono); 0 mg cholesterol; 4 g carbohydrate; 0 g added sugars; 16 g protein; 2 g fiber; 131 mg sodium; 303 mg potassium.

NUTRITION BONUS: Calcium (40% daily value), Magnesium (19% dv), Iron (18% dv).

This is one of the simplest ways to prepare tofu, yet the salty, tangy results will not disappoint. Eat it warm or cold, included in a quick stir-fry, served on a salad, tossed with some cold peanut noodles or just on its own as a snack.

1   **14-ounce package extra-firm water-packed tofu, drained**
⅓   **cup reduced-sodium soy sauce**
⅓   **cup lime juice**
3   **tablespoons toasted sesame oil**

1. Pat tofu dry and cut into ½- to ¾-inch cubes. Combine soy sauce, lime juice and oil in a medium shallow dish or large sealable plastic bag. Add the tofu; gently toss to combine. Marinate in the refrigerator, gently stirring once or twice, for 1 hour or up to 4 hours.
2. Preheat oven to 450°F.
3. Remove the tofu from the marinade with a slotted spoon (discard marinade). Spread out on a large baking sheet, making sure the pieces are not touching. Roast, gently turning halfway through, until golden brown, about 20 minutes.

How Healthy Is Soy Really?

Packed with high-quality protein and fiber, soy in all its forms (tofu, edamame, soymilk, etc.) would seem to be a naturally healthful choice. Not always, say some experts. Here are the pros and cons. —*Amy Paturel, M.S., M.P.H.*

+ HEART Eating 25 grams of soy protein daily (about 1¼ cups of tofu or edamame) may help lower your "bad" LDL and total cholesterol levels, suggests a review of 30 studies. One hypothesis is that soy protein lowers cholesterol by helping the liver clear more LDL from the body.

+ PROSTATE Studies in Asia show that men who consume about two servings of soy per day are about 30 percent less likely to develop prostate cancer than those who eat less soy.

+ MENOPAUSE Soy is high in isoflavones, compounds that act as weak estrogens, and a new analysis of 17 studies shows consuming isoflavones from soy halves the frequency and severity of hot flashes.

— THYROID Soy isoflavones may inhibit your ability to make thyroid hormones (they play a role in everything from metabolism to body temperature), which over time could cause thyroid problems, such as hypothyroidism (a condition characterized by weight gain, fatigue and cold intolerance).

Other studies say that soy only affects thyroid function in those low in iodine—a deficiency rare in the U.S.

+/— BONES Because soy isoflavones can mimic estrogen (which helps maintain bone mass), eating soy should help protect against bone loss, but the bulk of the research has concluded that isoflavones do not prevent bone loss. Soybeans also contain phytic acid, a natural plant substance that interferes with the absorption of bone-building calcium.

+/— BREASTS While there have been concerns about soy and breast health, recent research shows that women who ate one daily serving of whole soyfoods—such as edamame or tofu—through adolescence lowered their breast-cancer risk later in life by up to 50 percent. Unfortunately, eating soy as an adult does not decrease risk.

Bottom line: A little soy—experts recommend eating just one to two servings a day—can be good for you. (One serving = ½ cup tofu or shelled edamame or 1 cup soymilk.)

Sesame-Maple Roasted Tofu & Snap Peas

Roasting cubes of tofu at high temperatures firms up the outside, crisps the edges and leaves the insides moist and creamy. In this quick but good-enough-for-company dinner, roasted tofu and crispy snap peas are tossed in a sweet and nutty tahini-maple sauce. Serve over soba or udon noodles.

1	14-ounce package extra-firm water-packed tofu, drained
1	medium red onion, sliced
2	teaspoons canola oil
2	teaspoons toasted sesame oil
1/4	teaspoon salt
1/4	teaspoon freshly ground pepper
1	tablespoon tahini (*see Note*)
1	tablespoon reduced-sodium soy sauce
2	teaspoons pure maple syrup
1	teaspoon cider vinegar
3	cups sugar snap peas, trimmed
1	tablespoon sesame seeds

1. Preheat oven to 450°F.
2. Pat tofu dry and cut into 1-inch cubes. Toss the tofu, onion, canola oil, sesame oil, salt and pepper in a large bowl. Spread on a large baking sheet. Roast until the tofu is lightly golden on top and the onions are browning in spots, 15 to 20 minutes.
3. Whisk tahini, soy sauce, maple syrup and vinegar in a small bowl until combined. Remove the tofu from the oven, add snap peas and drizzle with the maple sauce; stir to combine. Sprinkle with sesame seeds. Return to the oven and continue roasting until the peas are crisp-tender, 8 to 12 minutes more.

ACTIVE TIME: 20 minutes
TOTAL: 45 minutes

MAKES: 4 servings, about 1¼ cups each

H✂W H♥H
PER SERVING: 192 calories; 12 g fat (2 g sat, 4 g mono); 0 mg cholesterol; 12 g carbohydrate; 2 g added sugars; 11 g protein; 3 g fiber; 300 mg sodium; 337 mg potassium.
NUTRITION BONUS: Vitamin C (62% daily value), Calcium (26% dv), Iron (19% dv), Magnesium (15% dv).

NOTE: Tahini is a thick paste of ground sesame seeds. Look for it in large supermarkets in the Middle Eastern section or near other nut butters.

Red-Cooked Tofu with Mushrooms

ACTIVE TIME: 45 minutes
TOTAL: 1 hour

MAKES: 4 servings, about 1 1/2 cups each

H✖W   H♥H
PER SERVING: 169 calories; 6 g fat
(1 g sat, 2 g mono); 0 mg cholesterol;
18 g carbohydrate; 1 g added sugars;
12 g protein; 4 g fiber; 709 mg sodium;
532 mg potassium.
NUTRITION BONUS: Calcium (23% daily
value), Magnesium (17% dv), Iron
(16% dv).

NOTE: **Vegetarian "oyster" sauce** is made
from mushroom extract and is great
for adding depth of flavor to vegetarian
stir-fries. Vegetarian "stir-fry sauce,"
also made from mushrooms, can be
used as a substitute.

"Red-cooking" is a traditional Chinese braising technique using soy sauce, which turns the food a gorgeous reddish brown color. A quick version of the technique is used here to transform mushrooms and tofu into a rich, earthy, saucy dish. Serve over steamed brown rice or as a soup.

1   14-ounce package firm water-packed tofu, cut into 1-inch-thick slabs
6   dried shiitake *or* Chinese black mushrooms
1   cup hot water
2   cups "no-chicken" broth (*see Note, page 218*) *or* vegetable broth
2   tablespoons reduced-sodium soy sauce
1 1/2 tablespoons vegetarian "oyster" sauce (*see Note*)
1   tablespoon Shao Hsing rice wine *or* dry sherry (*see Notes, page 219*)
1   teaspoon sugar
1   teaspoon canola oil
1   medium leek, white part only, halved lengthwise, rinsed well and cut into
        1-inch lengths
1   tablespoon minced garlic
8   ounces white mushrooms, trimmed and halved
4   ounces fresh shiitake mushrooms, stemmed and halved
1   tablespoon cornstarch mixed with 2 tablespoons water

1. Fold a clean kitchen towel and place it on a cutting board or large plate. Set tofu on the towel. Put another folded clean towel over the tofu and place a flat, heavy weight (such as a skillet) on top; drain for 30 minutes.
2. Meanwhile, place dried shiitakes (or black mushrooms) in a measuring cup, cover with hot water and set aside for 20 minutes. Drain, reserving the soaking liquid. Discard the mushroom stems and cut the caps in half. Set aside.
3. Stir the reserved mushroom-soaking liquid, broth, soy sauce, "oyster" sauce, rice wine (or sherry) and sugar in a small bowl until the sugar has dissolved.
4. Cut the pressed tofu into 1/2-inch cubes. Heat oil in a wok or large nonstick skillet over medium-high heat until shimmering. Add the reserved mushrooms, leek and garlic; cook, stirring, until fragrant, 10 to 15 seconds. Add the broth mixture and bring to a boil. Add the tofu, white mushrooms and fresh shiitakes and return to a boil. Reduce heat to maintain a gentle boil and simmer until the liquid is reduced by half, 10 to 15 minutes.
5. Stir cornstarch and water mixture. Add to the pan and cook, stirring, until the sauce is thickened, about 1 minute.

Garden-Fresh Stir-Fry with Seitan

ACTIVE TIME: 35 minutes
TOTAL: 35 minutes

MAKES: 4 servings, 1½ cups each

H✖W   H↑F   H♥H

PER SERVING: 327 calories; 12 g fat
(1 g sat, 7 g mono); 0 mg cholesterol;
32 g carbohydrate; 6 g added sugars;
20 g protein; 12 g fiber; 705 mg
sodium; 436 mg potassium.
NUTRITION BONUS: Vitamin A (241% daily
value), Vitamin C (137% dv).

NOTE: Seitan is processed wheat gluten
that is high in protein and has a meaty
texture. It can be found in natural-foods
stores or large supermarkets near the
tofu. The actual weight of the seitan in
a package varies depending on whether
water weight is included. Look for the
"drained weight" on the label. We used
two types of White Wave seitan: one
has a 1-pound 2-ounce water-packed
package containing "8 ounces drained"
seitan and one comes in a package
labeled "8 ounces" that actually contains
8 ounces of seitan.

When you're in the mood for a protein that's a bit more toothsome than tofu, seitan is a good bet. For a wide selection of varieties, look in Asian markets for mock duck, chicken and even mock squid and abalone. These flavored, textured wheat glutens are great for stir-fries, braises and curries. Here, seitan is cooked into a tasty stir-fry that takes less time to prepare than a trip to your local Chinese takeout joint. (Photograph: page 3.)

½   **cup dry sherry *or* Shao Hsing rice wine (*see Notes, page 219*)**
½   **cup water**
2   **tablespoons brown sugar**
2   **tablespoons lime juice**
2   **tablespoons hoisin sauce (*see Note, page 219*)**
2   **teaspoons cornstarch**
¼   **teaspoon salt**
2   **tablespoons canola oil, divided**
1   **pound water-packed seitan (*see Note*), preferably chicken-style,
      drained, patted dry and broken into bite-size pieces**
¼   **cup chopped unsalted peanuts**
2   **teaspoons minced fresh ginger**
4   **carrots, thinly sliced**
2   **bell peppers, thinly sliced**
¼   **cup chopped fresh cilantro (optional)**

1. Whisk sherry (or rice wine), water, brown sugar, lime juice, hoisin, cornstarch and salt in a small bowl.
2. Heat 1 tablespoon oil in a large nonstick skillet over medium-high heat. Add seitan; cook, stirring occasionally, until crispy, 4 to 6 minutes. Stir in the remaining 1 tablespoon oil, peanuts and ginger. Cook, stirring often, until fragrant, about 1 minute. Add carrots and bell peppers and cook, stirring constantly, about 1 minute.
3. Whisk the sauce and add to the pan; stir to coat. Reduce heat to medium, cover and cook until the vegetables are crisp-tender and the sauce is thickened, 3 to 4 minutes. Stir in cilantro, if using.

Tofu with Thai Curry Sauce

Canned or jarred curry pastes are truly one of the most versatile items to stock in your pantry. From one inexpensive ingredient you get instant, complex flavor to use as a foundation for soups, stews, marinades and more. In this incredibly quick dish, red curry paste is used to flavor a creamy curry sauce that gives humble tofu a spicy, satisfying kick. You can adjust the amount of curry paste depending on your taste for heat. Serve with brown basmati rice and lime wedges. (Photograph: page 130.)

SAUCE

- **1** cup "lite" coconut milk (*see Note*)
- **2** tablespoons chopped fresh cilantro
- **1** teaspoon red curry paste (*see Note, page 219*), or to taste
- **½** teaspoon brown sugar
- **½** teaspoon salt, or to taste

TOFU & VEGETABLES

- **1** 14-ounce package extra-firm water-packed tofu
- **2** teaspoons extra-virgin olive oil
- **4** cups baby spinach (about 6 ounces)
- **1** red bell pepper, sliced

1. **To prepare sauce:** Whisk coconut milk, cilantro, curry paste, brown sugar and salt in a small bowl.
2. **To prepare tofu:** Drain and rinse tofu; pat dry. Slice the block crosswise into eight ½-inch-thick slabs. Coarsely crumble each slice into smaller, uneven pieces.
3. Heat oil in a large nonstick skillet over medium-high heat. Add tofu and cook in a single layer, without stirring, until the pieces begin to turn golden brown on the bottom, 5 to 7 minutes. Then gently stir and continue cooking, stirring occasionally, until all sides are golden brown, 5 to 7 minutes more.
4. Add spinach, bell pepper and the curry sauce and cook, stirring, until the vegetables are just cooked, 1 to 2 minutes more.

ACTIVE TIME: 20 minutes
TOTAL: 20 minutes

MAKES: 4 servings, generous ¾ cup each

H✷W

PER SERVING: 162 calories; 11 g fat (4 g sat, 3 g mono); 0 mg cholesterol; 8 g carbohydrate; 1 g added sugars; 11 g protein; 3 g fiber; 365 mg sodium; 397 mg potassium.
NUTRITION BONUS: Vitamin C (102% daily value), Vitamin A (97% dv), Calcium (25% dv), Folate (22% dv), Magnesium (18% dv), Iron (17% dv).

NOTE: Refrigerate any leftover **coconut milk** for up to 1 week or freeze for up to 2 months. It will appear separated when thawed; simply mix until smooth.

Sesame-Crusted Tofu over Vegetables

ACTIVE TIME: 45 minutes

TOTAL: 1 3/4 hours

MAKES: 4 servings, about 1 1/2 cups each

H✖W   H⬆F   H❤H

PER SERVING: 232 calories; 12 g fat
(2 g sat, 4 g mono); 0 mg cholesterol;
19 g carbohydrate; 0 g added sugars;
14 g protein; 5 g fiber; 483 mg sodium;
1,006 mg potassium.
NUTRITION BONUS: Vitamin C (172%
daily value), Vitamin A (171% dv),
Calcium (44% dv), Folate (33% dv),
Iron & Potassium (29% dv), Magnesium
(23% dv).

NOTE: **Mirin** is a sweet, low-alcohol rice
wine essential in Japanese cooking.
Look for it in your supermarket with
other Asian ingredients.

Extra-firm tofu gets marinated, sesame-crusted and then sauced in this sophisticated stir-fry. The recipe packs enough vegetables that all you need to add is a little short-grain brown rice to make it a meal. (Photograph: page 214.)

TOFU & MARINADE

- 1   14-ounce package extra-firm water-packed tofu, drained
- 2   cloves garlic, minced
- 1/2   tablespoon grated *or* minced fresh ginger
- 1   teaspoon reduced-sodium soy sauce
- 1   teaspoon mirin (*see Note*) or dry sherry
- 1   teaspoon chile-garlic sauce (*see Note, page 218*)
- 1/2   teaspoon toasted sesame oil

SAUCE

- 1/2   cup water *or* vegetable broth
- 3   tablespoons reduced-sodium soy sauce
- 2   tablespoons mirin *or* sherry
- 2   teaspoons chile-garlic sauce
- 2   teaspoons cornstarch
- 1   teaspoon toasted sesame oil

VEGETABLES

- 2   tablespoons sesame seeds
- 1   tablespoon peanut oil, divided
- 3   cloves garlic, minced
- 1   tablespoon grated fresh ginger
- 1 1/2   pounds bok choy, trimmed and very coarsely chopped
- 1   red bell pepper, cut into 1-inch pieces
- 1   bunch scallions, trimmed and cut into 1-inch pieces
- 1 1/2   cups snow peas, trimmed

1. **To prepare tofu & marinade:** Fold a clean kitchen towel and place it on a cutting board or large plate. Set tofu on the towel. Put another folded clean towel over the tofu and place a flat, heavy weight (such as a skillet) on top; drain for 30 minutes.

2. Combine garlic, ginger, soy sauce, mirin (or sherry), chile-garlic sauce and sesame oil in a bowl. Cut the drained tofu into 1-inch cubes. Add to the marinade and toss to coat. Cover and let marinate in the refrigerator for 30 minutes.

3. **To prepare sauce:** Whisk water (or broth), soy sauce, mirin (or sherry), chile-garlic sauce, cornstarch and sesame oil in a small bowl. Set aside.

4. **To stir-fry tofu & vegetables:** Toss the tofu with sesame seeds in a large bowl. Heat 1½ teaspoons peanut oil in a large nonstick skillet over medium heat. Add the tofu and cook, turning often, until golden and crusty, 8 to 10 minutes. Cover and keep warm.

5. Heat the remaining 1½ teaspoons peanut oil in a wok or large nonstick skillet over medium-high heat. Add garlic and ginger; cook, stirring, until fragrant, about 30 seconds. Add bok choy, bell pepper, scallions and snow peas; cook, stirring, until the vegetables are crisp-tender, 5 to 7 minutes.

6. Make a well in the vegetables; whisk the reserved sauce and add to the center of the pan. Bring the sauce to a boil, stirring, until thickened. Toss the vegetables with the sauce. Transfer to a large shallow serving bowl and top with the tofu.

Stir-Fried Vegetables in Black Bean Sauce

This fragrant stir-fry could also be called triple-soy delight: a rich, complex sauce made from fermented black soybeans and soy sauce envelops tofu and crisp vegetables. Fermented black beans, which are preserved in salt and flavored with ginger, are available in Asian grocery stores, as is five-spice powder, a blend of cinnamon, aniseed, coriander, ginger and black pepper. Serve over rice noodles or brown rice.

2	14-ounce packages firm water-packed tofu, drained
4½	tablespoons Shao Hsing rice wine *or* sake (*see Notes, page 219*), divided
2½	tablespoons reduced-sodium soy sauce, divided
1	teaspoon Chinese five-spice powder (*see Note, page 218*)
½	teaspoon toasted sesame oil
½	cup vegetable broth *or* water
1	tablespoon cornstarch
2	teaspoons sugar
¼	teaspoon freshly ground pepper
1	tablespoon canola oil
6	cloves garlic, minced
2	tablespoons fermented black beans *or* 1 tablespoon black bean-garlic sauce (*see Notes*)
1½	tablespoons minced fresh ginger
1	teaspoon chile-garlic sauce (*see Note, page 218*)
1	red bell pepper, cut into thin strips
1	yellow bell pepper, cut into thin strips
2	cups snow peas, strings removed
2	cups chopped scallions greens

1. Cut each block of tofu in half horizontally, making two large slices about 1 inch thick. Fold a clean kitchen towel and place it on a cutting board or large plate. Set the tofu on the towel. Put another folded clean towel over the tofu and place a flat, heavy weight (such as a skillet) on top; drain for 30 minutes.
2. Stir together 2 tablespoons rice wine (or sake), 1 tablespoon soy sauce, five-spice powder and sesame oil in a medium bowl. Cut the drained tofu into 1-inch pieces. Add to the marinade and toss to coat. Cover and let stand at room temperature for 25 minutes.
3. Position a rack 4 to 6 inches from the heat source; preheat broiler. Line a large baking sheet with foil and spread the tofu on it in an even layer. Broil, turning once, until lightly browned and crisp, 8 to 10 minutes total.
4. Meanwhile, stir together 1½ tablespoons rice wine (or sake), the remaining 1½ tablespoons soy sauce, broth (or water), cornstarch, sugar and pepper in a small bowl. Place next to the stove.
5. Heat oil in a large nonstick skillet or wok over medium-high heat. Add garlic, black beans (or black bean-garlic sauce), ginger and chile-garlic sauce and cook, stirring, until fragrant, 10 to 15 seconds. Add bell peppers and cook, stirring, for 1 minute. Add snow peas and the remaining 1 tablespoon rice wine (or sake) and cook, stirring, for 30 seconds. Add scallion greens and the reserved sauce mixture and cook, stirring, until thickened, about 45 seconds. Add the tofu and toss to coat.

ACTIVE TIME: 55 minutes

TOTAL: 1 hour 20 minutes

MAKES: 4 servings, about 2 cups each

H✕W   H⬆F   H❤H

PER SERVING: 273 calories; 12 g fat (2 g sat, 5 g mono); 0 mg cholesterol; 24 g carbohydrate; 2 g added sugars; 18 g protein; 5 g fiber; 793 mg sodium; 650 mg potassium.

NUTRITION BONUS: Vitamin C (200% daily value), Calcium (42% dv), Vitamin A (38% dv), Iron (30% dv), Folate (24% dv), Magnesium (23% dv), Potassium (18% dv).

NOTES:

Fermented black beans, oxidized soybeans that are salt-dried, have a savory, salty and slightly bitter flavor. They are frequently used in Chinese stir-fries, marinades and sauces. Before using, they should be soaked in water for 10 to 30 minutes to get rid of excess salt. When purchasing fermented black beans, look for shiny and firm beans (avoid dull and dry beans with salt spots). Once open, store airtight in the refrigerator for up to 1 year.

Black bean-garlic sauce, made from pureed salted and fermented black soybeans, is a widely used condiment in Chinese cooking and can be found with the Asian food in most supermarkets.

Vegan Migas

Crumbled soft tofu is often used to make satisfying, egg-free scrambles so it's a natural for a vegan interpretation of migas, a traditional Tex-Mex dish made with eggs and strips of corn tortillas. In this version, fresh chiles, chipotle and cilantro balance the neutrality of the tofu. Serve with a side of black beans.

ACTIVE TIME: 30 minutes
TOTAL: 30 minutes

MAKES: 4 servings

H✗W   H↑F   H♥H
PER SERVING: 334 calories; 14 g fat (2 g sat, 6 g mono); 0 mg cholesterol; 42 g carbohydrate; 0 g added sugars; 14 g protein; 7 g fiber; 391 mg sodium; 655 mg potassium.
NUTRITION BONUS: Folate (60% daily value), Vitamin C (40% dv), Vitamin A (30% dv), Calcium (29% dv), Magnesium (26% dv), Potassium (19% dv), Iron (18% dv).

1	14-ounce package soft tofu, preferably water-packed
1	teaspoon plus 1 tablespoon canola oil, divided
3	corn tortillas, preferably stale, torn into strips
	Pinch of ground turmeric
1-2	jalapeño *or* serrano chiles, finely diced, seeded if less heat is desired
½	teaspoon ground chipotle chile *or* smoked paprika (*see Notes, pages 218-219*), or more to taste
4	scallions, trimmed and chopped
½	teaspoon kosher salt
¼	cup chopped fresh cilantro
2	plum tomatoes, diced
½	cup shredded nondairy cheese
1	cup Salsa Ranchera (*page 23*) *or* other salsa
8	corn tortillas, warmed (*see Note, page 219*)

1. Drain tofu in a fine-meshed sieve over a bowl.
2. Meanwhile, heat 1 teaspoon oil in a medium nonstick skillet over medium heat. Add tortilla strips and cook, stirring frequently, until golden and crispy, 7 to 9 minutes. Transfer to a plate.
3. Add the remaining 1 tablespoon oil to the pan and return to medium heat. When hot, crumble the tofu into the pan in various-sized pieces to resemble scrambled eggs. Stir in turmeric, chiles to taste, ground chipotle (or paprika) and scallions; season with salt. Cook, stirring often, until the water remaining in the tofu has cooked away, but not so long that the tofu turns hard, 4 to 6 minutes. It should remain tender, like eggs.
4. Add cilantro, tomatoes, cheese and the tortilla strips. Cook, stirring, until the cheese has melted, 1 to 2 minutes. Divide among 4 plates, using a slotted spoon so that liquid remains in the pan. Serve with Salsa Ranchera (or other salsa) and warm tortillas.

Smothered Tempeh Sandwich

For this hot and hearty sandwich, toasty slices of whole-grain bread are topped with slabs of tempeh cooked with red wine and mushrooms and topped with melted provolone cheese (or your favorite nondairy cheese). For variety, choose among the different soy, grain and rice blends of tempeh that are available at most well-stocked markets.

- 1   8-ounce package tempeh (*see Note*)
- 1   tablespoon canola oil
- 10 ounces mushrooms, sliced
- 1   small red onion, thinly sliced
- 1/4 teaspoon salt
- 1   cup dry red wine
- 4   ounces sliced provolone cheese
- 8   thin slices whole-wheat bread, toasted

1. Cut tempeh in half widthwise, then slice each piece horizontally to make 4 thin slices total.
2. Heat oil in a large nonstick skillet over medium-high heat. Add mushrooms, onion and salt and cook, stirring often, until golden brown, about 10 minutes. Reduce heat to medium and stir in wine. Add the tempeh slices and spoon some of the mushroom mixture over them; cook until the tempeh is heated through and the wine has evaporated, about 5 minutes. Remove from the heat, top with cheese, cover and let stand until the cheese melts, about 1½ minutes.
3. To assemble sandwiches, divide the tempeh among half the toasted bread. Top with the mushroom mixture and the remaining toasted bread. Serve immediately.

ACTIVE TIME: 30 minutes
TOTAL: 30 minutes

MAKES: 4 servings

H↑F
PER SERVING: 152 calories; 19 g fat (6 g sat, 7 g mono); 20 mg cholesterol; 33 g carbohydrate; 2 g added sugars; 26 g protein; 5 g fiber; 595 mg sodium; 598 mg potassium.
NUTRITION BONUS: Calcium (33% daily value), Iron (21% dv), Magnesium & Potassium (17% dv).

NOTE: **Tempeh** is a chewy, nutty, fermented soybean loaf. Find it (plain or with added grains) near refrigerated tofu in natural-foods stores and many large supermarkets. We particularly like SoyBoy 5 Grain and Lightlife Flax tempeh.

Sesame-Honey Tempeh & Quinoa Bowl

ACTIVE TIME: 30 minutes
TOTAL: 30 minutes

MAKES: 4 servings, ½ cup each quinoa and slaw & ¾ cup tempeh

H↑F   H♥H

PER SERVING: 536 calories; 27 g fat (5 g sat, 9 g mono); 0 mg cholesterol; 53 g carbohydrate; 13 g added sugars; 28 g protein; 5 g fiber; 588 mg sodium; 899 mg potassium.
NUTRITION BONUS: Vitamin A (182% daily value), Magnesium (46% dv), Iron (32% dv), Folate (27% dv), Potassium (26% dv), Calcium (21% dv), Zinc (19% dv).

The big nutty flavor of tempeh is a stark contrast with the relatively mild flavor of tofu. Here we toss tempeh with a simple honey-sesame sauce and serve it over quinoa and shredded carrots for a satisfying and protein-packed meal.

QUINOA & CARROT SLAW

1½	**cups water**
¾	**cup quinoa (see "Wholesome Grains," page 123), rinsed**
2	**cups grated carrots (about 3 large)**
2	**tablespoons rice vinegar**
2	**tablespoons sesame seeds, toasted (see Note, page 219)**
1	**tablespoon toasted sesame oil**
1	**tablespoon reduced-sodium soy sauce**

SESAME-HONEY TEMPEH

2	**tablespoons toasted sesame oil**
2	**8-ounce packages tempeh (see Note, page 143), crumbled into bite-size pieces**
3	**tablespoons honey *or* agave syrup**
3	**tablespoons reduced-sodium soy sauce**
2	**tablespoons water**
1	**teaspoon cornstarch**
2	**scallions, sliced**

1. **To prepare quinoa:** Bring 1½ cups water to a boil in a small saucepan. Add quinoa and return to a boil. Reduce to a low simmer, cover and cook until the water is absorbed, 10 to 14 minutes. Uncover and let stand.
2. **To prepare carrot slaw:** Meanwhile, combine carrots, rice vinegar, sesame seeds, 1 tablespoon sesame oil and 1 tablespoon soy sauce in a medium bowl. Set aside.
3. **To prepare tempeh:** Heat 2 tablespoons sesame oil in a large nonstick skillet over medium heat. Add tempeh and cook, stirring frequently, until beginning to brown, 7 to 9 minutes.
4. Combine honey (or agave syrup), 3 tablespoons soy sauce, 2 tablespoons water and cornstarch in a small bowl. Add to the pan and cook, stirring, until the sauce has thickened and coats the tempeh, about 1 minute.
5. Divide the quinoa among 4 bowls and top each with ½ cup carrot slaw and ¾ cup tempeh mixture. Sprinkle with scallions.

Grilled Curried Tofu with Sweet & Spicy Tamarind Chutney

ACTIVE TIME: 30 minutes
TOTAL: 30 minutes

TO MAKE AHEAD: Cover and refrigerate the chutney (Step 2) for up to 1 week.

MAKES: 8 servings, 2 slices tofu & 2-3 tablespoons chutney each

H✷W H♥H

PER SERVING: 211 calories; 6 g fat (1 g sat, 2 g mono); 0 mg cholesterol; 33 g carbohydrate; 4 g added sugars; 9 g protein; 3 g fiber; 158 mg sodium; 211 mg potassium.
NUTRITION BONUS: Calcium (21% daily value).

NOTES:

Tamarind is a tropical tree that produces a sour-sweet fruit in a brown pod, with edible pulp. It's used in Caribbean, Asian and Indian curries, beverages and desserts. Purchase either tamarind concentrate or pulp from Asian or other ethnic markets (or from *amazon.com*). We found Thai brands work best in this recipe; Indian brands were too thick, dense and strong in flavor.

To make your own "concentrate":
Combine ¼ cup tamarind pulp and 1 cup hot water in a bowl. Let stand for 20 minutes. Break up the paste and mix it with the water with a fork. Pass the mixture through a fine sieve set over a bowl, pressing to collect as much of the pulp as possible. Discard solids.

Here, extra-firm tofu, which can easily stand up to the rigors of the grill, is seasoned with curry powder and cooked until golden. The real secret to the fantastic flavor of this dish lies in the sweet, spicy and tangy tamarind chutney served on the side for dipping. If you have extra chutney left over, try a dollop of it on a cracker with a bit of cream cheese. (Photograph: page 130.)

- **1** cup tamarind concentrate (*see Notes*)
- **10** small dates (about 2½ ounces), pitted and coarsely chopped
- **2** tablespoons agave syrup (*see Note, page 218*)
- **1** teaspoon finely grated fresh ginger
- **½** teaspoon ground cumin
- **½** teaspoon salt, divided
  Pinch-¼ teaspoon cayenne pepper (optional)
- **2** 14-ounce packages water-packed firm *or* extra-firm tofu, drained
- **1** tablespoon grapeseed oil *or* canola oil
- **1** teaspoon curry powder
- **¼** teaspoon freshly ground pepper

1. Preheat grill to high.
2. Blend tamarind concentrate, dates, agave syrup, ginger, cumin, ¼ teaspoon salt and cayenne to taste (if using) in a blender until smooth.
3. Cut each block of tofu crosswise into eight ½-inch-thick slices. Lightly brush each slice with oil and season on both sides with a light sprinkle of curry powder, the remaining ¼ teaspoon salt and pepper.
4. Oil the grill rack (*see Note, page 219*). Grill the tofu slices until golden and heated through, 2 to 3 minutes on each side. Serve hot with the tamarind chutney for dipping.

Minted Tomato, Onion & Glazed Tofu Kebabs

In this recipe we start by pressing the tofu and letting it drain. That helps it really absorb the marinade and also gives you firmer results, which is helpful with grilled preparations like these kebabs. The glaze for the kebabs is made with kecap manis, *a sweet Indonesian soy sauce, which is an excellent pantry item to have for basting sauces and stir-fries. It can be purchased in most Asian markets or you can make a mock* kecap manis *with soy sauce and molasses.* (Photograph: page 130.)

1	14-ounce package extra-firm water-packed tofu, drained
1	tablespoon lime juice
1	tablespoon reduced-sodium soy sauce
1	teaspoon minced fresh ginger
16	fresh mint leaves
4	plum tomatoes, quartered and seeded
1	onion, peeled, quartered and separated into layers
2	jalapeño peppers, seeded and cut into ½-inch pieces
¼	cup *kecap manis* (see Note)

1. Cut tofu in half horizontally, making two large slices about 1 inch thick. Fold a clean kitchen towel and place it on a cutting board or large plate. Set the tofu on the towel. Put another folded clean towel over the tofu and place a flat, heavy weight (such as a skillet) on top; drain for 15 minutes; remove the weight and cut the tofu into 1½-inch pieces.
2. Preheat grill to medium-high.
3. Combine lime juice, soy sauce and ginger in a medium bowl. Add tofu and toss to coat. Cover and marinate in the refrigerator for 15 minutes.
4. Tuck a mint leaf into each tomato quarter and thread onto 4 or 8 skewers alternately with tofu, onion and jalapeños. (Discard any remaining marinade.)
5. Oil the grill rack (*see Note, page 219*). Grill the kebabs, turning occasionally, for 7 minutes. Brush with *kecap manis* and grill until the vegetables are softened and the tofu is well glazed, about 3 minutes more.

ACTIVE TIME: 15 minutes
TOTAL: 40 minutes

EQUIPMENT: 4 or 8 metal or bamboo skewers

MAKES: 4 servings

H)(W   H♥H
PER SERVING: 178 calories; 6 g fat (1 g sat, 4 g mono); 0 mg cholesterol; 20 g carbohydrate; 12 g added sugars; 11 g protein; 2 g fiber; 546 mg sodium; 348 mg potassium.
NUTRITION BONUS: Vitamin C (25% daily value), Calcium (19% dv), Iron & Magnesium (16% dv).

NOTE: **Kecap manis** is a thick, palm sugar–sweetened soy sauce. It's used as a flavoring, marinade or condiment in Indonesian cooking. Find it in Asian food markets or online at *importfood.com.* To substitute for *kecap manis,* whisk 1 part molasses with 1 part reduced-sodium soy sauce.

158

150

159

161

EGGS & DAIRY

Eggs and dairy provide protein and the vitamin A we need to keep our eyes strong, but they also deliver saturated fat (dairy) and dietary cholesterol (eggs). To keep dishes with eggs and dairy healthy, we often choose low-fat dairy, and when we use cheeses, we typically go for ones with the biggest flavor so we can use the smallest amounts and still make an impact. With eggs, we often use a combination of egg whites and whole eggs to cut down on calories and dietary cholesterol.

Spanish Tortilla

ACTIVE TIME: 25 minutes
TOTAL: 40 minutes

TO MAKE AHEAD: Store airtight in the refrigerator for up to 1 day.

MAKES: 6 servings

H✕W   H♥H

PER SERVING: 175 calories; 9 g fat (3 g sat, 4 g mono); 217 mg cholesterol; 10 g carbohydrate; 0 g added sugars; 12 g protein; 2 g fiber; 433 mg sodium; 212 mg potassium.

NUTRITION BONUS: Vitamin A (36% daily value).

NOTES:
Look for **precooked diced potatoes** in the refrigerated section of most supermarket produce departments.

Mild-flavored sheep's-milk **Manchego cheese** is available in well-stocked supermarkets or specialty stores.

In Spain, a tortilla *is a potato-and-egg dish cooked in a skillet traditionally using lots and lots of olive oil. Our version uses less oil, so it's lower in calories, and if you use precooked diced potatoes, it's faster too. To complete the Spanish theme, serve with slices of toasted bread that have been rubbed with garlic and topped with chopped, fresh tomatoes.*

3 **teaspoons extra-virgin olive oil, divided**
1 **small onion, thinly sliced**
1 **cup precooked diced red potatoes (*see Notes*)**
1 **tablespoon chopped fresh thyme *or* 1 teaspoon dried**
½ **teaspoon smoked paprika (*see Note, page 219*)**
6 **large eggs**
4 **large egg whites**
½ **cup shredded Manchego (*see Notes*) *or* Jack cheese**
3 **cups baby spinach, roughly chopped**
½ **teaspoon salt**
½ **teaspoon freshly ground pepper**

1. Heat 2 teaspoons oil in a medium nonstick skillet over medium heat. Add onion and cook, stirring, until translucent, 3 to 4 minutes. Add potatoes, thyme and paprika and cook for 2 minutes more.
2. Lightly whisk eggs and egg whites in a large bowl. Gently stir the potato mixture into the eggs along with cheese, spinach, salt and pepper until combined. Wipe the pan clean; add the remaining 1 teaspoon oil and heat over medium heat. Pour in the egg mixture, cover and cook until the edges are set and the bottom is browned, 4 to 5 minutes (it will still be moist in the center).
3. To flip the tortilla, run a spatula gently around the edges to loosen them. Invert a large plate over the pan and turn out the tortilla onto it. Slide the tortilla back into the pan and continue cooking until completely set in the middle, 3 to 6 minutes. Serve warm or cold.

Artichoke & Parmesan Frittata

ACTIVE TIME: 20 minutes
TOTAL: 20 minutes

MAKES: 4 servings

H✗W   H♥H

PER SERVING: 163 calories; 9 g fat
(3 g sat, 4 g mono); 167 mg cholesterol;
9 g carbohydrate; 0 g added sugars;
13 g protein; 3 g fiber; 413 mg sodium;
306 mg potassium.
NUTRITION BONUS: Folate (28% daily
value), Calcium (15% dv).

*A slice of frittata, a salad and some crusty bread makes a nice lunch or light supper.
This 20-minute frittata combines convenient frozen artichokes and Parmesan cheese.
To add another savory layer, throw in a few tablespoons of chopped oil-cured olives.*

3	**large eggs**
2	**large egg whites**
1/2	**cup freshly grated Parmesan cheese, divided**
1	**tablespoon finely chopped fresh parsley**
1/4	**teaspoon salt**
	Freshly ground pepper to taste
2	**teaspoons extra-virgin olive oil**
1	**small onion, finely chopped**
3	**cloves garlic, minced**
2	**cups chopped frozen artichoke hearts, thawed, *or* canned, rinsed**

1. Position oven rack in upper third of oven; preheat broiler.
2. Lightly beat eggs and egg whites together in a bowl. Stir in ¼ cup Parmesan, parsley, salt and pepper; set aside.
3. Heat oil in a large broiler-safe nonstick skillet (*see Note, page 218*) over medium heat. Add onion and cook, stirring occasionally, until softened, 2 to 3 minutes. Add garlic and continue cooking until fragrant, about 1 minute. Add artichoke hearts and cook, stirring, until heated through, 3 to 4 minutes.
4. Spread artichoke mixture evenly over bottom of skillet. Pour the reserved egg mixture into skillet and tilt to distribute it evenly. Reduce heat to medium-low and cook, undisturbed, until eggs are set on the bottom but the top is still runny, 3 to 5 minutes.
5. Sprinkle remaining ¼ cup Parmesan over frittata. Place the pan under the broiler. Broil until the top is set and turning golden brown, about 2 minutes. Loosen the frittata and slide it onto a serving platter. Serve immediately.

Chile, Potato & Cheese Omelet

Ready-to-use frozen hash browns and canned chopped green chiles keep this piquant omelet under the quick-enough-for-weeknights time limit. That's not to say it wouldn't make a delicious breakfast or brunch entree as well. Bump up the heat, if you like, by using spicy pepper Jack cheese and serve with your favorite salsa and some warmed corn tortillas.

ACTIVE TIME: 25 minutes
TOTAL: 25 minutes

MAKES: 2 servings

H❋W

PER SERVING: 276 calories; 15 g fat (6 g sat, 6 g mono); 228 mg cholesterol; 20 g carbohydrate, 0 g added sugars; 17 g protein; 3 g fiber; 765 mg sodium; 519 mg potassium.

NUTRITION BONUS: Vitamin C (53% daily value), Calcium (22% dv), Folate (21% dv), Vitamin A (18% dv), Iron (17% dv).

- **2 large eggs**
- **2 large egg whites**
- **Freshly ground pepper to taste**
- **1/3 cup shredded Monterey Jack cheese**
- **1/4 cup chopped fresh cilantro**
- **1/2 tablespoon extra-virgin olive oil**
- **3/4 cup frozen hash browns *or* diced cooked potatoes**
- **1/4 teaspoon salt**
- **1 4-ounce can chopped green chiles**
- **4 scallions, trimmed and chopped**

1. Position oven rack in upper third of oven; preheat broiler.
2. Whisk eggs, egg whites and pepper in a bowl until blended. Stir in cheese and cilantro.
3. Heat oil in a 9-inch broiler-safe nonstick skillet (*see Note, page 218*) over medium heat. Add potatoes and season with salt and pepper. Cook, stirring frequently, until potatoes soften and begin to brown, 4 to 5 minutes. Remove from heat; stir in chiles and scallions. Pour egg mixture over vegetables; return to heat and cook, shaking pan occasionally, until the edges are set and the omelet is lightly browned on the bottom, 3 to 4 minutes.
4. Place the pan under the broiler. Broil until the top is set and lightly browned, 2 to 3 minutes. Loosen the omelet and slide it onto a serving platter. Serve immediately.

Pocket Eggs with Soy-Sesame Sauce

These aromatic, crispy fried eggs are crusted in flavorful basil, scallions and black sesame seeds before being basted in a fragrant soy-sesame sauce. Serve over brown rice or, if you can get them, with the kind of thin Chinese pancakes used for Mu Shu dishes or Peking Duck. Add a side of steamed Chinese broccoli or baby bok choy to complete the meal.

- **2 tablespoons reduced-sodium soy sauce**
- **1 teaspoon toasted sesame oil**
- **1½ teaspoons rice vinegar**
- **1 tablespoon minced scallion greens**
- **4 teaspoons canola oil**
- **4 large eggs**
- **2 teaspoons black sesame seeds (*see Note*)**
- **1 tablespoon dried basil**
- **¼ teaspoon ground white pepper**

1. Combine soy sauce, sesame oil, vinegar and scallion in a small bowl. Set aside.
2. Heat canola oil in a medium nonstick skillet over medium heat and swirl to coat. Crack 2 eggs into a small bowl; crack the remaining 2 eggs into a second small bowl.
3. Working quickly, pour 2 eggs on one side of the pan and the other 2 on the other side. The egg whites will flow together, forming one large piece.
4. Sprinkle sesame seeds, basil and pepper over the eggs. Cook until the egg whites are crispy and brown on the bottom and the yolks are firmly set, about 3 minutes. Keeping them in one piece, flip the eggs using a wide spatula and cook until the whites turn crispy and brown on the other side, 1 to 2 minutes more.
5. Pour the reserved sauce over the eggs. Simmer for 30 seconds, turning the eggs once to coat both sides with sauce. Serve in wedges, drizzled with the pan sauce.

ACTIVE TIME: 15 minutes
TOTAL: 15 minutes

MAKES: 4 servings

H✂W   H♥H
PER SERVING: 139 calories; 12 g fat (2 g sat, 6 g mono); 212 mg cholesterol; 2 g carbohydrate; 0 g added sugars; 7 g protein; 1 g fiber; 338 mg sodium; 117 mg potassium.

NOTE: Black sesame seeds are slightly more flavorful and aromatic than white sesame seeds. Find them in the Asian-foods section of the supermarket or substitute the white variety if they aren't available.

Florentine Hash Skillet

ACTIVE TIME: 10 minutes
TOTAL: 10 minutes

MAKES 1 serving

H✖W

PER SERVING: 226 calories; 15 g fat
(5 g sat, 7 g mono); 226 mg cholesterol;
12 g carbohydrate; 0 g added sugars;
13 g protein; 3 g fiber; 374 mg sodium;
352 mg potassium.
NUTRITION BONUS: Vitamin A (191% daily
value), Folate (35% dv), Calcium
(23% dv), Iron (15% dv).

NOTE: Shredded cooked potatoes
can be found in the refrigerated
produce section or dairy section
of most supermarkets.

One pan, 10 minutes and classic flavor—that's the winning combination for this super-quick, all-in-one-skillet meal that's loaded with ready-to-use hash browns, spinach, egg and cheese. This is a great easy solution when you're just cooking for yourself. If you want to double it, just use a medium nonstick skillet and double the ingredients.

1 teaspoon extra-virgin olive oil
1/2 cup frozen hash browns *or* precooked shredded potatoes (*see Note*)
1/2 cup frozen chopped spinach
1 large egg
  Pinch of salt
  Pinch of freshly ground pepper
2 tablespoons shredded sharp Cheddar cheese

Heat oil in a small nonstick skillet over medium heat. Layer potatoes and spinach into the pan. Crack egg on top and sprinkle with salt, pepper and cheese. Cover, reduce heat to medium-low and cook until the potatoes are starting to brown on the bottom, the egg is set and the cheese is melted, 4 to 7 minutes.

Spinach & Feta Soufflé

ACTIVE TIME: 40 minutes

TOTAL: 1 ¼ hours

EQUIPMENT: 2-quart soufflé dish or deep, straight-sided casserole dish

MAKES: 4 servings

H✖W

PER SERVING: 219 calories; 8 g fat (4 g sat, 3 g mono); 122 mg cholesterol; 23 g carbohydrate; 0 g added sugars; 14 g protein; 2 g fiber; 642 mg sodium; 635 mg potassium.

NUTRITION BONUS: Vitamin A (122% daily value), Folate (39% dv), Vitamin C (33%), Calcium (28% dv), Magnesium & Potassium (18% dv), Iron (15% dv).

This elegant spinach and feta soufflé gets its inspiration from spanakopita, *the classic Greek pie made with phyllo pastry. While soufflés have a reputation for being tricky to make, they're actually quite easy. Serve with olive oil-roasted potatoes and a tomato-cucumber salad tossed in a lemony dressing.* (Photograph: page 148.)

2	**tablespoons fine dry breadcrumbs**
8	**cups fresh spinach (about 8 ounces), stemmed and washed**
1½	**teaspoons canola oil**
1	**medium onion, finely chopped**
1	**clove garlic, finely chopped**
1½	**cups low-fat milk, divided**
⅓	**cup cornstarch**
2	**large egg yolks**
½	**cup crumbled feta cheese**
2	**tablespoons chopped fresh mint** *or* **dill**
½	**teaspoon salt, divided**
½	**teaspoon freshly ground pepper**
6	**large egg whites**

1. Position rack in lower third of oven; preheat to 375°F. Coat a 2-quart soufflé dish or similar deep, straight-sided casserole dish with cooking spray. Sprinkle with breadcrumbs, tapping out the excess.
2. Heat a large skillet over medium heat. Add spinach with the water still clinging to the leaves and cook, stirring, just until wilted, 2 to 3 minutes. Transfer to a colander to drain. Squeeze out excess liquid and chop.
3. Wipe out the pan, add oil and heat over medium heat. Add onion and garlic and cook, stirring, until softened, 2 to 4 minutes. Add the chopped spinach and cook, stirring, until heated through and quite dry, about 2 minutes.
4. Heat 1 cup milk in a heavy medium saucepan until steaming. Dissolve cornstarch in the remaining ½ cup cold milk in a small bowl. Add to the hot milk and cook, whisking constantly, until thickened and smooth, 2 to 3 minutes. Remove from the heat and let cool slightly. Add egg yolks, one at a time, whisking until incorporated. Stir in the reserved spinach mixture, feta, mint (or dill), ¼ teaspoon salt and pepper.
5. Beat egg whites in a large mixing bowl with an electric mixer on medium speed until foamy. Add the remaining ¼ teaspoon salt; gradually increase speed to high and beat until stiff (but not dry) peaks form.
6. Whisk about one-third of the beaten egg whites into the spinach mixture to lighten it. Fold the spinach mixture back into the remaining whites with a rubber spatula. Turn into the prepared dish and smooth the top.
7. Bake the soufflé until puffed and the top feels firm to the touch, 35 to 40 minutes. Serve immediately.

Mini Chile Relleno Casseroles

These mini Tex-Mex casseroles are quick-cooking—the secret is in the individual-size servings, which take about half the time in the oven compared to a full-size baking dish. Plus, everyone loves getting their own little ramekin, especially when it's filled with all the cheesy, peppery flavors of a chile relleno. Serve with salsa and some warmed flour tortillas. (Photograph: page 148.)

2	**4-ounce cans diced green chiles, drained and patted dry**
3/4	**cup frozen corn, thawed and patted dry**
4	**scallions, thinly sliced**
1	**cup shredded reduced-fat Cheddar cheese**
1 1/2	**cups nonfat milk**
6	**large egg whites**
4	**large eggs**
1/4	**teaspoon salt**

1. Preheat oven to 400°F. Coat eight 6-ounce or four 10-ounce heatproof ramekins with cooking spray and place on a baking sheet.
2. Equally divide green chiles, corn and scallions among the ramekins. Top each with cheese. Whisk milk, egg whites, eggs and salt in a medium bowl until combined. Divide the egg mixture evenly among the ramekins.
3. Bake the mini casseroles until the tops begin to brown and the eggs are set, about 25 minutes for 6-ounce ramekins and about 35 minutes for 10-ounce ramekins.

ACTIVE TIME: 10 minutes
TOTAL: 35-45 minutes

EQUIPMENT: Eight 6-ounce or four 10-ounce heatproof ramekins

MAKES: 4 servings, two 6-ounce or one 10-ounce casserole each

PER SERVING: 209 calories; 7 g fat (3 g sat, 3 g mono); 219 mg cholesterol; 14 g carbohydrate; 0 g added sugars; 23 g protein; 2 g fiber; 633 mg sodium; 447 mg potassium.
NUTRITION BONUS: Calcium (27% daily value), Vitamin C (25% dv), Folate (18% dv), Vitamin A (15% dv).

Egg Smarts

EGGS FOR HEALTH
One large egg contains 72 calories, 5 grams of fat and 6 grams of protein. Egg yolks are an excellent source of choline—an essential nutrient that is important for brain and nerve function and may help prevent memory loss associated with aging.

SIZE AND COLOR: CRACKING THE CODE
Eggs range in size from Jumbo to Pee Wee. Size depends on the breed and age of the hen. The color of the eggshell varies with the bird's feathers and earlobes. White eggs come from white hens with white earlobes, brown eggs come from red hens with red earlobes. The color of the eggshell does not affect nutrition.

UNSCRAMBLING THE OMEGA-3 MYSTERY
People shelling out extra cash for omega-3-enhanced eggs should be aware that most of the omega-3s are ALA (an omega-3 fat found in flax, walnuts and canola), not the EPA and DHA found in fatty fish, the type that most nutrition experts emphasize for heart health.

GET A GOOD EGG
Eggs lose water through their shells during storage. When moisture leaves the egg, the air space within the shell enlarges. To test for freshness, place whole eggs in a bowl of water. A fresher egg will hover closer to the bottom of the bowl. If the egg floats to the top, discard it. It's past its prime. Or you can just go by the expiration date on the carton.

Roasted Ratatouille with Eggs & Cheese

ACTIVE TIME: 25 minutes
TOTAL: 1 hour 40 minutes

TO MAKE AHEAD: Prepare through Step 4, cover and refrigerate for up to 2 days. Reheat before continuing.

MAKES: 4 servings

H✕W   H↑F

PER SERVING: 372 calories; 21 g fat (6 g sat, 11 g mono); 227 mg cholesterol; 28 g carbohydrate; 0 g added sugars; 19 g protein; 6 g fiber; 490 mg sodium; 484 mg potassium.
NUTRITION BONUS: Vitamin C (58% daily value), Folate (32% dv), Calcium (28% dv), Vitamin A (25% dv).

Ratatouille on its own makes a delightful entree, but add some eggs and mozzarella cheese and you have a truly satisfying meal. Keep a close eye on the eggs while they're in the oven or they'll go from soft and tender to hard and rubbery before you can say hockey puck.

1   **small eggplant (about 12 ounces), trimmed, peeled and cut into ¹/₂-inch pieces**
1   **medium onion, cut into ¹/₂-inch pieces**
1   **small zucchini, cut into ¹/₂-inch pieces**
1   **small red bell pepper, cut into ¹/₂-inch pieces**
2   **cloves garlic, minced**
2   **tablespoons plus 2 teaspoons extra-virgin olive oil, divided**
¹/₄ **teaspoon salt**
    Freshly ground pepper to taste
1   **28-ounce can plum tomatoes, with juice**
2   **tablespoons torn fresh basil leaves, plus more for garnish**
1   **tablespoon finely chopped fresh parsley**
4   **large eggs**
4   **ounces part-skim mozzarella, thinly sliced and cut into ¹/₄-inch strips**
4   **¹/₂-inch-thick slices Italian bread, preferably whole-wheat**

1. Preheat oven to 400°F. Lightly coat a large rimmed baking sheet with cooking spray.
2. Combine eggplant, onion, zucchini, bell pepper and garlic in a large bowl; drizzle with 2 tablespoons oil; toss to coat. Spread the vegetables on the prepared baking sheet. Season with salt and pepper.
3. Roast the vegetables, stirring often, until lightly browned and tender, about 45 minutes. Transfer the vegetables to a 9-by-13-inch baking dish. Cut tomatoes into chunks. Stir the tomatoes (and their juices), basil and parsley into the vegetables. Cover with foil.
4. Bake until the ratatouille is hot and bubbling, about 20 minutes. Remove from the oven.
5. With a large spoon, make four evenly spaced indentations in the hot ratatouille. Carefully break an egg into each indentation. Sprinkle cheese over the vegetables and eggs. Bake, uncovered, until the eggs are set and the cheese is melted, 8 to 10 minutes.
6. While the eggs are baking, toast bread and drizzle each slice with ¹/₂ teaspoon oil. Divide bread slices among 4 plates or shallow soup bowls.
7. To serve, lift an egg and some ratatouille from the baking dish and place on top of a slice of toasted bread. Spoon the remaining vegetables and juices around the edges, distributing evenly. Garnish with more basil, if desired.

Summer Vegetable Crêpes

Savory stuffed crêpes make a delicious and quick weeknight supper, especially if you use store-bought crêpes. Here they're filled with ricotta cheese, green beans, zucchini and corn and topped with a chive-cream sauce, but you can use any savory filling that suits you. Try a sautéed mushroom and crumbled tofu blend in a reduced-fat sour cream sauce or perhaps sautéed spinach, red onion and shredded Swiss cheese. (Photograph: page 148.)

ACTIVE TIME: 30 minutes
TOTAL: 30 minutes

MAKES: 4 servings

PER SERVING: 304 calories; 17 g fat (8 g sat, 6 g mono); 46 mg cholesterol; 25 g carbohydrate; 0 g added sugars; 15 g protein; 3 g fiber; 684 mg sodium; 463 mg potassium.
NUTRITION BONUS: Vitamin C (37% daily value), Calcium (34% dv), Vitamin A (23% dv), Folate (15% dv).

NOTE: "Ready-to-use" **crêpes** are fast and convenient. Look for them in the produce section of the market or near refrigerated tortillas. For a whole-wheat crêpe recipe, go to *eatingwell.com*.

- ⅓ cup reduced-fat sour cream
- ½ cup chopped fresh chives, divided, plus more for garnish
- 3 tablespoons low-fat milk
- 2 teaspoons lemon juice
- ¾ teaspoon salt, divided
- 1 tablespoon extra-virgin olive oil
- 2 cups chopped zucchini
- 1¼ cups chopped green beans
- 1 cup fresh corn kernels (from 1 large ear; *see Note, page 218*)
- 1 cup part-skim ricotta cheese
- ½ cup shredded Monterey Jack cheese
- ¼ teaspoon freshly ground pepper
- 4 9-inch "ready-to-use" crêpes (*see Note*)

1. Stir sour cream, ¼ cup chives, milk, lemon juice and ¼ teaspoon salt in a small bowl until combined. Set aside.
2. Heat oil in a large nonstick skillet over medium-high heat. Add zucchini, green beans and corn and cook, stirring, until beginning to brown, 6 to 8 minutes. Reduce heat to low; stir in ricotta, Monterey Jack, the remaining ¼ cup chives, the remaining ½ teaspoon salt and pepper. Cook, stirring gently, until the cheese is melted, 1 to 2 minutes. Remove from the heat.
3. To roll crêpes, place one on a piece of parchment or wax paper (or leave it on the piece of plastic separating the crêpes in the package). Spoon one-fourth of the vegetable-cheese mixture (about ¾ cup) down the center of the crêpe. Use the paper (or plastic) to help you gently roll the crêpe around the filling. Place the crêpe seam-side down on a dinner plate. Repeat with the remaining crêpes and filling. Serve each crêpe topped with 2 tablespoons of the reserved sauce and more chives, if desired.

164

173

176

170

CASSEROLES, TARTS & GRATINS

The recipes in this chapter are great for get-togethers or for a Sunday-night supper with the family. You might consider taking some of the more casual dishes, like the Zucchini Rice Casserole, to a summer potluck, while others, like the Roasted Vegetable Galette with Olives, would be at home as the star of a holiday meal. Several of the recipes take a little more time and effort to assemble, but while they're baking you'll have time to make a salad, steam some vegetables or just relax.

Tomato & Spinach Dinner Strata

ACTIVE TIME: 45 minutes

TOTAL: 3¾ hours

TO MAKE AHEAD: Prepare through Step 5; refrigerate for up to 1 day.

MAKES: 8 servings

H✖W   H↑F

PER SERVING: 317 calories; 15 g fat (6 g sat, 5 g mono); 99 mg cholesterol; 26 g carbohydrate; 1 g added sugars; 20 g protein; 5 g fiber; 683 mg sodium; 640 mg potassium.

NUTRITION BONUS: Vitamin A (104% daily value), Calcium (41% dv), Folate (26% dv), Magnesium (20% dv), Potassium & Zinc (18% dv).

This yummy lasagna-inspired casserole has cheese, vegetables, eggs and marinara sauce but uses sturdy whole-grain bread instead of noodles, which makes it even easier to make. Its hearty look hides the fact that it's made with all low-fat, healthful ingredients. Of course, it makes a great brunch entree as well—don't let the name fool you. (Photograph: page 162.)

4	teaspoons extra-virgin olive oil, divided
1	medium onion, chopped
8	ounces mushrooms, thinly sliced
½	teaspoon freshly ground pepper, divided
¼	teaspoon salt
1	15-ounce container part-skim ricotta cheese
1	10-ounce package frozen chopped spinach, thawed and squeezed dry, *or* 1 ½ pounds fresh spinach, cooked, squeezed dry and chopped
⅛	teaspoon freshly grated nutmeg
2	cups prepared marinara sauce, divided
6	slices whole-grain sandwich bread, preferably day-old
1	cup shredded part-skim mozzarella cheese
3	large eggs
1	cup low-fat milk
¼	cup freshly grated Parmesan cheese
2	tablespoons chopped fresh parsley

1. Coat a 7-by-11-inch (or similar-size) baking dish with cooking spray.
2. Heat 2 teaspoons oil in a large nonstick skillet over medium heat. Add onion and cook, stirring often, until softened but not browned, 5 to 8 minutes. Transfer to a bowl. Add the remaining 2 teaspoons oil to the pan; increase heat to medium-high. Add mushrooms and cook, stirring, until the moisture has evaporated, 4 to 5 minutes. Transfer to the bowl with the onions, add ¼ teaspoon pepper and salt and stir to combine.
3. Combine ricotta, spinach, nutmeg and the remaining ¼ teaspoon pepper in another bowl.
4. Spoon 1 cup marinara sauce into the prepared baking dish. Break each slice of bread into 4 roughly equal pieces; arrange half the bread on the sauce (the bread doesn't have to completely cover the sauce). Spoon the ricotta mixture over the bread. Arrange the remaining bread over the ricotta. Scatter the mushroom mixture over the bread. Top with mozzarella. Spoon the remaining marinara sauce over the top. The pan will be very full.
5. Whisk eggs and milk in a small bowl. Pour the mixture slowly over the casserole, poking the filling gently with the tip of a knife until the egg mixture is evenly distributed and the bread is saturated. Coat a piece of foil with cooking spray on one side and cover the casserole, sprayed-side down. Refrigerate for at least 2 hours or up to 1 day.
6. Preheat oven to 375°F. Bake the strata, uncovered, for 40 minutes. Sprinkle with Parmesan and bake until puffed and golden brown, 10 minutes more. Let stand for 10 minutes. Serve sprinkled with parsley.

Grits & Greens Casserole

Convenient prepared salsa and extra-sharp Cheddar give quite a bit of zip to this casserole combo of two classic Southern sides. In the summer this is great served with a simple sliced-tomato salad.

  2 **teaspoons extra-virgin olive oil**
  1 **small onion, diced**
  4 **cloves garlic, minced**
  2 **cups "no-chicken" broth (*see Note, page 218*) *or* vegetable broth, divided**
 ¼ **teaspoon salt**
16 **cups chopped collard greens *or* kale, stems removed (about 1 large bunch, 1½-2 pounds)**
  2 **cups water, plus more as needed**
  1 **cup grits (*not* instant)**
 ¾ **cup shredded extra-sharp Cheddar cheese, divided**
 ¼ **cup prepared salsa**
  1 **large egg, lightly beaten**

1. Preheat oven to 400°F. Coat an 8-inch-square baking dish with cooking spray.
2. Heat a large Dutch oven over medium-low heat; add oil, onion and garlic and cook, stirring often, until fragrant and starting to brown in spots, 2 to 8 minutes. Add 1 cup broth and salt; bring to a boil over high heat. Add collards (or kale); stir until wilted down to about one-third the volume and bright green, 1 to 2 minutes. Cover, reduce heat to medium-low and simmer, stirring occasionally, until tender, 18 to 20 minutes. Adjust heat during cooking to maintain a simmer, and add water, ¼ cup at a time, if the pan seems dry.
3. Meanwhile, bring 2 cups water and the remaining 1 cup broth to a boil in a large saucepan. Pour in grits in a steady stream, whisking constantly. Bring to a simmer, whisking constantly. Reduce heat to medium-low and cook, whisking often, until thick, about 5 minutes. Combine ½ cup cheese, salsa and egg in a small bowl. Remove the grits from the heat and quickly stir in the cheese mixture until combined.
4. Working quickly, spread about half the grits in the prepared baking dish. Top with greens, spreading evenly. Spread the remaining grits over the greens. Sprinkle with the remaining ¼ cup cheese.
5. Bake the casserole until hot and bubbling, about 20 minutes. Let stand for about 10 minutes before serving.

ACTIVE TIME: 50 minutes
TOTAL: 1¼ hours

TO MAKE AHEAD: Prepare through Step 4, cover and refrigerate for up to 1 day. Bake at 400°F until bubbling, about 30 minutes.

MAKES: 6 servings, about 1 cup each

H✖W H⬆F H♥H

PER SERVING: 238 calories; 8 g fat (3 g sat, 2 g mono); 50 mg cholesterol; 33 g carbohydrate; 0 g added sugars; 10 g protein; 5 g fiber; 442 mg sodium; 269 mg potassium.

NUTRITION BONUS: Vitamin A (136% daily value), Vitamin C (60% dv), Folate (57% dv), Calcium (26% dv).

Cheese Enchiladas with Red Chile Sauce

ACTIVE TIME: 45 minutes

TOTAL: 1 1/4 hours

TO MAKE AHEAD: Cover and refrigerate the sauce (Step 1) for up to 3 days.

MAKES: 8 servings

H↑F

PER SERVING: 305 calories; 14 g fat (6 g sat, 4 g mono); 30 mg cholesterol; 35 g carbohydrate; 0 g added sugars; 12 g protein; 7 g fiber; 606 mg sodium; 308 mg potassium.
NUTRITION BONUS: Vitamin A (58% daily value), Calcium (27% dv).

NOTE: Unlike most commercial chile powder, which is a blend of spices, **New Mexican ground red chile** is just straight ground New Mexican chiles. Look for it in the bulk-spice section at natural-foods stores or online from *thespicehouse.com*. Or use whole dried New Mexican chiles (available in well-stocked supermarkets) to grind your own chile powder in a spice mill or clean coffee grinder. Ancho chile powder can also be used as a substitute.

These absolutely addictive enchiladas are all about the potent red sauce, so it's essential to use the best chile powder you can get your hands on. Shop for spices at your local natural-foods store, especially if they sell them in bulk. The variety is likely to be greater and you can buy only as much as needed, which means the remainder won't end up stale and flavorless in your cupboard.

RED CHILE SAUCE

- 2 teaspoons canola oil
- 1/2 cup minced white onion
- 1 clove garlic, minced
- 1/2 cup mild-to-medium-hot red New Mexican chile powder (*see Note*)
- 2 cups vegetable broth
- 1 cup water
- 1/2 teaspoon dried oregano, preferably Mexican
- 1/2 teaspoon salt

ENCHILADAS

- 1 15-ounce can pinto beans, rinsed and mashed, *or* nonfat refried beans
- 2 tablespoons low-fat plain yogurt
- 12 corn tortillas, blue corn if available
- 2 cups shredded sharp Cheddar cheese, divided
- 1/4 cup minced white onion, plus more for garnish

1. **To prepare sauce:** Heat oil in a medium saucepan over medium heat. Add 1/2 cup onion; cook, stirring, until it begins to soften, about 1 minute. Stir in garlic and continue cooking until the onion is translucent and soft, about 2 minutes more. Stir in chile powder. Add broth, water, oregano and salt. Bring to a boil. Reduce heat to a simmer and cook until thickened and reduced by about one-third, about 20 minutes. (The sauce should be thick enough to coat a spoon lightly.)

2. **To prepare enchiladas:** Preheat oven to 400°F. Coat a 7-by-11-inch (or similar-size 2-quart) baking dish with cooking spray.

3. Combine beans and yogurt in a small bowl.

4. Spread about 1/4 cup of the sauce in the baking dish. Arrange 4 tortillas in the dish, overlapping them to cover the bottom. Top with half the bean mixture, using the back of a spoon to spread it thin. Scatter 2/3 cup cheese and 2 tablespoons onion on top of the beans. Top with one-third of the remaining sauce, 4 tortillas, the remaining bean mixture, 2/3 cup cheese and the remaining 2 tablespoons onion. Spread half of the remaining sauce on top and cover with the remaining 4 tortillas. Top with the remaining sauce and the remaining 2/3 cup cheese.

5. Bake the enchiladas until hot and bubbling, 15 to 20 minutes. Let stand for 5 minutes before serving. Serve with additional minced onion, if desired.

Bean & Hominy Potpie

The Latin section of your supermarket is a great place to find a wide variety of canned beans, spices and interesting ingredients like the hominy that's featured in this Southwestern-inspired potpie. To make this casserole even more weeknight-friendly, prepare the filling ahead of time and refrigerate in the baking dish. When ready to serve, simply top with tortillas and cheese and bake, adding a few extra minutes to the cooking time to make sure everything's heated through.

ACTIVE TIME: 45 minutes

TOTAL: 1¼ hours

EQUIPMENT: 2- to 3-quart baking dish

MAKES: 6 servings, about 1½ cups each

H✖W   H⬆F   H❤H

PER SERVING: 336 calories; 9 g fat (3 g sat, 4 g mono); 10 mg cholesterol; 56 g carbohydrate; 0 g added sugars; 11 g protein; 11 g fiber; 667 mg sodium; 724 mg potassium.

NUTRITION BONUS: Vitamin A (176% daily value), Vitamin C (49% dv), Magnesium & Potassium (21% dv), Calcium (20% dv), Folate & Iron (18% dv).

FILLING

- 2 teaspoons extra-virgin olive oil
- 1 large onion, thinly sliced
- 3 cloves garlic, minced
- 2 jalapeño peppers, seeded and minced
- 1 tablespoon paprika
- 1 teaspoon ground cumin
- 1 teaspoon dried oregano
- ¼ teaspoon ground cinnamon
  Pinch of ground cloves
- 1 pound butternut squash, peeled, seeded and diced (about 3 cups)
- 1 14-ounce can crushed tomatoes
- 1 cup vegetable broth
- 1 15-ounce can pinto beans, rinsed
- 1 15-ounce can yellow *or* white hominy, rinsed
- ¼ teaspoon salt
  Freshly ground pepper to taste

TOPPING

- 1 tablespoon extra-virgin olive oil
- ¼ teaspoon salt
- 8 corn tortillas
- ½ cup shredded sharp Cheddar cheese

1. Preheat oven to 400°F.
2. **To prepare filling:** Heat 2 teaspoons oil in a large skillet over medium heat. Add onion and cook, stirring, until softened, about 3 minutes. Add garlic and jalapeños and cook, stirring, 1 minute more. Add paprika, cumin, oregano, cinnamon and cloves; cook, stirring, until fragrant, about 1 minute. Add squash, tomatoes and broth; bring to a simmer. Simmer, covered, until the squash is just tender, 10 to 12 minutes. Add beans and hominy. Season with salt and pepper. Transfer the mixture to a 2- to 3-quart baking dish.
3. **To prepare topping:** Combine 1 tablespoon oil and ¼ teaspoon salt in a small bowl; brush on both sides of tortillas. Cut the tortillas into ¾-inch strips and cut the strips in half. Scatter the tortilla strips over the filling.
4. Bake the potpie in the center of the oven until the filling is bubbling, 25 to 30 minutes. Sprinkle cheese on top and return to the oven until melted, 1 to 3 minutes.

Root Vegetable Gratin

ACTIVE TIME: 30 minutes

TOTAL: 1 1/4 hours

MAKES: 8 servings

H✂W   H↑F

PER SERVING: 285 calories; 13 g fat
(5 g sat, 6 g mono); 24 mg cholesterol;
33 g carbohydrate; 0 g added sugars;
12 g protein; 6 g fiber; 350 mg sodium;
676 mg potassium.
NUTRITION BONUS: Vitamin A (200% daily
value), Vitamin C (32% dv), Calcium
(31% dv), Folate (29% dv), Potassium
(19% dv).

NOTE: You can **peel root vegetables**,
such as beets, carrots and parsnips,
with a vegetable peeler, but for
tougher-skinned roots like celeriac,
rutabaga and turnips, removing the
peel with a knife can be easier.
Cut off one end of the root to create a
flat surface to keep it steady on the
cutting board. Follow the contour of
the vegetable with your knife. If you
use a vegetable peeler on the tougher
roots, peel around each vegetable
at least three times to ensure all the
fibrous skin has been removed.

*This gratin is defined by the sweet, earthy taste of the roots balanced with the creamy,
almost nutty Gruyère cheese. Serve with warm garlic bread and a salad. For a more
substantial variation, crack some whole eggs on top of the gratin to bake for the last
10 minutes or so.*

3	**pounds assorted root vegetables, peeled (*see Note*) and cut into** 1/8-**inch-thick slices**
3	**tablespoons extra-virgin olive oil, divided**
1	**cup thinly sliced shallots**
1 1/3	**cups low-fat milk, divided**
3	**tablespoons all-purpose flour**
1 1/2	**cups finely shredded Gruyère cheese, divided**
1	**tablespoon chopped fresh thyme *or* 1 teaspoon dried**
1/2	**teaspoon salt**
1/4	**teaspoon freshly ground pepper**
1	**cup fresh whole-wheat breadcrumbs (*see Note, page 218*)**

1. Preheat oven to 400°F. Coat a 9-by-13-inch baking dish with cooking spray.
2. If using parsnips, quarter lengthwise and remove the woody core before cutting into 1/8-inch thick slices. Cook vegetables in a large pot of boiling water until barely tender, about 5 minutes. Drain.
3. Heat 2 tablespoons oil in a medium saucepan over medium heat. Add shallots and cook, stirring occasionally, until light brown, 3 to 4 minutes. Add 1 cup milk and bring to a simmer. Combine flour and the remaining 1/3 cup milk in a small bowl to make a smooth paste; stir into the hot milk and cook, whisking constantly, until the sauce bubbles and thickens, 1 to 2 minutes. Remove from the heat. Stir in 3/4 cup cheese, thyme, salt and pepper.
4. Combine breadcrumbs, the remaining 3/4 cup cheese and 1 tablespoon oil in a bowl.
5. Layer the vegetable slices in the prepared baking dish. Pour the cheese sauce over the top and top with the breadcrumb mixture.
6. Bake the gratin until it is bubbling and the top is golden, 30 to 40 minutes. Let cool for 10 minutes before serving.

Zucchini Rice Casserole

ACTIVE TIME: 40 minutes

TOTAL: 2 hours

TO MAKE AHEAD: Prepare through Step 4; cool, cover and refrigerate for up to 1 day. To finish, bake at 375°F until the casserole is hot and the cheese is melted, about 45 minutes.

MAKES: 10 servings, about 1 cup each

H❯❮W

PER SERVING: 236 calories; 9 g fat (5 g sat, 3 g mono); 23 mg cholesterol; 29 g carbohydrate; 0 g added sugars; 10 g protein; 3 g fiber; 461 mg sodium; 320 mg potassium.

NUTRITION BONUS: Vitamin C (57% daily value), Vitamin A (23% dv), Calcium (22% dv).

We pack extra vegetables into this cheesy baked rice casserole. Plus we substitute brown rice for white and reduce the cheese by half. If you're bringing it to a potluck, plan to reheat it before serving.

1½	**cups long-grain brown rice**
3	**cups "no-chicken" broth (*see Note, page 218*) *or* vegetable broth**
4	**cups diced zucchini *and/or* summer squash (about 1 pound)**
2	**red *or* green bell peppers, chopped**
1	**large onion, diced**
¾	**teaspoon salt**
1½	**cups low-fat milk**
3	**tablespoons all-purpose flour**
2	**cups shredded pepper Jack cheese, divided**
1	**cup corn kernels, fresh *or* frozen (thawed)**
4	**ounces reduced-fat cream cheese (Neufchâtel)**
¼	**cup chopped pickled jalapeños**

1. Preheat oven to 375°F.
2. Pour rice into a 9-by-13-inch baking dish. Bring broth to a simmer in a small saucepan. Stir hot broth into the rice along with zucchini (and/or squash), bell peppers, onion and salt. Cover with foil. Bake for 45 minutes. Remove foil and continue baking until the rice is tender and most of the liquid is absorbed, 35 to 45 minutes more.
3. Meanwhile, whisk milk and flour in a small saucepan. Cook over medium heat until bubbling and thickened, 3 to 4 minutes. Reduce heat to low. Add 1½ cups Jack cheese and corn and cook, stirring, until the cheese is melted.
4. When the rice is done, stir in the cheese sauce. Sprinkle the remaining ½ cup Jack cheese on top and dollop cream cheese by the teaspoonful over the casserole. Top with jalapeños.
5. Return the casserole to the oven and bake until the cheese is melted, about 10 minutes. Let stand for about 10 minutes before serving.

Roasted Vegetable Galette with Olives

Roasted vegetables give this impressive-looking tart a sweet-savory flavor. The autumnal mix of produce makes it an obvious choice for a Thanksgiving entree, but the recipe is quite adaptable, so you can experiment with whatever is in season. (Photograph: page 162.)

CRUST
- 1¼ **cups all-purpose flour**
- 1 **cup whole-wheat pastry flour** (*see Note, page 218*)
- 2 **teaspoons baking powder**
- 1 **teaspoon sugar**
- ½ **teaspoon salt**
- ⅓ **cup water**
- ¼ **cup extra-virgin olive oil**
- ½ **cup finely chopped pitted Kalamata olives**

FILLING (*see Note*)
- 1½ **cups diced peeled carrots**
- 1½ **cups diced peeled parsnips**
- 1½ **cups diced peeled butternut squash**
- 1 **cup diced peeled beets**
- 2 **tablespoons extra-virgin olive oil, divided**
- 2 **teaspoons chopped fresh rosemary** *or* ½ **teaspoon dried**
- ½ **teaspoon salt, or to taste** **Freshly ground pepper to taste**
- 1 **head garlic**
- 1 **cup crumbled creamy goat cheese (4 ounces), divided**
- 1 **egg mixed with 1 tablespoon water for glazing**

ACTIVE TIME: 1 hour
TOTAL: 2¼ hours

TO MAKE AHEAD: Refrigerate crust (Step 1) for up to 2 days.

MAKES: 8 servings

H♦F
PER SERVING: 382 calories; 20 g fat (6 g sat, 12 g mono); 41 mg cholesterol; 41 g carbohydrate; 1 g added sugars; 10 g protein; 5 g fiber; 693 mg sodium; 371 mg potassium.
NUTRITION BONUS: Vitamin A (142% daily value), Folate (27% dv), Calcium (25% dv), Vitamin C (22% dv).

NOTE: The **vegetables for the filling** should be cut to a uniform size so they cook evenly. Aim for ¾-inch pieces.

1. **To prepare crust:** Combine all-purpose flour, whole-wheat flour, baking powder, sugar and salt in a food processor; pulse several times. Mix water and oil; sprinkle over the dry ingredients and pulse just until blended. Add olives and pulse to mix. (*Alternatively, combine dry ingredients in a large bowl. Make a well in the center and add the water-oil mixture, stirring until well blended. Stir in olives.*) Press the dough into a disk; if it seems dry, add a little more water. Wrap in plastic wrap and refrigerate for 30 minutes or longer.
2. Preheat oven to 400°F. Coat a large baking sheet with cooking spray.
3. **To prepare filling:** Combine carrots, parsnips, squash, beets, 1 tablespoon oil, rosemary, salt and pepper in a large bowl; toss to coat. Spread the vegetables on the prepared baking sheet. Cut the tip off the head of garlic. Set on a square of foil, sprinkle with a tablespoon of water and pinch the edges of the foil together. Place the packet on the baking sheet with the vegetables. Roast, stirring the vegetables every 10 minutes, until they are tender and beginning to brown and the garlic is soft, about 35 minutes. (The garlic may take a little longer.)
4. Transfer the vegetables to a bowl. Carefully unwrap the garlic and let cool slightly. Squeeze the garlic cloves into a small bowl; add the remaining 1 tablespoon oil and mash with a fork. Add the mashed garlic to the roasted vegetables and toss to mix. Add ¾ cup goat cheese and toss to coat.
5. **To assemble galette:** Roll the dough into a rough 14-inch circle about ¼ inch thick. Coat a baking sheet with cooking spray and place the dough on it. Arrange the roasted vegetables on the dough, leaving a 2-inch border all around. Fold the border up and over the filling to form a rim, pleating as you go. Scatter the remaining ¼ cup goat cheese over the vegetables. Stir egg and water briskly; brush lightly over the crust.
6. Bake the galette at 400° until the crust is golden, 30 to 35 minutes. Let cool for 10 minutes. Serve warm.

Rustic Mushroom Tart

Sautéed wild mushrooms are blended with ricotta and goat cheese plus fresh herbs to make the filling for this quick-to-make, yet impressive tart. Our method of brushing olive oil and sprinkling breadcrumbs between the layers of phyllo allows you to skip some of the oil (or butter) typically used with phyllo and still get a flaky, crispy texture. This recipe also makes a great appetizer—just cut it into smaller portions. Make sure you plan ahead and have your phyllo dough defrosted before you start preparing the tart.

ACTIVE TIME: 30 minutes

TOTAL: 1 hour

MAKES: 6 servings

PER SERVING: 309 calories; 18 g fat (6 g sat, 10 g mono); 19 mg cholesterol; 26 g carbohydrate; 0 g added sugars; 10 g protein; 2 g fiber; 459 mg sodium; 259 mg potassium.

NUTRITION BONUS: Folate (18% daily value).

- ¾ cup part-skim ricotta cheese
- ½ cup soft goat cheese (2 ounces)
- 2 teaspoons chopped fresh rosemary
  Freshly ground pepper to taste
- 1 tablespoon butter
- 4 cups mixed wild mushrooms, coarsely chopped
- 1 large leek, white part only, halved lengthwise, thinly sliced and thoroughly washed
- ½ teaspoon salt
- ¼ cup dry white wine
- 10 sheets (14x18-inch) *or* 20 sheets (9x14-inch) phyllo dough, thawed according to package directions
- ¼ cup extra-virgin olive oil
- ¼ cup plain dry breadcrumbs

1. Combine ricotta, goat cheese, rosemary and pepper in a bowl. Set aside.
2. Heat butter in a large skillet over medium-high heat. Add mushrooms, leek and salt and cook, stirring, until the leek starts to soften and the mushrooms release their juices, about 3 minutes. Pour in wine and simmer until the liquid has evaporated, about 2 minutes. Set aside.
3. Preheat oven to 400°F. Line a large baking sheet (approximately 12 by 17 inches) with parchment paper. Lay one large sheet of phyllo on the prepared pan. (If using the smaller size, slightly overlap two sheets on the pan to form a rectangle.) Keep the remaining phyllo covered with plastic wrap (or wax paper) and a damp kitchen towel.
4. Lightly coat the phyllo with oil using a pastry brush. Sprinkle with 1 teaspoon breadcrumbs. Repeat this step, layering the remaining phyllo on top. Carefully roll about ¾ inch of each side toward the center to form the outer rim of the tart.
5. Spread the reserved cheese mixture evenly over the phyllo. Top with the reserved mushroom mixture.
6. Bake the tart until the crust is brown and crispy, 25 to 30 minutes. Let cool in the pan on a wire rack for 5 minutes. To serve, lift the parchment paper and slide the tart onto a cutting board or large platter. Serve warm.

Tomato Phyllo Tart

ACTIVE TIME: 30 minutes
TOTAL: 1 hour 20 minutes

TO MAKE AHEAD: Bake the tart, cover and refrigerate for up to 8 hours. Reheat at 350°F for 10 to 15 minutes, or until warmed through. Garnish with basil just before serving.

MAKES: 6 servings

H✗W

PER SERVING: 289 calories; 18 g fat (5 g sat, 11 g mono); 18 mg cholesterol; 24 g carbohydrate; 0 g added sugars; 7 g protein; 2 g fiber; 544 mg sodium; 224 mg potassium.
NUTRITION BONUS: Folate (19% daily value).

Think of this dish as a sort of Mediterranean pizza with a phyllo-dough crust. This beautiful tart will surely impress your guests, but it only takes 30 minutes to get in the oven. Try it with different toppings, such as black olive pesto, caramelized onions and crumbles of goat cheese. Frozen phyllo dough needs to be defrosted according to package directions before use—be sure to plan ahead. (Photograph: page 162.)

12	sheets (14x18-inch) *or* 24 sheets (9x14-inch) phyllo dough, thawed according to package directions
1/4	cup extra-virgin olive oil
1	tablespoon plain dry breadcrumbs
2	tablespoons prepared pesto
3/4	cup crumbled feta cheese
1	large red tomato, cut into 1/4-inch slices
1	large yellow tomato, cut into 1/4-inch slices
1/2	teaspoon kosher salt, or to taste
	Freshly ground pepper to taste
10-12	small basil leaves

1. Preheat oven to 400°F. Line a large baking sheet (approximately 12 by 17 inches) with parchment paper. Lay one large sheet of phyllo on the prepared pan. (If using the smaller size, slightly overlap two sheets on the pan to form a rectangle.) Keep the remaining phyllo covered with plastic wrap (or wax paper) and a damp kitchen towel.

2. Lightly coat the phyllo surface with oil using a pastry brush. Sprinkle with 1/4 teaspoon breadcrumbs. Repeat this step, layering the remaining phyllo on top. Brush the final sheet with oil. Carefully roll about 3/4 inch of each side toward the center to form the outer rim of the tart.

3. Brush pesto evenly on the surface of the phyllo. Sprinkle about half of the crumbled feta cheese over the pesto. Arrange tomato slices, alternating colors, over the feta; season with salt and pepper. Sprinkle the remaining cheese over the top.

4. Bake the tart until the crust is brown and crispy, 30 to 35 minutes. Let cool in the pan on a wire rack for 5 minutes. To serve, lift the parchment paper and slide the tart onto a cutting board or large platter. Scatter basil leaves on top. Serve warm or at room temperature.

Leek & Gruyère Quiche

Nutty Gruyère is the classic Alpine melting cheese used in quiche or fondue. Here, it's blended with low-fat milk, plus nonfat evaporated milk and more egg whites than yolks to get a lighter quiche. If you want to cut down on the prep time, use a store-bought prepared pie shell; look for one without trans fats. Serve this quiche with Mixed Green Salad with Grapefruit & Cranberries (page 36).

ACTIVE TIME: 45 minutes
TOTAL: 1½ hours

TO MAKE AHEAD: Prepare crust (Steps 2-3), wrap and refrigerate for up to 2 days.

MAKES: 8 servings

H✕W

PER SERVING: 244 calories; 13 g fat (4 g sat, 6 g mono); 70 mg cholesterol; 21 g carbohydrate; 0 g added sugars; 11 g protein; 1 g fiber; 292 mg sodium; 239 mg potassium.

NUTRITION BONUS: Calcium (24% daily value), Folate (19% dv), Vitamin A (17% dv).

CRUST
- 1 tablespoon butter
- 3 tablespoons canola oil
- 1 cup all-purpose flour
- ¼ teaspoon salt
- 1-2 tablespoons ice water

FILLING
- 2 teaspoons extra-virgin olive oil
- 8 ounces leeks, white and light green part only, thinly sliced and thoroughly washed (about 2 cups)
- 2 large eggs
- 4 large egg whites
- ¾ cup nonfat *or* low-fat milk
- ¾ cup evaporated nonfat milk
- ¼ teaspoon salt
- ¼ teaspoon freshly ground pepper
- ¼ teaspoon freshly grated nutmeg
  Pinch of cayenne pepper
- 1 teaspoon Dijon mustard
- 1 tablespoon fine dry breadcrumbs
- ¾ cup shredded Gruyère cheese
- 1 tablespoon freshly grated Parmesan cheese

1. Position rack in lower third of oven; preheat to 425°F.
2. **To prepare crust:** Melt butter in a small saucepan over low heat. Cook butter, swirling the pan, until it is a light nutty brown, about 30 seconds. Pour into a small bowl and let cool. Stir in canola oil.
3. Whisk flour and ¼ teaspoon salt in a medium bowl. Slowly stir in the butter-oil mixture with a fork until it is crumbly. Gradually stir in enough ice water for the dough to hold together. Gather the dough into a ball.
4. Place the dough between two sheets of plastic wrap and flatten into a disk. Roll into a 12-inch circle. Remove the top plastic sheet and invert dough into a 9-inch pie pan. Remove the remaining plastic. Fold edges under at the rim and crimp.
5. Line the dough with a piece of foil or parchment paper large enough to lift out easily; fill evenly with pie weights or dried beans. Bake for 7 minutes. Remove foil (or paper) and weights and bake just until lightly browned, 3 to 5 minutes more. (The crust will not be fully baked.) Cool on a wire rack. Reduce oven temperature to 350°.
6. **To prepare filling:** Meanwhile, heat olive oil in a large nonstick skillet over low heat. Add leeks and cook, stirring occasionally, until soft and wilted, 15 minutes. Set aside to cool.
7. Whisk eggs and egg whites in a large bowl. Add milk, evaporated milk, salt, pepper, nutmeg and cayenne, stirring gently to avoid creating bubbles.
8. **To assemble & bake quiche:** Spread mustard over the bottom of the prebaked crust; sprinkle evenly with breadcrumbs. Top with Gruyère, then the leeks. Carefully pour in the egg mixture. Sprinkle with Parmesan. Bake until just set and a knife inserted in the center comes out clean, 25 to 30 minutes. Transfer to a wire rack and let cool for at least 10 minutes before slicing.

Tomato-Corn Pie

Sliced ripe tomatoes and fresh corn (a winning combo) float in a cheesy, yet light egg custard to create a delicious quiche-like pie. The easy-to-make whole-wheat crust is versatile and would be great for any savory pie.

CRUST

3/4	cup whole-wheat pastry flour (*see Notes*)
3/4	cup all-purpose flour
1/2	teaspoon salt
1/2	teaspoon freshly ground pepper
1/3	cup extra-virgin olive oil
5	tablespoons cold water

FILLING

3	large eggs
1	cup low-fat milk
1/2	cup shredded sharp Cheddar cheese, divided
2	medium tomatoes, sliced
1	cup fresh corn kernels (about 1 large ear; *see Notes*) *or* frozen
1	tablespoon chopped fresh thyme *or* 1 teaspoon dried
1/2	teaspoon salt, divided
1/4	teaspoon freshly ground pepper

1. **To prepare crust:** Combine whole-wheat flour, all-purpose flour and 1/2 teaspoon each salt and pepper in a large bowl. Make a well in the center, add oil and water and gradually stir them in to form a soft dough. Wrap the dough in plastic and chill in the refrigerator for 15 minutes.
2. Preheat oven to 400°F.
3. Roll the dough into a 12-inch circle on a lightly floured surface. Transfer to a 9-inch pie pan, preferably deep-dish, and press into the bottom and up the sides. Trim any overhanging crust. Line the dough with a piece of foil or parchment paper large enough to lift out easily; fill evenly with pie weights or dry beans. Bake for 20 minutes. Remove the foil (or paper) and weights. Let cool on a wire rack for at least 10 minutes or up to 1 hour.
4. **To prepare filling:** Whisk eggs and milk in a medium bowl. Sprinkle half the cheese over the crust, then layer half the tomatoes evenly over the cheese. Sprinkle with corn, thyme, 1/4 teaspoon each salt and pepper and the remaining cheese. Layer the remaining tomatoes on top and sprinkle with the remaining 1/4 teaspoon salt. Pour the egg mixture over the top.
5. Bake the pie until a knife inserted in the center comes out clean, 40 to 50 minutes. Let cool for 20 minutes before serving.

ACTIVE TIME: 25 minutes
TOTAL: 2 hours

TO MAKE AHEAD: Prepare the crust (Step 1), wrap tightly and refrigerate for up to 3 days or freeze for up to 6 months. Cover and refrigerate the baked pie for up to 1 day.

EQUIPMENT: 9-inch pie pan, preferably deep-dish

MAKES: 8 servings

H✹W

PER SERVING: 258 calories; 14 g fat (4 g sat, 9 g mono); 88 mg cholesterol; 24 g carbohydrate; 0 g added sugars; 8 g protein; 2 g fiber; 379 mg sodium; 217 mg potassium.
NUTRITION BONUS: Folate (15% daily value).

NOTES:

Look for **whole-wheat pastry flour** in large supermarkets and natural-foods stores. Store it in the freezer.

To remove corn kernels from the cob, stand an ear of corn on one end and slice the kernels off with a sharp knife.

198

189

182

182

SIDES

When it comes to side dishes we tend toward large servings of vegetables because, after all, they're packed with vitamins, minerals, fiber, antioxidants and other nutrients. Plus they're relatively low in calories, so you can eat a lot without overeating, calorie-wise. For more calorie-dense "starchy" sides, like grains and potatoes, we keep serving sizes conservative and we skip refined grains when possible and opt for whole grains (e.g., bulgur, quinoa or brown rice), which may help protect against cancer, heart disease and diabetes.

Corn & Basil Cakes

ACTIVE TIME: 30 minutes
TOTAL: 30 minutes

MAKES: 5 servings, 2 cakes each

H)(W   H♥H
PER SERVING: 180 calories; 9 g fat
(1 g sat, 5 g mono); 86 mg cholesterol;
21 g carbohydrate; 0 g added sugars;
7 g protein; 2 g fiber; 329 mg sodium;
250 mg potassium.

Sweet corn and fresh basil bring the quintessential flavors of summer to these easy-to-make fritters. Serve with a dab of crème fraîche on top. (Photograph: page 180.)

½ cup white whole-wheat flour (*see Note, page 218*) *or* all-purpose flour
½ cup low-fat milk
2 large eggs
2 tablespoons canola oil, divided
½ teaspoon baking powder
½ teaspoon salt
¼ teaspoon freshly ground pepper
2 cups fresh corn kernels (about 2 large ears; *see Note, page 218*) *or* frozen
½ cup chopped fresh basil

1. Whisk flour, milk, eggs, 1 tablespoon oil, baking powder, salt and pepper in a medium bowl until smooth. Stir in corn and basil.
2. Brush a large nonstick skillet lightly with some of the remaining 1 tablespoon oil; heat over medium heat until hot (but not smoking). Cook 4 cakes at a time, using about ¼ cup batter for each, making them about 3 inches wide. Cook until the edges are dry, about 2 minutes. Flip and cook until golden brown on the other side, 1 to 3 minutes more. Repeat with the remaining oil and batter, making 10 cakes total. Reduce the heat as necessary to prevent burning.

Asparagus with Curry Butter

ACTIVE TIME: 20 minutes
TOTAL: 20 minutes

MAKES: 4 servings, about ½ cup each

H)(W   H♥H
PER SERVING: 67 calories; 5 g fat
(2 g sat, 2 g mono); 5 mg cholesterol;
6 g carbohydrate; 0 g added sugars;
3 g protein; 2 g fiber; 161 mg sodium;
262 mg potassium.
NUTRITION BONUS: Folate (40% daily value), Vitamin A (24% dv), Vitamin C (15% dv).

Nobody can accuse asparagus of being a pushover—its assertive, grassy flavor is an able match for curry and lemon in this dish. (Photograph: page 180.) NOTE: *Check the ingredient label on your curry powder: if it has added salt (as some do), you may want to omit the salt in the recipe or add salt to taste.*

2 teaspoons butter, melted
1 teaspoon curry powder (*see Note, above*)
½ teaspoon lemon juice
¼ teaspoon salt, or to taste
2 teaspoons extra-virgin olive oil
1 shallot, finely diced
1 bunch asparagus (about 1 pound), trimmed and cut into 1-inch pieces

1. Combine butter, curry powder, lemon juice and salt in a small bowl.
2. Heat oil in a large nonstick skillet over medium heat. Add shallot; cook, stirring, until softened, about 2 minutes. Add asparagus; cook, stirring, until just tender, 3 to 5 minutes. Stir the curry butter into the asparagus; toss to coat.

Roasted Asparagus Salad with Citrus Dressing

Fresh citrus juices, honey and a dash of Dijon mustard give this fat-free dressing the perfect bright flavors to go with summery asparagus, tomatoes and watercress. But don't forget to use this dressing on salads and vegetables in the winter when citrus fruits are in high season. If you can find Meyer lemons, use their juice instead of the lemon and orange juices for a real tangy-fruity treat.

- **2 bunches asparagus (2 pounds), trimmed**
- **1 pint cherry *or* pear tomatoes, red *or* mixed colors**
- **1 tablespoon extra-virgin olive oil**
- **3/4 teaspoon salt, divided**
- **Freshly ground pepper to taste**
- **1 tablespoon fresh lemon juice**
- **1 tablespoon fresh orange juice**
- **1 tablespoon honey *or* agave syrup**
- **1/2 teaspoon Dijon mustard**
- **2 bunches watercress, tough stems removed (about 4 cups lightly packed)**
- **2 tablespoons finely chopped fresh dill**

1. Preheat oven to 450°F.
2. Place asparagus in a large bowl. Add tomatoes and oil and toss to coat. Spread in a heavy roasting pan or rimmed baking sheet, spooning the tomatoes between and on top of the asparagus. Sprinkle with ½ teaspoon salt and add a generous grinding of pepper. Roast until the asparagus is crisp-tender and the tomatoes are warmed and slightly crinkled, about 15 minutes. Set aside until ready to serve.
3. Whisk lemon juice, orange juice, honey (or agave syrup), mustard and the remaining ¼ teaspoon salt in a medium bowl until blended. Reserve half of the dressing in a small bowl.
4. Add watercress to the medium bowl; toss to coat. Spread the watercress on a platter. Arrange the roasted asparagus on the watercress and top with tomatoes. Drizzle the reserved dressing over the asparagus and tomatoes; sprinkle with dill. Serve warm or at room temperature.

ACTIVE TIME: 20 minutes
TOTAL: 35 minutes

TO MAKE AHEAD: Prepare through Step 2 up to 2 hours ahead. Cover and refrigerate the dressing (Step 3) for up to 5 days.

MAKES: 6 servings

H✖W   H♥H
PER SERVING: 61 calories, 3 g fat (0 g sat, 2 g mono); 0 mg cholesterol; 9 g carbohydrate; 3 g added sugars; 3 g protein; 2 g fiber; 319 mg sodium, 372 mg potassium.
NUTRITION BONUS: Vitamin C (40% daily value), Vitamin A (38% dv), Folate (31% dv).

Packet-Roasted Balsamic Green Beans & Peppers

ACTIVE TIME: 20 minutes
TOTAL: 40 minutes

MAKES: 4 servings

H❌W   H⬆F   H❤H
PER SERVING: 199 calories; 15 g fat
(2 g sat, 8 g mono); 0 mg cholesterol;
15 g carbohydrate; 2 g added sugars;
4 g protein; 4 g fiber; 333 mg sodium;
391 mg potassium.
NUTRITION BONUS: Vitamin C (150% daily
value), Vitamin A (50% dv), Folate
(16% dv).

NOTE: To toast pine nuts, place in a small
dry skillet and cook over medium-low
heat, stirring constantly, until fragrant
and lightly browned, 2 to 4 minutes.

Foil packets are a great way to cook vegetables on the grill without having to worry about losing half your batch through the grates. Here, Dijon mustard, maple syrup and balsamic vinegar give green beans and bell peppers a sweet and zesty flair that will taste great over pasta or grilled tofu. No maple syrup? No problem—use a touch of brown sugar instead.

- 2 **tablespoons extra-virgin olive oil**
- 2 **teaspoons Dijon mustard**
- 2 **teaspoons pure maple syrup**
- 2 **cloves garlic, minced**
- 1/2 **teaspoon salt**
- 12 **ounces green beans** *and/or* **yellow wax beans**
- 2 **bell peppers, thinly sliced lengthwise**
- 1/3 **cup toasted pine nuts (*see Note*)**
- 2 **tablespoons balsamic vinegar**

1. Preheat grill to medium.
2. To prepare packets, start with eight 20- to 24-inch-long pieces of foil. Layer two sheets for each of four packets (the double layers will help protect the contents from burning).
3. Mix oil, mustard, syrup, garlic and salt in a large bowl. Add beans and peppers; toss to coat.
4. Place one-fourth of the vegetable mixture (about 1 cup) on half of each double layer of foil, leaving at least a 1-inch border around the edges for folding. Sprinkle with pine nuts. Fold the foil over the ingredients and tightly seal the packets by crimping and folding the edges together.
5. Grill for 10 to 12 minutes, rotating the packets to another spot on the grill about halfway through to ensure even cooking. Let the packets rest unopened for 5 minutes. Drizzle the vegetables with vinegar just before serving.

Provençal Summer Vegetables

This gorgeous layered dish of baked tomatoes, eggplant and summer squash is as versatile as it is flavorful. Serve it as a summery side or turn it into a light supper by nestling it between some slices of crusty bread with a little bit of fresh arugula to create a tasty sandwich.

4	tablespoons extra-virgin olive oil, divided
2	cups thinly sliced leeks, rinsed and well drained
5	cloves garlic, thinly sliced
1/2	teaspoon salt, divided
1/2	teaspoon freshly ground pepper, divided
1/2	cup dry white wine
3	large tomatoes (about 1 1/2 pounds), sliced 1/4 inch thick
1	small summer squash *or* zucchini, sliced diagonally 1/4 inch thick
1	small eggplant, sliced 1/4 inch thick
1/3	cup finely shredded Pecorino Romano *or* Parmesan cheese
1	tablespoon chopped fresh marjoram *or* 1 teaspoon dried

1. Preheat oven to 425°F.
2. Heat 2 tablespoons oil in a large skillet over medium heat. Add leeks, garlic, 1/4 teaspoon each salt and pepper and cook, stirring, until soft and beginning to brown, about 6 minutes. Add wine and cook, stirring, 1 minute more. Transfer the mixture to a shallow 2-quart baking dish.
3. Layer tomatoes, summer squash (or zucchini) and eggplant slices in an alternating shingle pattern over the leek mixture (they will overlap quite a bit). If you have extra vegetable slices, save them for another use. Sprinkle the vegetables with the remaining 1/4 teaspoon each salt and pepper and drizzle with the remaining 2 tablespoons oil.
4. Bake the vegetables for 1 1/4 hours. Sprinkle cheese and marjoram over the top. Continue baking until the edges are browned and the vegetables are very tender, about 15 minutes more. Let cool for about 5 minutes before serving.

ACTIVE TIME: 25 minutes
TOTAL: 2 1/4 hours

MAKES: 6 servings, about 2/3 cup each

H✱W   H⬆F
PER SERVING: 185 calories; 12 g fat (3 g sat, 7 g mono); 9 mg cholesterol; 13 g carbohydrate; 0 g added sugars; 5 g protein; 4 g fiber; 323 mg sodium; 457 mg potassium.
NUTRITION BONUS: Vitamin C (33% daily value), Vitamin A (28% dv).

◄ Thyme-Braised Brussels Sprouts

Fresh thyme is a fine match for the powerful flavor of Brussels sprouts in this easy braise. Look for petite baby sprouts, which tend to be more sweet and tender than big ones.

- 1 **tablespoon extra-virgin olive oil**
- 2 **shallots, sliced**
- 1 **pound Brussels sprouts, trimmed**
- 1 **cup "no-chicken" broth (*see Note, page 218*) or vegetable broth**
- 1½ **teaspoons chopped fresh thyme *or* ½ teaspoon dried**
- ¼ **teaspoon salt**
- ¼ **teaspoon freshly ground pepper**

Heat oil in a large skillet over medium-high heat. Add shallots and Brussels sprouts and cook, stirring often, until the shallots are starting to brown and the Brussels sprouts are browned in spots, 2 to 4 minutes. Stir in broth, thyme, salt and pepper; cover and reduce heat to medium-low. Cook until the Brussels sprouts are tender, 10 to 15 minutes.

ACTIVE TIME: 10 minutes
TOTAL: 20 minutes

MAKES: 4 servings, ¾ cup each

H✖W   H↑F   H♥H
PER SERVING: 89 calories; 4 g fat (1 g sat, 3 g mono); 0 mg cholesterol; 12 g carbohydrate; 0 g added sugars; 4 g protein; 4 g fiber; 288 mg sodium; 429 mg potassium.
NUTRITION BONUS: Vitamin C (130% daily value), Vitamin A (25% dv), Folate (19% dv).

Roasted Cauliflower with Blue Cheese Vinaigrette

A quartered head of cauliflower, roasted then drizzled with a blue cheese vinaigrette, makes a dramatic but simple-to-prepare side.

- 1 **large head cauliflower, leaves trimmed**
- 2 **teaspoons plus 1 tablespoon extra-virgin olive oil, divided**
- ⅛ **teaspoon plus ¼ teaspoon salt, divided**
- 2 **tablespoons crumbled blue cheese**
- 1 **tablespoon white-wine vinegar**
- 1 **tablespoon water**
- 1 **tablespoon minced scallion greens**
- ¼ **teaspoon freshly ground pepper**

1. Position rack in lower third of oven; preheat to 450°F. Coat a large rimmed baking sheet with cooking spray.
2. Cut cauliflower into quarters. Remove any extra woody core from the ends, but keep the quarters intact. Brush with 2 teaspoons oil and sprinkle with ⅛ teaspoon salt. Place cut-side down on the prepared baking sheet.
3. Roast the cauliflower for 15 minutes. Turn so the opposite cut sides are down. Continue roasting until tender, 15 to 20 minutes more.
4. Meanwhile, combine the remaining 1 tablespoon oil, the remaining ¼ teaspoon salt, blue cheese, vinegar, water, scallion greens and pepper in a small bowl. Serve the roasted cauliflower drizzled with the vinaigrette.

ACTIVE TIME: 10 minutes
TOTAL: 45 minutes

MAKES: 4 servings

H✖W   H♥H
PER SERVING: 90 calories, 7 g fat (2 g sat, 5 g mono); 3 mg cholesterol; 5 g carbohydrate; 0 g added sugars; 3 g protein; 2 g fiber; 304 mg sodium; 281 mg potassium.
NUTRITION BONUS: Vitamin C (72% daily value).

Quick Cucumber Kimchi

ACTIVE TIME: 30 minutes
TOTAL: 40 minutes (plus 12-24 hours marinating time)

TO MAKE AHEAD: Cover and refrigerate for up to 1 week.

MAKES: 1 1/2 cups

H✖W   H♥H
PER 1/4-CUP SERVING: 28 calories; 0 g fat (0 g sat, 0 g mono); 0 mg cholesterol; 7 g carbohydrate; 1 g added sugars; 10 g protein; 0 g fiber; 263 mg sodium; 75 mg potassium.

NOTE: Korean chile powder (also called gochugaru or Korean "crushed red pepper") is made from thin red peppers that are sun-dried on woven mats or strung together and hung from the eaves of thatch-roofed houses throughout the countryside. Find it in Korean or Asian markets or online from *koamart.com*. Store, airtight, in the refrigerator or freezer indefinitely.

Here's a cool and refreshing version of Korea's favorite national dish, made with crispy cucumbers instead of cabbage. Serve this spicy, garlicky pickle like a condiment or as part of a salad plate. (Photograph: page 8.)

2   pickling cucumbers *or* other small cucumbers (about 8 ounces)
1   teaspoon kosher salt
2   cloves garlic, finely chopped
2   scallions, white and light green parts only, finely chopped
1   1/4-inch piece fresh ginger, peeled and finely chopped
2   tablespoons rice vinegar
1   tablespoon Korean chile powder (*see Note*)
2   teaspoons sugar
1/2   teaspoon reduced-sodium soy sauce

1. Cut cucumbers in half lengthwise and then crosswise into 1/8-inch-thick half moons. Place in a medium bowl and mix thoroughly with salt. Let stand at room temperature for about 30 minutes.
2. Meanwhile, combine garlic, scallions, ginger, vinegar, chile powder, sugar and soy sauce in a medium nonreactive bowl (*see Note, page 219*).
3. Drain the cucumbers (discard the liquid). Stir the cucumbers into the vinegar mixture. Cover and refrigerate for 12 to 24 hours before serving.

Roasted Portobello Caps

These supersized stuffed mushrooms have all the flavor of traditional stuffed mush-rooms, but without all the high-fat ingredients. Serve as a side or topped with poached eggs to make a Portobello Benedict for a deluxe brunch. (Photograph: page 180.)

- 4 large portobello mushrooms, stems removed
- ¼ teaspoon salt, divided
  Freshly ground pepper to taste
- ¼ cup plain dry breadcrumbs
- 2 tablespoons grated Parmesan cheese
- 1 tablespoon minced fresh parsley
- 1 tablespoon extra-virgin olive oil

1. Preheat oven to 450°F. Coat a rimmed baking sheet or roasting pan with cooking spray.
2. Place mushroom caps, gill-side up, on the prepared pan. Sprinkle with ⅛ tea-spoon salt and pepper. Roast until tender, about 20 minutes.
3. Meanwhile, combine breadcrumbs, Parmesan, parsley, oil, the remaining ⅛ teaspoon salt and pepper in a small bowl. Remove the mushrooms from the oven and top each cap with about 2 tablespoons of the breadcrumb mixture, spreading evenly. Return to the oven and roast until the breadcrumbs are browned, about 5 minutes.

ACTIVE TIME: 10 minutes
TOTAL: 40 minutes

MAKES: 4 servings

PER SERVING: 94 calories; 5 g fat (1 g sat, 3 g mono); 2 mg cholesterol; 9 g carbohydrate; 0 g added sugars; 4 g protein; 2 g fiber; 244 mg sodium; 435 mg potassium.

Brown Sugar-Glazed Beets

Beets are already the candy of the root vegetable world so why not celebrate it and give them a brown sugar and orange juice glaze? Try this easy treatment with steamed carrots, turnips or rutabaga as well. (Photograph: page 214.)

- 3 cups cubed beets, ½- to 1-inch cubes
- 3 tablespoons dark brown sugar
- 2 tablespoons orange juice
- 1 tablespoon butter
- ¼ teaspoon salt
- ¼ teaspoon freshly ground pepper

1. Place beets in a steamer basket over 1 inch of boiling water in a large pot. Cover and steam over high heat until tender, 10 to 15 minutes.
2. Combine brown sugar, orange juice, butter, salt and pepper in a large nonstick skillet. Cook over medium heat until the sugar and butter are melted and starting to bubble. Stir in beets. Cook until most of the liquid has evaporated and the beets are coated with glaze, 6 to 8 minutes. Serve hot or warm.

ACTIVE TIME: 15 minutes
TOTAL: 15 minutes

MAKES: 6 servings, about ½ cup each

PER SERVING: 74 calories; 2 g fat (1 g sat, 1 g mono); 5 mg cholesterol; 14 g carbohydrate; 4 g added sugars; 2 g protein; 2 g fiber; 164 mg sodium; 277 mg potassium.
NUTRITION BONUS: Folate (18% daily value).

◀ Sesame-Seasoned Spinach

This sesame-and-garlic-seasoned spinach is inspired by the Korean style of adding bold flavors to vegetables.

1/4 **cup water**
1 **pound baby spinach (about 20 cups)**
1 **tablespoon toasted sesame seeds (*see Note, page 219*)**
2 **teaspoons reduced-sodium soy sauce**
2 **teaspoons toasted sesame oil**
1 **small clove garlic, minced**

1. Place water in a very large pot or Dutch oven and bring to a boil over high heat. Add spinach and cook, stirring frequently, until completely wilted, 2 to 3 minutes. Transfer to a colander and let stand until cool enough to handle. Squeeze out excess water.
2. Coarsely chop the spinach. Place in a bowl and mix in sesame seeds, soy sauce, sesame oil and garlic. Serve at room temperature.

ACTIVE TIME: 20 minutes
TOTAL: 30 minutes

MAKES: 4 servings, about 1/2 cup each

PER SERVING: 56 calories; 4 g fat (1 g sat, 1 g mono); 0 mg cholesterol; 4 g carbohydrate; 0 g added sugars; 3 g protein; 2 g fiber; 151 mg sodium; 425 mg potassium.
NUTRITION BONUS: Vitamin A (183% daily value), Folate (32% dv), Iron & Magnesium (19% dv), Vitamin C (15% dv).

Spicy Broccoli Salad

A simple Asian-style vinaigrette is all it takes to turn steamed broccoli along with some crisp onion and bell pepper into a spicy vegetable salad. If you like, double the dressing and toss in some premarinated, diced tofu to make this a main-course salad.

1 1/2 **pounds broccoli**
3 **tablespoons chopped red bell pepper**
3 **tablespoons chopped red onion**
3 **tablespoons rice-wine vinegar *or* distilled white vinegar**
1 **tablespoon toasted sesame oil**
2 **teaspoons light brown sugar**
1 **teaspoon crushed red pepper**
1/4 **teaspoon salt**

1. Cut off broccoli florets. Trim and peel stems; cut into 1/2-inch-thick slices. Place the broccoli florets and stems in a steamer basket over boiling water; cover and steam until crisp-tender, 2 to 3 minutes. Refresh under cold water. Drain well.
2. Stir together bell pepper, onion, vinegar, oil, brown sugar and crushed red pepper in a serving bowl. Add the broccoli and toss to combine. Season with salt.

ACTIVE TIME: 15 minutes
TOTAL: 15 minutes

MAKES: 4 servings, 1 cup each

PER SERVING: 108 calories; 4 g fat (1 g sat, 1 g mono); 0 mg cholesterol; 16 g carbohydrate; 2 g added sugars; 5 g protein; 5 g fiber; 338 mg sodium; 574 mg potassium.
NUTRITION BONUS: Vitamin C (270% daily value), Vitamin A (29% dv), Folate (28% dv), Potassium (16% dv).

Herbed Lemon Orzo

ACTIVE TIME: 10 minutes
TOTAL: 25 minutes

MAKES: 4 servings, about 1 cup each

H❌W H⬆F H❤H
PER SERVING: 239 calories; 3 g fat
(0 g sat, 1 g mono); 0 mg cholesterol;
45 g carbohydrate; 0 g added sugars;
8 g protein; 10 g fiber; 147 mg sodium;
17 mg potassium.

Adding some freshly grated lemon zest and chopped fresh parsley is a remarkably simple way of taking orzo from bland to grand. Try serving with Minted Tomato, Onion & Glazed Tofu Kebabs (page 147).

1½	**cups orzo, preferably whole-wheat**
3	**tablespoons chopped fresh parsley**
1½	**teaspoons extra-virgin olive oil**
1	**teaspoon freshly grated lemon zest**
¼	**teaspoon salt**
	Freshly ground pepper to taste

Cook orzo in a large pot of boiling water until just tender, 7 to 9 minutes or according to package directions. Drain and transfer to a serving bowl. Stir in parsley, oil and lemon zest. Season with salt and pepper.

Couscous with Currants

ACTIVE TIME: 25 minutes
TOTAL: 25 minutes

MAKES: 12 servings

H❌W H⬆F H❤H
PER SERVING: 172 calories; 4 g fat
(1 g sat, 3 g mono); 0 mg cholesterol;
32 g carbohydrate; 0 g added sugars;
5 g protein; 5 g fiber; 108 mg sodium;
163 mg potassium.
NUTRITION BONUS: Vitamin C (18% daily value).

Couscous is a pasta that comes in a variety of sizes ranging from small grains to peppercorn-size pearls. Here it is mixed with currants, plum tomatoes and a lemony, roasted-garlic dressing. This dish is best served at room temperature.

3	**cups water**	1	**teaspoon Dijon mustard**
2	**cups whole-wheat couscous**	¼	**teaspoon sugar**
½	**cup currants**	¼	**teaspoon freshly ground pepper**
¾	**teaspoon salt, divided**	6	**plum tomatoes, diced**
3	**cloves garlic, unpeeled**	½	**cup finely chopped scallions**
¼	**cup lemon juice**		**(about 5 scallions)**
3	**tablespoons extra-virgin olive oil**	½	**cup chopped fresh parsley**

1. Bring water to a boil in a medium saucepan. Stir in couscous, currants and ½ teaspoon salt. Remove from the heat, cover and let stand until the water has been absorbed and the couscous is tender, at least 5 minutes.
2. Meanwhile, heat a cast-iron or other heavy skillet over medium heat. Add garlic and cook, turning occasionally, until blackened in spots and tender, about 10 minutes. Slip the cloves from their skins and trim the tough ends.
3. Combine the roasted garlic, lemon juice, oil, mustard and sugar in a blender or food processor; blend until smooth. Season with the remaining ¼ teaspoon salt and pepper.
4. Fluff the couscous with a fork. Add tomatoes, scallions and parsley. Drizzle with the lemon dressing and toss lightly to coat.

Roasted Fennel & Farro Salad

Nutty-flavored farro, an ancient variety of wheat, is combined with sweet roasted fennel and bell peppers in this simple whole-grain salad. Enjoy the leftovers for lunch the next day.

1 cup farro *or* wheat berries (*see Note*)	1/2 teaspoon salt
2 bulbs fennel, trimmed, cored and coarsely chopped	1/2 teaspoon freshly ground pepper
2 medium yellow *and/or* orange bell peppers, chopped	1/4 cup oil-cured *or* Kalamata olives, chopped
2 tablespoons extra-virgin olive oil	2 tablespoons white balsamic *or* white-wine vinegar
	2 teaspoons chopped fresh thyme

1. Preheat oven to 400°F.
2. Place farro (or wheat berries) in a large saucepan; add enough water to cover by 2 inches. Bring to a boil. Cover, reduce heat to a simmer, and cook until tender, 15 to 20 minutes for farro, about 1 hour for wheat berries.
3. Meanwhile, toss fennel and bell peppers with oil, salt and pepper in a large roasting pan. Roast, stirring occasionally, until lightly browned and tender, 35 to 40 minutes.
4. Drain the farro (or wheat berries); transfer to a large bowl. Stir in the roasted vegetables, olives, vinegar and thyme. Serve warm, room temperature or cold.

ACTIVE TIME: 35 minutes
TOTAL: 1 hour 5 minutes

TO MAKE AHEAD: Cover and refrigerate for up to 2 days.

MAKES: 6 servings, about 1 cup each

H✕W   H↑F   H♥H

PER SERVING: 213 calories; 8 g fat (1 g sat, 5 g mono); 0 mg cholesterol; 33 g carbohydrate; 0 g added sugars; 5 g protein; 6 g fiber; 352 mg sodium; 417 mg potassium.
NUTRITION BONUS: Vitamin C (138% daily value).

NOTE: Look for **farro**, a type of whole-grain wheat, and **wheat berries** in the bulk section or near other grains in natural-foods stores.

Bulgur Salad with Asian Accents

This satisfying salad combines bulgur with Asian flavors and spicy sprouts.

1 2/3 cups water	1 tablespoon toasted sesame oil
1 1/4 cups bulgur (*see Note, page 218*)	1 tablespoon finely chopped fresh ginger
2 cups lightly packed radish sprouts (3 ounces)	1 1/2 teaspoons chile-garlic sauce (*see Note, page 218*)
1 bunch scallions, chopped	1 teaspoon honey *or* agave syrup
1/4 cup rice-wine vinegar	1/4 cup toasted cashews (*see Note, page 219*)
1 1/2 tablespoons reduced-sodium soy sauce	

1. Bring water to a boil in a saucepan; stir in bulgur, remove from the heat, cover and set aside until the water has been absorbed, about 30 minutes. Spread the bulgur out on a baking sheet to cool to room temperature, about 15 minutes.
2. Combine the cooled bulgur, sprouts and scallions in a serving bowl.
3. Whisk vinegar, soy sauce, sesame oil, ginger, chile-garlic sauce and honey (or agave syrup) in a small bowl. Pour over the salad and toss well. Sprinkle the salad with cashews.

ACTIVE TIME: 15 minutes
TOTAL: 50 minutes

TO MAKE AHEAD: The salad can be made without the sprouts up to 2 hours ahead and kept, covered, in the refrigerator; add sprouts just before serving.

MAKES: 4 servings, 1 1/4 cups each

H↑F   H♥H

PER SERVING: 266 calories; 8 g fat (2 g sat, 4 g mono); 0 mg cholesterol; 44 g carbohydrate; 2 g added sugars; 8 g protein; 9 g fiber; 419 mg sodium; 325 mg potassium.
NUTRITION BONUS: Magnesium (28% daily value), Vitamin C (16% dv).

Mustard Greens & Bulgur

The delightful, pungent flavor of mustard greens meets its match when combined with nutty bulgur wheat, a double hit of walnuts (oil and toasted nuts) and sweet dates in this hearty dish. If you like, turn this side into a light meal by adding a can of drained, rinsed chickpeas and some crumbles of goat cheese on top.

1	cup bulgur (*see Note, page 218*)
2	tablespoons chopped walnuts
6	teaspoons walnut oil *or* extra-virgin olive oil, divided
2	shallots, chopped
1	tablespoon finely chopped garlic
12	cups thinly sliced mustard greens (about 1 bunch), tough stems removed
1/3	cup chopped pitted dates
2-3	tablespoons water
4	teaspoons white-wine vinegar
1/2	teaspoon salt

1. Prepare bulgur according to package directions or place in a medium bowl, cover generously with hot water and let soak for about 30 minutes.
2. Transfer the bulgur to a colander and rinse under cool water; drain. Toast walnuts in a small dry skillet over medium-low heat, stirring, until lightly browned and fragrant, 2 to 3 minutes.
3. Place 5 teaspoons oil and shallots in a large skillet over medium-low heat. Cook until the shallots start to brown, 4 to 6 minutes. Add garlic and cook, stirring, until fragrant, about 15 seconds. Add mustard greens, dates and 2 tablespoons water and cook, stirring occasionally, until the greens are tender and the water evaporates (add another tablespoon of water if the pan is dry before the greens are tender), about 4 minutes. Stir in vinegar, salt and the prepared bulgur; cook until heated through, about 1 minute. Drizzle with the remaining 1 teaspoon oil and sprinkle with the walnuts before serving.

ACTIVE TIME: 40 minutes
TOTAL: 40 minutes

MAKES: 6 servings, about 2/3 cup each

H✕W   H↑F   H♥H
PER SERVING: 195 calories; 7 g fat (1 g sat, 1 g mono); 0 mg cholesterol; 31 g carbohydrate; 0 g added sugars; 7 g protein; 9 g fiber; 227 mg sodium; 584 mg potassium.
NUTRITION BONUS: Vitamin A (237% daily value), Vitamin C (132% dv), Folate (56% dv), Magnesium (21% dv), Potassium (17% dv).

Nina's Mexican Rice

ACTIVE TIME: 15 minutes
TOTAL: 30 minutes

MAKES: 6 servings, about 2/3 cup each

H✕W   H♥H

PER SERVING: 196 calories; 5 g fat
(0 g sat, 3 g mono); 0 mg cholesterol;
33 g carbohydrate; 0 g added sugars;
4 g protein; 2 g fiber; 417 mg sodium;
206 mg potassium.
NUTRITION BONUS: Folate (26% daily
value), Vitamin A (19% dv).

BROWN RICE VARIATION: Use 1 cup long-
grain brown rice and 1 3/4 cups broth.
In Step 2, simmer for **45** minutes.
Remove the rice from the heat and let
stand, covered, for **15** minutes before
adding the vegetables.

*This tomatoey, south-of-the-border-style rice gets an extra-toasty flavor from the simple
step of browning the rice in a bit of oil before adding the other ingredients.*

2   tablespoons canola oil
1   cup long-grain white rice (*see Brown Rice Variation*)
1/2   cup finely chopped onion
1/4   teaspoon salt
1   tablespoon minced garlic
1   8-ounce can tomato sauce
1 1/2   cups vegetable broth
1/2   cup frozen mixed vegetables (such as corn, peas and carrots), thawed

1. Heat a large heavy saucepan with a tight-fitting lid over medium heat. Add oil
   and rice and cook, stirring, until the rice is just beginning to brown, 4 to 5
   minutes. Add onion and salt and cook, stirring, until the onion begins to
   soften, about 2 minutes. Add garlic and cook, stirring, until fragrant, 1 minute
   more. Pour tomato sauce over the rice and cook, stirring, for 1 minute.
2. Stir in broth and bring to a boil. Reduce to a simmer, cover and cook until
   the rice is cooked, about 15 minutes. Stir in vegetables and serve.

Goat Cheese Grits with Fresh Corn

ACTIVE TIME: 20 minutes
TOTAL: 20 minutes

MAKES: 6 servings, about 2/3 cup each

H✕W

PER SERVING: 156 calories; 5 g fat
(3 g sat, 1 g mono); 11 mg cholesterol;
23 g carbohydrate; 0 g added sugars;
6 g protein; 1 g fiber; 277 mg sodium;
124 mg potassium.
NUTRITION BONUS: Folate (15% daily value).

NOTE: Look for quick **grits** near oatmeal
and other hot cereals or near cornmeal
in the baking aisle.

*Tangy goat cheese and chives bring a savory quality to mellow grits studded with
kernels of sweet fresh corn.*

3   cups water
1/2   teaspoon salt
1/4   teaspoon freshly ground pepper
3/4   cup quick grits (*not* instant; *see Note*)
1   cup fresh corn kernels (about 1 large ear; *see Note, page 218*) *or* frozen
3/4   cup crumbled goat cheese (3 ounces), divided
1/4   cup thinly sliced fresh chives *or* scallion greens

Bring water, salt and pepper to a boil in a large saucepan. Slowly pour in grits,
stirring constantly. Stir in corn; return to a simmer. Reduce heat to medium-low,
cover and cook, stirring once or twice, until thickened, about 5 minutes. Remove
from the heat, stir in half the goat cheese and let stand for 5 minutes. Stir in chives
(or scallions). Serve each portion sprinkled with some of the remaining cheese.

Cheesy Baked Mashed Potatoes

The creamy yellow flesh of Yukon Gold potatoes gives mashed potatoes a velvety texture and lovely flavor. In this recipe, we shred the cooked potatoes on a box grater rather than mashing them with a potato masher. This results in a light, fluffy texture. The potatoes are then baked in a casserole to give them a light golden crust. Use the sharpest Cheddar cheese you can find to get a bold cheesy flavor.

ACTIVE TIME: 30 minutes
TOTAL: 2 hours

TO MAKE AHEAD: Cover and refrigerate for up to 2 days.

MAKES: 8 servings

H✳W   H↑F
PER SERVING: 205 calories; 5 g fat (3 g sat, 1 g mono); 15 mg cholesterol; 31 g carbohydrate; 0 g added sugars; 11 g protein; 5 g fiber; 671 mg sodium; 808 mg potassium.
NUTRITION BONUS: Vitamin C (62% daily value), Potassium (23% dv).

3	pounds large Yukon Gold *or* russet potatoes (about 6), scrubbed but not peeled
6	large cloves garlic, unpeeled
1 1/2	cups low-fat cottage cheese
1/2	cup reduced-fat sour cream
1 1/2	teaspoons salt
1/4	teaspoon freshly ground pepper
1	bunch scallions, trimmed and sliced
1/2	cup shredded Cheddar cheese, preferably extra-sharp
1/4	teaspoon paprika

1. Preheat oven to 350°F. Lightly coat a 2-quart baking dish with cooking spray.
2. Place potatoes and garlic in a large saucepan and cover with cold water. Bring to a simmer over medium heat. Reduce the heat to low and cook until the potatoes are barely tender, 15 to 20 minutes. Drain and let stand until cool enough to handle, about 20 minutes. Peel the potatoes and shred them into a large bowl; set aside.
3. Squeeze the garlic cloves from their skins into a food processor. Add cottage cheese and process until completely smooth. Add sour cream, salt and pepper and process briefly to combine. Add the cottage cheese mixture and scallions to the shredded potatoes and mix well. Turn into the prepared baking dish and sprinkle with Cheddar and paprika. Bake until golden brown, 30 to 40 minutes.

Potato Salad

ACTIVE TIME: 30 minutes
TOTAL: 1 hour

MAKES: 8 servings, 1 cup each

H✂W   H⬆F   H❤H
PER SERVING: 206 calories; 8 g fat
(2 g sat, 2 g mono); 13 mg cholesterol;
32 g carbohydrate; 1 g added sugars;
4 g protein; 3 g fiber; 322 mg sodium;
738 mg potassium.
NUTRITION BONUS: Vitamin C (28% daily
value), Potassium (21% dv).

This tasty potato salad has the best of both worlds—the potatoes get infused with vinegar like German-style and tossed in mayonnaise and sour cream like American-style.

2½	**pounds red potatoes**	¼	**teaspoon salt**
¼	**cup cider vinegar, divided**		**Freshly ground pepper to taste**
1	**cup low-fat mayonnaise**	¾	**cup chopped red onion**
½	**cup reduced-fat sour cream**	¾	**cup chopped celery**
1	**tablespoon Dijon mustard**	⅓	**cup chopped fresh parsley**

1. Put potatoes in a large pot and add cold water to cover. Bring to a simmer over medium heat and cook until just tender, about 15 minutes.
2. Drain the potatoes. When cool enough to handle, dice the potatoes and gently toss them with 2 tablespoons of the vinegar in a large bowl. Let cool to room temperature.
3. Whisk mayonnaise, sour cream, mustard and the remaining 2 tablespoons vinegar in a bowl. Season with salt and pepper.
4. Add the dressing to the potatoes. Add onion, celery and parsley and toss gently to combine.

Twice-Baked Potatoes

ACTIVE TIME: 15 minutes
TOTAL: 1¼ hours

MAKES: 4 servings

H✂W   H⬆F   H❤H
PER SERVING: 182 calories; 2 g fat
(1 g sat, 1 g mono); 54 mg cholesterol;
34 g carbohydrate; 0 g added sugars;
8 g protein; 4 g fiber; 430 mg sodium;
875 mg potassium.
NUTRITION BONUS: Vitamin C (35% daily
value), Potassium (25% dv).

Our twice-baked potatoes aren't drowning in fat and calories, yet still have all the comfort-food qualities of traditional versions. Serve as a side or paired with a salad as a light supper. (Photograph: page 180.)

2	**large russet potatoes**	1½	**tablespoons chopped fresh dill**
½	**cup low-fat cottage cheese**	½	**teaspoon salt**
1	**large egg yolk**	¼	**teaspoon freshly ground pepper**
2	**scallions, chopped**		

1. Pierce potatoes all over with a fork and microwave on Medium, turning once, until soft, about 20 minutes. (*Alternatively, place pierced potatoes directly on oven rack and bake at 450°F for 50 to 60 minutes.*) Let cool.
2. Preheat oven to 400°F.
3. Halve the cooled potatoes lengthwise and scoop out the insides into a medium bowl, leaving a ¼-inch shell. Place the shells in a baking dish. Mash the insides with a potato masher. Puree cottage cheese and egg yolk in a food processor. Add scallions, dill, salt and pepper; pulse until just blended. Stir the mixture into the mashed potato until combined. Mound the filling into the shells.
4. Bake the filled shells until heated through, 20 to 30 minutes.

Quick & Spicy Refried Beans

Refried beans are great to have on hand. Spread them on a tortilla, add cheese and you've got a quesadilla. Top whole-grain toast with refrieds and a little salsa and you've got a great savory breakfast. This easy version has all the great flavor of traditional refried beans without the added fat.

 1 **tablespoon extra-virgin olive oil**
½ **cup finely chopped onion**
 2 **cloves garlic, minced**
 4 **teaspoons chili powder**
 1 **teaspoon ground cumin**
¼ **teaspoon ground chipotle pepper (optional)**
 2 **15-ounce cans black beans** *or* **pinto beans, rinsed,** *or* **2½ cups cooked beans (***see "How to Cook Beans," page 127***)**
2-3 **tablespoons water (optional)**

Heat oil in a large saucepan over medium heat. Add onion and cook, stirring occasionally, until softened, about 3 minutes. Add garlic, chili powder, cumin and chipotle (if using). Cook, stirring constantly, for 1 minute. Add beans and cook until heated through, 2 to 3 minutes. Remove from the heat and mash to desired consistency with a potato masher. Add water if necessary to achieve desired consistency.

ACTIVE TIME: 15 minutes
TOTAL: 15 minutes

TO MAKE AHEAD: Cover and refrigerate for up to 3 days.

MAKES: 4 servings, ½ cup each

PER SERVING: 177 calories; 4 g fat (1 g sat, 3 g mono); 0 mg cholesterol; 28 g carbohydrate; 0 g added sugars; 8 g protein; 9 g fiber; 142 mg sodium; 470 mg potassium.
NUTRITION BONUS: Folate (21% daily value), Iron (17% dv), Vitamin A (15% dv).

213

209

205

212

DESSERTS

Desserts get a bad rap because they're often full of sugar and usually pretty high in calories. But that doesn't mean you need to abandon them to stay healthy—just eat them in moderation. And go for lightened desserts like the ones in this chapter. Strawberry sherbet (*page 207*) made with nonfat buttermilk and the little peanut butter and chocolate truffles (*page 204*) are a good place to start.

▶ Maple-Cinnamon Applesauce

ACTIVE TIME: 20 minutes
TOTAL: 50 minutes

TO MAKE AHEAD: Refrigerate for up to 2 weeks or freeze for up to 6 months.

MAKES: about 3½ cups

H✂W   H♥H

PER 1/2-CUP SERVING: 86 calories; 0 g fat (0 g sat, 0 g mono); 0 mg cholesterol; 23 g carbohydrate; 3 g added sugars; 0 g protein; 2 g fiber; 1 mg sodium; 144 mg potassium.

You might not always think of applesauce as a to-die-for dessert, but if you start with fresh fall apples and add the magic of pure maple syrup and a touch of cinnamon, your results will be too good to be relegated to the role of side dish or snack.

- 6 McIntosh *or* other tart apples, peeled and cut into 1-inch pieces
- 2 Golden Delicious *or* other sweet apples, peeled and cut into 1-inch pieces
- ¼ cup water
- 2 tablespoons pure maple syrup
- ½ teaspoon ground cinnamon

Combine apple pieces and water in a large saucepan. Bring to a boil, then reduce heat to maintain a simmer. Cover and cook, stirring once or twice, until the apples are very soft and falling apart, about 30 minutes. Mash the apples to the desired consistency and stir in maple syrup and cinnamon.

Quick Mini Chocolate Cheesecakes

ACTIVE TIME: 10 minutes
TOTAL: 10 minutes

TO MAKE AHEAD: Store airtight in the refrigerator for up to 2 days.

MAKES: 1 dozen mini cheesecakes

H✂W   H♥H

PER CHEESECAKE: 61 calories; 3 g fat (1 g sat, 1 g mono); 3 mg cholesterol; 8 g carbohydrate; 5 g added sugars; 2 g protein; 0 g fiber; 48 mg sodium; 38 mg potassium.

NOTE: To **melt chocolate**, microwave on Medium for 1 minute. Stir, then continue microwaving on Medium, stirring every 20 seconds, until melted. Or place chocolate in the top of a double boiler over hot, but not boiling, water. Stir until melted.

Here we stir a little melted chocolate into ricotta cheese for a cheesecake-like topping for chocolate wafer cookies.

- ¼ cup semisweet *or* bittersweet chocolate chips, melted (*see Note*)
- ½ cup part-skim ricotta
- 12 chocolate wafer cookies
- 1 tablespoon 100% fruit jam, such as raspberry or cherry

Combine melted chocolate and ricotta in a small bowl. Spoon a scant 1 tablespoon of the mixture on each chocolate wafer and top with ¼ teaspoon jam.

Peanut Butter & Pretzel Truffles

ACTIVE TIME: 15 minutes
TOTAL: 2 hours

TO MAKE AHEAD: Store airtight in the refrigerator for up to 2 weeks.

MAKES: 20 truffles

PER TRUFFLE: 64 calories; 4 g fat (1 g sat, 2 g mono); 1 mg cholesterol; 5 g carbohydrate; 2 g added sugars; 2 g protein; 1 g fiber; 53 mg sodium; 65 mg potassium.

Peanut butter, pretzels and chocolate chips—what could possibly be bad about combining those three ingredients in a simple-to-make confection?

- ½ **cup crunchy natural peanut butter**
- ¼ **cup finely chopped salted pretzels**
- ½ **cup milk chocolate chips**

Combine peanut butter and pretzels in a small bowl. Chill in the freezer until firm, about 15 minutes. Roll the peanut butter mixture into 20 balls (about 1 teaspoon each). Place on a baking sheet lined with parchment or wax paper and freeze until very firm, about 1 hour. Place chocolate chips in a small bowl and microwave on Medium for 1 minute. Stir, then continue microwaving on Medium, stirring every 20 seconds, until melted. Roll the frozen balls in the melted chocolate. Refrigerate until the chocolate is set, about 30 minutes.

Dairy-Free Banana Rice Pudding

ACTIVE TIME: 30 minutes
TOTAL: 3½ hours (including 2 hours chilling time)

TO MAKE AHEAD: Prepare through Step 3, cover and refrigerate for up to 1 day. Finish with Step 4 just before serving.

MAKES: 8 servings, generous ½ cup each

H❭❬W   H⬆F   H❤H
PER SERVING: 201 calories; 2 g fat (0 g sat, 0 g mono); 0 mg cholesterol; 47 g carbohydrate; 6 g added sugars; 3 g protein; 3 g fiber; 184 mg sodium; 221 mg potassium.

This vegan banana rice pudding calls for fragrant basmati rice and cinnamon to give it an aromatic quality.

- 1 **cup brown basmati rice**
- 2 **cups water**
- ½ **teaspoon salt**
- 3 **cups plus 1 tablespoon vanilla rice milk, divided**
- ⅓ **cup light brown sugar**
- ½ **teaspoon ground cinnamon, plus more for garnish**
- 1 **tablespoon cornstarch**
- 4 **ripe bananas, divided**
- 1 **teaspoon vanilla extract**

1. Combine rice, water and salt in a medium saucepan; bring to a boil. Reduce heat to low, cover and cook until the liquid is fully absorbed, 45 to 50 minutes.
2. Stir in 3 cups rice milk, brown sugar and ½ teaspoon cinnamon and bring to a lively simmer. Cook, stirring occasionally, for 10 minutes. Stir cornstarch and the remaining 1 tablespoon rice milk in a small bowl until smooth; add to the pudding. Continue cooking, stirring often, until the mixture is the consistency of porridge, about 10 minutes. Remove from the heat.
3. Mash 2 bananas in a small bowl. Stir the mashed bananas and vanilla into the pudding. Transfer to a large bowl, press plastic wrap directly onto the surface of the pudding and refrigerate until cold, at least 2 hours.
4. Just before serving, slice the remaining 2 bananas. Top each serving with a few slices of banana and sprinkle with cinnamon, if desired.

Chocolate-Raspberry Frozen Yogurt Pops

Thick, Greek-style yogurt makes an excellent creamy base for these tangy, colorful raspberry pops. Also try this recipe with other frozen berries or even icy chunks of peaches, mango or banana.

  2 cups fresh *or* frozen raspberries
  2 cups nonfat *or* low-fat plain yogurt, preferably Greek-style
3-5 tablespoons sugar
  ½ cup mini chocolate chips

1. Puree raspberries, yogurt and sugar to taste in a food processor until smooth.
2. Divide the mixture among freezer-pop molds, stopping about 1 inch from the top. Evenly divide chocolate chips among the molds. Stir the chips into the raspberry mixture, stirring out any air pockets at the same time. Insert the sticks and freeze until completely firm, about 6 hours. Dip the molds briefly in hot water before unmolding.

ACTIVE TIME: 15 minutes
TOTAL: 6¼ hours

TO MAKE AHEAD: Freeze for up to 3 weeks

MAKES: about 10 (3-ounce) freezer pops

EQUIPMENT: Ten 3-ounce (or similar-size) freezer-pop molds

H❌W H❤H
PER SERVING: 93 calories; 3 g fat (2 g sat, 1 g mono); 0 mg cholesterol; 14 g carbohydrate; 9 g added sugars; 5 g protein; 2 g fiber; 18 mg sodium; 69 mg potassium.

Melon & Apple Granita

This refreshing melon-and-apple granita takes only 10 minutes to get into the freezer and has absolutely no added sugar in it. You can vary the color by using either green honeydew or orange cantaloupe and although the mixed berry topping is quite striking, you could also use diced peaches and plums or even fresh figs if they're available (Photograph: page 200.)

  4 cups cubed ripe melon
  1 cup unsweetened apple juice
  ¼ cup lime juice

  1 cup fresh blueberries
  1 cup fresh raspberries
      Fresh mint leaves for garnish

1. Combine melon, apple juice and lime juice in a blender; puree until smooth. Pour the mixture into a 9-by-13-inch glass or metal pan.
2. Place the pan on a level surface in your freezer. Freeze, stirring and scraping with a fork every 30 minutes, moving the frozen edges in toward the slushy center and crushing any lumps, until the granita is firm but not frozen solid, 3 to 4 hours.
3. Remove from the freezer; use a metal spatula or large spoon to break up the frozen ice into small slivers. Pack into an airtight plastic container and freeze for at least 1 hour more.
4. Remove from the freezer about 20 minutes before serving to soften slightly. Use a wide spoon or ice cream scoop to scrape the granita into shallow bowls. Sprinkle blueberries and raspberries over each portion and garnish with mint leaves, if desired.

ACTIVE TIME: 10 minutes
TOTAL: 4½ hours (including freezing time)

TO MAKE AHEAD: Freeze for up to 1 week. Remove about 20 minutes before serving to soften slightly.

MAKES: 8 servings, about ¾ cup granita & ¼ cup fruit each

H❌W H❤H
PER SERVING: 65 calories; 0 g fat (0 g sat, 0 g mono); 0 mg cholesterol; 16 g carbohydrate; 0 g added sugars; 1 g protein; 2 g fiber; 17 mg sodium; 272 mg potassium.
NUTRITION BONUS: Vitamin C (40% daily value).

◄ Strawberry Sherbet

We use nonfat buttermilk to give this berry sherbet a decidedly tangy edge, but if you like it sweeter, increase the sugar a bit. Try this with raspberries or peaches as well.

 2 cups chopped fresh *or* frozen (*not* thawed) strawberries
   (about 10 ounces), divided
 ½ cup sugar
 2½ cups nonfat buttermilk
 ½ cup half-and-half
 2 teaspoons lemon juice
 1 teaspoon vanilla extract
   Pinch of salt

1. Combine 1 cup berries and sugar in a small bowl and let sit, stirring occasionally until the sugar has begun to dissolve, about 10 minutes. Transfer the berry mixture to a food processor or blender and process until smooth.
2. Meanwhile, combine buttermilk, half-and-half, lemon juice, vanilla and salt in a medium bowl. Press the strawberry mixture through a fine-mesh sieve into the bowl. Stir, cover and chill for at least 2 hours or up to 1 day.
3. Whisk the sherbet mixture and pour into the canister of an ice cream maker. Freeze according to manufacturer's directions. During the last 5 minutes of freezing, add the remaining 1 cup chopped berries. If necessary, place the sherbet in the freezer to firm up before serving. (If the sherbet becomes very hard in the freezer, soften it in the refrigerator for about 30 minutes before scooping.)

ACTIVE TIME: 20 minutes
TOTAL: 2 hours 50 minutes (including chilling time)

TO MAKE AHEAD: Prepare through Step 2 up to 1 day ahead. Freeze sherbet in an airtight container for up to 4 days.

EQUIPMENT: Ice cream maker

MAKES: 8 servings, ½ cup each

H✖W   H♥H
PER SERVING: 112 calories; 2 g fat (1 g sat, 1 g mono); 7 mg cholesterol; 21 g carbohydrate; 13 g added sugars; 4 g protein; 1 g fiber; 94 mg sodium; 105 mg potassium.
NUTRITION BONUS: Vitamin C (42% daily value).

Cherry-Vanilla Bean Milkshake

We developed this recipe using bagged frozen cherries because they help to make the shake thick and frosty, but that doesn't mean you can't use fresh ones when they're in season. Just pit and pop them in the freezer for a few hours before blending. For a nutty variation, swap almond milk for the nonfat milk.

 1 10-ounce bag frozen pitted cherries (about 2¼ cups)
 1 cup reduced-fat "light" vanilla ice cream *or* nonfat frozen yogurt
 1 cup nonfat milk
 ½ vanilla bean, split lengthwise, *or* 1 teaspoon vanilla extract

Place cherries, ice cream (or frozen yogurt) and milk in a blender. With the tip of a sharp knife, scrape all the black paste from inside the vanilla bean into the blender (or add vanilla extract); blend until smooth. Stop and stir once or twice if necessary to completely blend.

ACTIVE TIME: 10 minutes
TOTAL: 10 minutes

MAKES: 2 servings, about 1½ cups each

H↑F   H♥H
PER SERVING: 276 calories; 4 g fat (2 g sat, 1 g mono); 23 mg cholesterol; 51 g carbohydrate; 11 g added sugars; 9 g protein; 3 g fiber; 108 mg sodium; 636 mg potassium.
NUTRITION BONUS: Calcium (27% daily value), Potassium (18% dv).

Italian Hazelnut Cookies

ACTIVE TIME: 15 minutes
TOTAL: 2 hours

TO MAKE AHEAD: Store in an airtight container for up to 1 week.

MAKES: about 2½ dozen cookies

EQUIPMENT: Parchment paper or nonstick baking mats

PER COOKIE: 92 calories; 5 g fat (0 g sat, 4 g mono); 0 mg cholesterol; 10 g carbohydrate; 8 g added sugars; 2 g protein; 1 g fiber; 46 mg sodium; 69 mg potassium.

NOTE: **Toast whole hazelnuts** on a baking sheet in a 350°F oven, stirring occasionally, until fragrant, 7 to 9 minutes. Let the nuts cool for a few minutes, then rub together in a clean kitchen towel to remove most of the papery skins.

These crispy treats are a tradition in the Piedmont region of Italy, and although they may look rather ordinary, their sweet, nutty flavor is anything but. Egg whites keep the cookies light while plenty of toasted hazelnuts make them rich with heart-healthy monounsaturated fat.

2	cups hazelnuts, toasted and skinned (*see Note*)
1¼	cups sugar
4	large egg whites
½	teaspoon salt
1	teaspoon vanilla extract

1. Position 2 racks as close to the center of the oven as possible; preheat to 325°F. Line 2 baking sheets with parchment paper or nonstick baking mats.
2. Pulse nuts and sugar in a food processor until finely ground. Scrape into a large bowl.
3. Beat egg whites and salt in another large bowl with an electric mixer on high speed until stiff peaks form. Using a rubber spatula, gently fold the egg whites into the nut mixture. Add vanilla and gently but thoroughly mix until combined.
4. Drop the batter by the tablespoonful 2 inches apart on the prepared baking sheets.
5. Bake the cookies until golden brown, switching the pans back to front and top to bottom halfway through, 25 to 30 minutes. Let cool on the baking sheets for 5 minutes. Gently transfer the cookies to a wire rack to cool completely. When the baking sheets are thoroughly cooled, repeat with the remaining batter.

Cranberry Upside-Down Cake

This homey little cake really shows off the cranberries, which glisten on top when you turn it over onto a serving plate. Make it in the fall when cranberries are fresh and in season. Serve warm with whipped cream or vanilla frozen yogurt. (Photograph: page 200.) *(Recipe adapted from* The Art of Simple Food *by Alice Waters.)*

¾ **cup packed light brown sugar**
4 **tablespoons unsalted butter, softened, divided**
2 **tablespoons plus ¼ cup fresh orange juice, divided**
1 **12-ounce bag fresh *or* frozen (thawed) cranberries (about 3 cups)**
¾ **cup whole-wheat pastry flour (*see Note, page 218*)**
¾ **cup all-purpose flour**
2 **teaspoons baking powder**
¼ **teaspoon salt**
2 **large eggs, at room temperature (*see Note*)**
⅓ **cup canola oil**
1 **cup granulated sugar**
1 **teaspoon vanilla extract**
½ **cup low-fat milk, at room temperature**
  Whipped cream for garnish

1. Preheat oven to 350°F.
2. Heat brown sugar, 2 tablespoons butter and 2 tablespoons orange juice in a large (12-inch) cast-iron or other ovenproof skillet over medium heat, stirring constantly, until the butter melts and the mixture starts to bubble. Let cool. Coat the sides of the skillet with cooking spray.
3. Bring the remaining ¼ cup orange juice and cranberries to a simmer in a medium saucepan, stirring often, until about half the cranberries have popped. Pour evenly over the cooled brown sugar mixture in the skillet.
4. Whisk whole-wheat flour, all-purpose flour, baking powder and salt in a medium bowl.
5. Separate egg whites and yolks. Place the yolks in a large bowl and add the remaining 2 tablespoons butter, oil, granulated sugar and vanilla. Beat with an electric mixer or stand mixer on medium-high speed until light and fluffy. Stir in the flour mixture alternately with milk, using a rubber spatula, starting and ending with the flour. Stir just until the flour is incorporated. Beat the egg whites in a clean dry mixing bowl with clean dry beaters on medium-high speed until they hold soft peaks. Fold one-third of the egg whites into the batter, then gently fold in the rest until almost no white streaks remain. Spread the batter over the cranberries.
6. Bake until the top is golden brown and the cake pulls away from the sides of the pan, 30 to 40 minutes. Let cool in the pan on a wire rack for 15 minutes. Run a knife around the edge of the pan and carefully invert the cake onto a serving plate. Let cool for at least 30 minutes more before serving. Serve warm or at room temperature. Garnish with whipped cream, if desired.

ACTIVE TIME: 30 minutes
TOTAL: 1 hour 50 minutes (including 15 minutes cooling time)

TO MAKE AHEAD: Prepare up to 8 hours ahead; serve at room temperature or warm in a 300°F oven.

MAKES: 10 servings

H↑F
PER SERVING: 356 calories; 13 g fat (4 g sat, 6 g mono); 55 mg cholesterol; 56 g carbohydrate; 36 g added sugars; 4 g protein; 3 g fiber; 181 mg sodium; 114 mg potassium.
NUTRITION BONUS: Vitamin C (15% daily value).

NOTE: To bring an **egg to room temperature,** set it on the counter for 15 minutes or submerge it (in the shell) in a bowl of lukewarm (not hot) water for 5 minutes.

Raspberry Spoonbread

ACTIVE TIME: 30 minutes

TOTAL: 1½ hours

MAKES: 8 servings

H↑F

PER SERVING: 263 calories; 6 g fat
(3 g sat, 2 g mono); 114 mg cholesterol;
46 g carbohydrate; 22 g added sugars;
6 g protein; 4 g fiber; 217 mg sodium;
216 mg potassium.
NUTRITION BONUS: Vitamin C (20% daily
value).

A spoonbread is a traditional Southern cornmeal-based dish. Often it's a savory side dish; here we sweeten it with maple syrup and raspberries for an irresistible dessert.

1 **cup cornmeal, preferably stone-ground (medium *or* finely ground)**
1 **cup nonfat buttermilk**
2/3 **cup pure maple syrup**
2 **tablespoons butter**
1/2 **teaspoon salt**
4 **large eggs, separated**
1/4 **cup all-purpose flour**
2 **teaspoons vanilla extract**
1/4 **cup sugar**
3 **cups fresh raspberries, divided**
8 **tablespoons nonfat plain Greek-style yogurt (optional)**

1. Preheat oven to 375°F. Coat an 8-inch-square baking dish (or other 2-quart ovenproof dish) with cooking spray.
2. Combine cornmeal, buttermilk, maple syrup, butter and salt in a large saucepan. Cook over medium-high heat, whisking constantly, until the mixture bubbles and thickens. Remove from the heat. Whisk egg yolks in a large bowl. Whisking constantly so the eggs won't scramble, add ½ cup of the hot cornmeal mixture until completely combined. Scrape in the remaining cornmeal mixture and whisk until smooth. Whisk in flour and vanilla until smooth.
3. Beat egg whites in another large bowl with an electric mixer on high speed until soft peaks form. Gradually sprinkle in sugar, continuing to beat until soft glossy peaks form. Fold the whites into the cornmeal mixture. Fold in 2 cups raspberries. Spoon the batter into the prepared dish.
4. Bake until puffed, golden brown on top and the center is set, 35 to 40 minutes. The spoonbread will be slightly wobbly and soft when it is completely cooked. Let cool for 20 minutes. Serve warm, topped with some of the remaining raspberries and yogurt, if using.

Glazed Chocolate-Pumpkin Bundt Cake

ACTIVE TIME: 30 minutes

TOTAL: 3 ½ hours (including cooling time)

EQUIPMENT: 12-cup Bundt pan

MAKES: 16 servings

TO MAKE AHEAD: Prepare through Step 4 up to 1 day ahead. Glaze and garnish (Step 5) shortly before serving.

H✖W H↑F H♥H

PER SERVING: 236 calories; 5 g fat (1 g sat, 3 g mono); 13 mg cholesterol; 47 g carbohydrate; 28 g added sugars; 4 g protein; 3 g fiber; 237 mg sodium; 102 mg potassium.

NUTRITION BONUS: Vitamin A (80% daily value).

What makes this chocolate cake so moist and delicious? The secret's in the canned pureed pumpkin, which replaces much of the fat in this recipe. Buttermilk does double duty as well, helping to keep the cake moist and tender, while also adding a touch of tang to the decorative glaze. (Photograph: page 200.)

CAKE

- 1 cup all-purpose flour
- ¾ cup whole-wheat pastry flour (*see Note, page 218*)
- 1 cup granulated sugar
- ¾ cup unsweetened cocoa powder (not Dutch-process)
- 1 ½ teaspoons baking powder
- 1 ½ teaspoons baking soda
- 1 teaspoon pumpkin pie spice
- ¼ teaspoon salt
- 1 cup nonfat buttermilk
- 1 15-ounce can unsweetened pumpkin puree
- ¾ cup packed dark brown sugar
- 1 large egg, at room temperature (*see Note, page 218*)
- 1 large egg white, at room temperature
- ¼ cup canola oil
- ¼ cup light corn syrup
- 1 tablespoon vanilla extract

GLAZE & GARNISH

- ½ cup packed confectioners' sugar
- 1 tablespoon nonfat buttermilk
- 2 tablespoons mini chocolate chips *or* toasted chopped nuts (*see Note, page 219*)

1. **To prepare cake:** Preheat oven to 350°F. Coat a 12-cup Bundt pan with cooking spray.
2. Whisk all-purpose flour, whole-wheat flour, granulated sugar, cocoa, baking powder, baking soda, pumpkin pie spice and salt in a medium bowl.
3. Blend 1 cup buttermilk, pumpkin puree and brown sugar in a large bowl with an electric mixer on low speed. Beat in whole egg and egg white. Stir in oil, corn syrup and vanilla. Gradually add the dry ingredients, stirring until just combined. Transfer the batter to the prepared pan.
4. Bake the cake until a wooden skewer inserted in the center comes out with only a few moist crumbs attached, 1 to 1¼ hours. Let cool on a wire rack for 15 minutes. Remove from the pan and let cool completely on the rack, about 2 hours.
5. **To glaze & garnish cake:** Combine confectioners' sugar and 1 tablespoon buttermilk in a small bowl, stirring until completely smooth. Place the cake on a serving plate and drizzle the glaze over the top; garnish with chocolate chips (or chopped nuts) while the glaze is still moist.

Chocolate Raspberry Tofu Pie

This chocolate raspberry pie gets an amazing smooth, rich, creamy texture from pureed tofu. But no need to tell that tofu's the secret ingredient—we're sure no one will guess. (Photograph: page 200.)

1½ **cups chocolate chips (about 10-ounces)**
1 **12.3-ounce shelf-stable package firm silken tofu (*see Note*)**
1 **tablespoon pure maple syrup**
1 **teaspoon vanilla extract**
1 **cup frozen raspberries, thawed**
½ **cup confectioners' sugar**
1 **9-inch graham cracker pie crust**
Fresh raspberries for garnish

1. Put chocolate chips in a medium microwavable bowl. Microwave on Medium for 1 minute. Stir, then continue microwaving on Medium, stirring every 20 seconds, until melted.
2. Place tofu in a food processor or blender and process until smooth. Add the melted chocolate, maple syrup and vanilla. Process again until smooth. Add raspberries and confectioners' sugar and process until very smooth; scraping down the sides as necessary. Spread the mixture into the crust. Refrigerate until firm, at least 2 hours. Garnish with fresh raspberries, if desired.

ACTIVE TIME: 15 minutes

TOTAL: 2¼ hours (including 2 hours chilling time)

TO MAKE AHEAD: Loosely cover with plastic wrap and refrigerate for up to 3 days.

MAKES: 8 servings

H↑F

PER SERVING: 254 calories; 13 g fat (7 g sat, 4 g mono); 0 mg cholesterol; 36 g carbohydrate; 28 g added sugars; 5 g protein; 3 g fiber; 36 mg sodium; 238 mg potassium.

NOTE: Look for **shelf-stable silken tofu** in the Asian foods section or near shelf-stable soymilk in natural-foods stores and some well-stocked supermarkets. If you can't find it, refrigerated silken tofu can be used in its place in this recipe. It's usually sold in a 1-pound container, but you'll only need 1⅓ cups for this recipe.

138

189

118

RESOURCES

In this section you'll find all the keys to using this book. Have a bunch of mushrooms? The 13 recipes that include mushrooms are listed on page 227 in the index. Are you wondering what "Shao Hsing" is in the ingredient list on page 139? In the Notes section (pages 218-219) you'll learn that it's a seasoned rice wine and you can find it in the Asian section of many well-stocked supermarkets. And if you want advice on some of the best things to keep stocked in your pantry to make vegetarian cooking as easy and fun as possible, turn to page 216.

The Healthy Pantry

While a good shopping list is the key to a quick and painless trip to the supermarket, a well-stocked pantry is the best way to ensure you'll have everything you need to cook once you get home. Our Healthy Pantry includes many of the items you need to prepare the recipes in this book plus a few other ingredients that will make impromptu meals easier.

OILS, VINEGARS & CONDIMENTS

Oils: extra-virgin olive, canola
Vinegars: balsamic, red-wine, white-wine, rice, cider
Asian condiments: reduced-sodium soy sauce, hoisin sauce, vegetarian "oyster" sauce, chile-garlic sauce, toasted sesame oil
Barbecue sauce
Hot sauce
Mustard: Dijon, whole-grain
Ketchup
Mayonnaise, low-fat

FLAVORINGS

Salt: kosher, iodized table
Black peppercorns
Herbs and spices, assorted dried
Onions
Garlic, fresh
Ginger, fresh
Olives: Kalamata, green
Capers
Lemons, limes, oranges

DRY GOODS

Pasta, whole-wheat (assorted shapes)
Barley: pearl, quick-cooking
Bulgur
Couscous, whole-wheat
Quinoa
Rice: brown, instant brown, wild
Dried beans and lentils
Flour: whole-wheat, whole-wheat pastry (store opened packages in the refrigerator or freezer), all-purpose
Rolled oats
Cornmeal
Breadcrumbs: plain dry, coarse whole-wheat
Crackers, whole-grain
Unsweetened cocoa powder
Bittersweet chocolate
Sweeteners: granulated sugar, brown sugar, honey, pure maple syrup
Tofu, shelf-stable

NUTS, SEEDS & FRUITS

(Store opened packages of nuts and seeds in the refrigerator or freezer.)
Nuts: walnuts, pecans, almonds, hazelnuts, peanuts, pine nuts
Natural peanut butter and/or other nut butters
Seeds: pepitas, sesame seeds, sunflower seeds
Tahini (sesame paste)
Dried fruits: apricots, prunes, cherries, cranberries, dates, figs, raisins

CANNED & BOTTLED GOODS

Broth: vegetable, "no-chicken" and mushroom
"Lite" coconut milk
Tomatoes, tomato paste
Beans: black, cannellini, kidney, pinto, great northern, chickpeas, lentils
Wine: red, white or nonalcoholic
Madeira
Sherry, dry

REFRIGERATOR ITEMS

Milk, low-fat or nonfat, and/or soymilk or rice milk
Buttermilk or buttermilk powder
Yogurt, plain and/or vanilla, low-fat or nonfat
Sour cream, reduced-fat or nonfat
Parmesan cheese, good-quality
Cheddar cheese, sharp
Eggs (large) or egg substitute, such as Egg Beaters
Orange juice
Tofu: water-packed, baked and/or seasoned
Tortillas: corn, whole-wheat

FREEZER BASICS

Fruit: berries, other fruit
Vegetables: peas, spinach, broccoli, corn, edamame

Quick Vegetable Broth

We like some commercial vegetable broths, but nothing beats homemade's fresh flavor.

4	quarts water	1	tomato, quartered
4	carrots, chopped	5	sprigs fresh parsley
2	medium onions, chopped	3	sprigs fresh thyme
2	leeks, washed and chopped		or ½ teaspoon dried
2	stalks celery	½	teaspoon kosher salt
8	mushrooms, sliced	1	bay leaf

Place all ingredients in a large pot. Bring to a boil over medium heat; cook, uncovered, for 30 minutes, skimming foam. Strain through a fine sieve. (Discard solids.)

ACTIVE TIME: 15 minutes
TOTAL: 45 minutes

TO MAKE AHEAD: Refrigerate for up to 2 days or freeze for up to 6 months.

MAKES: about 16 cups

ANALYSIS NOTE: After straining, the broth has negligible calories and nutrients except sodium (120 mg per cup).

Roasted Vegetable Broth

Roasting the vegetables yields rich and flavorful results; use it in any recipe that calls for vegetable broth.

6	large carrots	4	stalks celery, cut into 1-inch pieces
5	large onions		
1	bulb fennel, cored	½	bunch parsley (about 10 sprigs)
2	tablespoons canola oil	½	bunch thyme (about 8 sprigs)
2	tablespoons tomato paste	12	black peppercorns
1	cup dry white wine, divided	6	cloves garlic, crushed and peeled
20	cups water	4	bay leaves

1. Preheat oven to 425°F.
2. Cut carrots, onions and fennel into 1-inch pieces. Combine in a large roasting pan. Toss with oil. Transfer half the vegetables to a second roasting pan. Roast the vegetables for 45 minutes, stirring every 15 minutes and switching the position of the pans each time you stir.
3. In one pan, push the vegetables to one side and spread tomato paste in the other side. Continue roasting (both pans) until the tomato paste begins to blacken, about 15 minutes more.
4. Transfer the roasted vegetables to a large stockpot. Pour ½ cup wine into each roasting pan and place each pan over two burners on the stovetop. Bring to a boil over medium-high heat. Cook, scraping up any browned bits, for 1 to 2 minutes. Add the contents of the roasting pans to the stockpot, along with water, celery, parsley, thyme, peppercorns, garlic and bay leaves. Cover and bring to a simmer. Uncover and simmer for 1 hour without stirring, adjusting heat as necessary to maintain the simmer.
5. Strain the broth through a colander, pressing on the solids to remove all liquid. Discard solids. If not using immediately, cool the broth before storing.

ACTIVE TIME: 30 minutes
TOTAL: 3 hours

TO MAKE AHEAD: Refrigerate for up to 1 week or freeze for up to 3 months.

EQUIPMENT: 2 roasting pans

MAKES: 16 cups

ANALYSIS NOTE: After straining and skimming, the broth has negligible calories and nutrients.

Notes from the Test Kitchen

AGAVE SYRUP: Agave syrup or nectar is the naturally sweet juice extracted from the agave plant. It has a lower glycemic index and is lower in calories than table sugar, but is even sweeter. Try it in place of honey or in moderation when substituting for table sugar. Look for it near other sweeteners in natural-foods stores.

BEETS, HOW TO PREP & STEAM: Trim greens and root end; peel with a vegetable peeler. Cut beets into 1-inch pieces. **To steam:** Place in a steamer basket over 1 inch of boiling water in a large pot. Cover and steam over high heat until tender, 10 to 15 minutes. **To steam in the microwave:** Place in a glass baking dish, add 2 tablespoons water, cover tightly and microwave on High until tender, 8 to 10 minutes. Let stand, covered, for 5 minutes.

BREADCRUMBS, HOW TO MAKE: To make your own **fresh** breadcrumbs, trim crusts from whole-wheat bread. Tear bread into pieces and process in a food processor until coarse crumbs form. To make **fine** breadcrumbs, process until very fine. To make **dry** breadcrumbs, spread coarse or fine breadcrumbs on a baking sheet and bake at 250°F until dry, 10 to 15 minutes. One slice of bread makes about ½ cup fresh breadcrumbs or about ⅓ cup dry breadcrumbs. For **store-bought** coarse dry breadcrumbs we like Ian's brand, labeled "Panko breadcrumbs." Find them at well-stocked supermarkets.

BROILER-SAFE NONSTICK SKILLET: Conventional nonstick cookware should not be used over high heat or under the broiler because the nonstick coating may break down and release potentially toxic fumes. There are several choices of nonstick cookware—marketed under names like "green cookware" or "eco-friendly cookware"—that are made with a high-heat-safe nonstick coating. When cooking under a broiler or over high heat, be sure your pan is rated for high temperatures. A cast-iron skillet is a good alternative to nonstick skillets.

BROTH, MUSHROOM: Look for mushroom broth in the natural-foods section of large supermarkets or natural-foods stores.

BROTH, "NO-CHICKEN": Chicken-flavored broth, sometimes called "No-Chicken Broth," is a vegetarian broth. It's preferable to vegetable broth in some recipes for its hearty, rich flavor. Look for it in the natural-foods section of most supermarkets.

BULGUR: Bulgur is made by parboiling, drying and coarsely grinding or cracking wheat berries. Don't confuse bulgur with cracked wheat. Since the parboiling step is skipped, cracked wheat must be cooked for up to an hour, whereas bulgur simply needs a quick soak in hot water for most uses. Look for it in the natural-foods section of large supermarkets, near other grains.

CHILE-GARLIC SAUCE: A blend of ground chiles, garlic and vinegar, chile-garlic sauce is commonly used to add heat and flavor to Asian soups, sauces and stir-fries. It can be found in the Asian section of large supermarkets (sometimes labeled as chili-garlic sauce or paste) and keeps up to 1 year in the refrigerator.

CHINESE FIVE-SPICE POWDER: Chinese five-spice powder is a blend of cinnamon, cloves, fennel seed, star anise and Szechuan peppercorns. Look for it in the spice section of the supermarket or with other Asian ingredients.

CHIPOTLE CHILES: **Chipotle chiles in adobo sauce** are smoked jalapeños packed in a flavorful sauce. Look for the small cans with the Mexican foods in large supermarkets. Once opened, they'll keep at least 2 weeks in the refrigerator or 6 months in the freezer. **Ground chipotle chile**, made from dried smoked jalapeños, can be found in the specialty-spice section of most supermarkets or online at *penzeys.com*.

CORN, HOW TO REMOVE KERNELS: Stand an ear of corn on one end and slice the kernels off with a sharp knife. One ear will yield about ½ cup kernels.

EGGS, HOW TO HARD-BOIL: Place eggs in a single layer in a saucepan; cover with water. Bring to a simmer over medium-high heat. Reduce heat to low and cook at the barest simmer for 10 minutes. Remove from heat, pour out hot water and cover with ice-cold water. Let cool before peeling.

EGGS, HOW TO POACH: Fill a large, straight-sided skillet or Dutch oven with 2 inches of water; bring to a boil. Add ¼ cup distilled white vinegar. Reduce to a gentle simmer: the water should be steaming and small bubbles should come up from the bottom of the pan. Working with one at a time, break an egg into a small bowl, submerge the lip of the bowl into the simmering water and gently add the egg. (Don't poach more than 4 at a time.) Cook for 4 minutes for soft set, 5 minutes for medium set and 8 minutes for hard set. Using a slotted spoon, transfer the eggs to a clean kitchen towel to drain for a minute before serving.

EGGS, ROOM TEMPERATURE: To bring an egg to room temperature, either set it out on the counter for 15 minutes or submerge it (in the shell) in a bowl of lukewarm (not hot) water for 5 minutes.

FERMENTED BLACK BEANS: Fermented black beans, oxidized soybeans that are salt-dried, have a savory, salty and slightly bitter flavor. They are frequently used in Chinese stir-fries, marinades and sauces. Before using, they should be soaked in water for 10 to 30 minutes to get rid of excess salt. When purchasing fermented black beans, look for shiny and firm beans. Once open, store in an airtight container in the refrigerator for up to 1 year.

FLOUR, WHITE WHOLE-WHEAT: White whole-wheat flour, made from a special variety of white wheat, is light in color and flavor but has the same nutritional properties as regular whole-wheat flour. It is available in large supermarkets and at natural-foods stores. Store in an airtight container in the freezer.

FLOUR, WHOLE-WHEAT PASTRY: Whole-wheat pastry flour is milled from soft wheat. It contains less gluten-forming potential than regular whole-wheat flour and helps ensure a tender result in delicate baked goods while providing the nutritional benefits of whole grains. Find it at large supermarkets and natural-foods stores. Store in an airtight container in the freezer.

GRILL RACK, HOW TO OIL: Oiling a grill rack before you grill foods helps ensure that the food won't stick. Oil a folded paper towel, hold it with tongs and rub it over the rack. (Do not use cooking spray on a hot grill.)

HOISIN SAUCE: Hoisin sauce is a dark brown, thick, spicy-sweet sauce made from soybeans and a complex mix of spices. Find it in the Asian section of your supermarket and in Asian markets.

NONREACTIVE PAN, BOWL OR BAKING DISH: A nonreactive bowl, pan or baking dish—stainless-steel, enamel-coated or glass—is necessary when cooking with acidic foods, such as lemon, to prevent the food from reacting with the pan. Reactive pans, such as aluminum and cast-iron, can impart off colors and/or flavors.

NUTS, HOW TO TOAST: To toast **whole nuts**, spread on a baking sheet and bake at 350°F, stirring once, until fragrant, 7 to 9 minutes. To toast **chopped nuts, small or sliced nuts,** cook in a small dry skillet over medium-low heat, stirring constantly, until fragrant and lightly brown, 2 to 4 minutes.

"OYSTER" SAUCE, VEGETARIAN: Vegetarian "oyster" sauce is made from mushroom extract and is great for adding depth of flavor to vegetarian stir-fries. Vegetarian "stir-fry sauce," also made from mushrooms, can be used as a substitute.

PAPRIKA: Paprika is a spice made from grinding dried red peppers. Paprika specifically labeled **Hungarian** delivers a fuller, richer flavor than regular paprika. **Smoked paprika** is made from smoke-dried red peppers and adds earthy, smoky flavor. It can be used in many types of savory dishes. Look for different types at large supermarkets, at *tienda.com* or *penzeys.com*.

PEPPERS, HOT: Hot peppers can "burn" your hands. Wear rubber gloves or wash your hands thoroughly after handling them.

PIZZA DOUGH: Look for fresh or frozen balls of whole-wheat pizza dough at your supermarket. Check the ingredient list to make sure the dough doesn't contain any hydrogenated oils.

POLENTA: Although you might have to ask your favorite grocery store clerk where to find the tubes of prepared polenta (we've found it refrigerated near both the tofu and the deli, and on the shelf by other grains or in the pasta aisle), it's worth seeking out this versatile timesaver and buying a few to have on hand. Our recipes were developed for plain polenta; most brands also make a variety of flavors, including sun-dried tomato and Italian herb (do note that flavored versions are often higher in sodium).

RED CURRY PASTE: Red curry paste is a blend of chile peppers, garlic, lemongrass and galangal (a root with a flavor similar to ginger). The heat and salt level can vary widely depending on brand. Be sure to taste as you go. Look for it in the Asian section of the supermarket or in specialty stores. Once opened, it will keep in the refrigerator for up to 1 year.

SAKE: Sake is a dry, Japanese rice wine generally available where other wines are sold.

SALSA, FRESH: Look for prepared fresh salsa in the supermarket refrigerator section near other dips and spreads. It has a nice bright flavor and is typically lower in sodium than jarred salsa.

SEEDS, HOW TO TOAST: To toast pumpkin seeds (pepitas), poppy seeds, sunflower seeds or sesame seeds, place in a small dry skillet and cook over medium-low heat, stirring constantly, until fragrant and lightly browned, 2 to 4 minutes.

SEITAN: Seitan is high-protein wheat gluten with a meaty texture. It can be found in natural-foods stores or large supermarkets near the tofu. The actual weight of the seitan in a package varies depending on whether water weight is included. Look for the "drained weight" on the label to make sure you're getting the amount you need for your recipe.

SHAO HSING: Shao Hsing (or Shaoxing) is a seasoned rice wine available in most Asian specialty markets and the Asian sections of some larger supermarkets.

SHERRY: Sherry is a type of fortified wine originally from southern Spain. Don't use the "cooking sherry" sold in many supermarkets—it can be surprisingly high in sodium. Instead, get dry sherry that's sold with other fortified wines at your wine or liquor store.

TAHINI: Tahini is a smooth, thick paste made from ground sesame seeds. Look for it in the Middle Eastern section or near other nut butters in large supermarkets.

TAMARIND: Tamarind is a tropical tree that produces a sour-sweet fruit in a brown pod, with edible pulp. It's used in Asian and Indian curries, beverages and desserts. Purchase either tamarind concentrate or pulp from Asian or other ethnic markets (or online from *amazon.com*). We found Thai brands of concentrate and pulp to work best in the recipe on page 146; Indian brands were too thick, dense and strong in flavor. To make your own "concentrate," combine 1/4 cup tamarind pulp and 1 cup hot water in a medium bowl. Let stand for 20 minutes. Break up the paste and mix it with the water with a fork. Pass the mixture through a fine sieve set over a bowl, pressing against the sieve to collect as much of the pulp as possible. Discard solids.

TEMPEH: Tempeh is a chewy, nutty, fermented soybean loaf. Find it (plain or with added grains) near refrigerated tofu in natural-foods stores and many large supermarkets. We particularly like SoyBoy 5 Grain and Lightlife Flax tempeh.

TOFU, BAKED: Precooked, seasoned "baked tofu" is firmer than water-packed tofu and comes in a wide variety of flavors. We like to use "teriyaki" or "Thai" in Asian-inspired dishes and "Italian" in Mediterranean-based recipes. If you like a smoky flavor, look for baked, smoked tofu and try it on sandwiches or in stir-fries.

TOMATOES, HOW TO PEEL: Make a small X in the bottom of each tomato and plunge into boiling water until the skins are slightly loosened, 30 seconds to 2 minutes. Transfer to a bowl of ice water for 1 minute. Peel with a paring knife, starting at the X.

TORTILLAS, HOW TO WARM: To warm tortillas, wrap in barely damp paper towels and microwave on High for 30 to 45 seconds or wrap in foil and bake at 300°F until steaming, 5 to 10 minutes.

Key to EATINGWELL Recipes & Nutritional Analyses

Icons identify recipes that are most appropriate for certain eating goals. Recipes with small serving sizes (e.g., salad dressings, cookies) don't qualify for icons. (For more on our nutritional analysis process and our complete guidelines on how we define each icon, visit *eatingwell.com/go/guidelines*.) A recipe marked…

H✘W [**Healthy Weight**] has reduced calories and limited saturated fat:

	CALORIES	SAT FAT
entrees	≤350	≤5g
side dishes, muffins, breads	≤250	≤3g
desserts	≤250	≤5g
dips, salsas (¼- to ⅓-cup serving)	≤100	≤2g
Combination meal*	≤420	≤7g
Complete meal**	≤500	≤7g

H♥F [**High Fiber**] provides significant total fiber: entrees/combination meals*/complete meals** have ≥5 grams of fiber per serving. All other recipes have ≥3 grams.

H♥H [**Healthy Heart**] has limited saturated fat:

	SAT FAT
entrees	≤3g
side dishes, muffins, breads, desserts	≤2g
dips, salsas (¼- to ⅓-cup serving)	≤1g
Combination meal*	≤5g
Complete meal**	≤7g

*Combination meal: A serving of protein plus a starch *or* vegetable serving.
**Complete meal: A serving of protein plus a starch *and* a vegetable.

⏱ is ready to eat in 45 minutes or less.

ACTIVE TIME includes prep time (the time it takes to chop, dice, puree, mix, combine, etc. before cooking begins). It also includes the time spent tending something on the stovetop, in the oven or on the grill—and getting it to the table. If you can't walk away from it for more than 10 minutes, we consider it active time.

TOTAL includes both active and inactive time and indicates the entire amount of time required for each recipe, start to finish.

TO MAKE AHEAD tells when a recipe or part of a recipe can be made in advance and gives storage instructions. If particular EQUIPMENT is needed to prepare a recipe, we tell you that too.

- All recipes are analyzed for nutrition content by a Registered Dietitian.
- We analyze for calories, total fat, saturated (sat) fat, monounsaturated (mono) fat, cholesterol, carbohydrate, added sugars, protein, fiber, sodium and potassium, using The Food Processor® SQL Nutrition Analysis Software from ESHA Research, Salem, Oregon. (Note: Nutrition information is updated regularly. The current analyses appear with the recipes on *eatingwell.com*.)
- When a recipe provides 15 percent or more of the Daily Value (dv) of a nutrient, it is listed as a nutrition bonus. These values are FDA benchmarks for adults eating 2,000 calories a day.
- Recipes are tested and analyzed with iodized table salt unless otherwise indicated.
- We estimate that rinsing with water reduces the sodium in some canned foods, such as beans, by 35 percent. (People on sodium-restricted diets can reduce or eliminate the salt in a recipe.)
- Garnishes and optional ingredients are not included in analyses.
- When a recipe gives a measurement range of an ingredient, we analyze the first amount.
- When alternative ingredients are listed, we analyze the first one suggested.
- We do not include trimmings or marinade that is not absorbed in analyses.

Special Indexes

Gluten-Free Index

These recipes do not include wheat, rye, barley or oats. But it's important to read the labels of processed foods, such as broths and condiments, to make sure they don't contain hidden sources of gluten. And not all serving suggestions are gluten free.

30 Minutes or Less
*Recipes marked with * are ready in 20 minutes or less.*

Recipe Index

Page numbers in italics indicate photographs.

Recipe Contributors

Bruce Aidells | Nina's Mexican
Rice, 196

Nancy Baggett | Spiced Eggplant-Lentil
Salad with Mango, 39; Vegetarian
Taco Salad, 43

Vanessa Barrington | Toasted Pita &
Bean Salad, 40; Bean Burgers with
Spicy Guacamole, 83

Rick Bayless | Vegetarian Tortilla
Soup, 62

Beth-Ann Bove | Individual Grilled
Pizzas with Pesto, Tomatoes
& Feta, 90

Marialisa Calta | Italian Hazelnut
Cookies, 208

James Chatto | White Bean Soup, 51

Ying Chang Compestine | Pocket Eggs
with Soy-Sesame Sauce, 155

Ruth Cousineau | Sweet & Sour
Barley-Bean Stew, 59

Kathy Farrell-Kingsley | Roasted
Vegetable Galette with Olives, 173

Ken Haedrich | Pecan & Mushroom
Burgers, 84; Southwestern Pumpkin
Burgers, 85

Susan Herr | Pickled Eggs, 26; Baked
Curried Brown Rice & Lentil Pilaf, 121

Cheryl & Bill Jamison | Green Olive
& Almond Spread, 20; Jícama &
Cucumber Salad with Red Chile
Dressing, 33; Cheese Enchiladas
with Red Chile Sauce, 166

Matthew G. Kadey | Packet-Roasted
Balsamic Green Beans &
Peppers, 184

Bharti Kirchner | Red Lentil &
Caramelized Onion Soup, 58;
Spicy Chickpea-Potato Stew, 63

Diane Kochilas | Butternut Squash
Pilaf, 114

Deborah Madison | Salsa Ranchera,
23; Braised Summer Vegetables
with a Green Herb Sauce, 54;
Vegan Migas, 141

Mary Marchese | French Onion
Pizza, 91

Perla Meyers | Spicy Kidney Bean &
Bell Pepper Ragout, 128

Jamie Purviance | Quick Cucumber
Kimchi, 188; Sesame-Seasoned
Spinach, 191

Elisabeth Redman | Chocolate
Raspberry Tofu Pie, 213

Victoria Abbott Riccardi | Chewy
Cheese Puffs, 22; Spinach with
Chickpeas, 27; Asparagus Salad
Topped with Poached Eggs, 42;
Portobello Paillards with Spinach,
White Beans & Caramelized Onions,
129; Sesame-Crusted Tofu over
Vegetables, 138; Glazed Chocolate-
Pumpkin Bundt Cake, 212

G. Franco Romagnoli | Islander Salad,
37; Orecchiette alla Carrettiera
("Wagon-Driver Style"), 95;
Mediterranean Baked Penne, 99;
Baked Tortellini, 105

Chris Schlesinger & John Willoughby
Eggplant Subs with Provolone, 71;
Tomato-Olive Relish, 71

Marie Simmons | Roasted Ratatouille
with Eggs & Cheese, 160; Roasted
Asparagus Salad with Citrus
Dressing, 183; Melon & Apple
Granita, 205

Nina Simonds | Red-Cooked Tofu
with Mushrooms, 134; Stir-Fried
Vegetables in Black Bean Sauce, 139

Corinne Trang | Grilled Curried
Tofu with Sweet & Spicy Tamarind
Chutney, 146

Mariana Velasquez | Tomato Phyllo
Tart, 176

Alice Waters | Cranberry Upside-Down
Cake, 209

Bruce Weinstein & Mark Scarbrough
Roasted Fennel & Farro Salad, 193

Other EATINGWELL Books

Available at *eatingwell.com/shop* and wherever fine books are sold.

The Simple Art of EatingWell: 400 Easy Recipes, Tips and Techniques for Delicious, Healthy Meals
(The Countryman Press, 2010) ISBN: 978-0-88150-935-9 (hardcover)

EatingWell on a Budget: 140 Delicious, Healthy, Affordable Recipes
(The Countryman Press, 2010) ISBN: 978-0-88150-913-7 (softcover)

EatingWell 500-Calorie Dinners: Easy, Delicious Recipes & Menus
(The Countryman Press, 2010) ISBN: 978-0-88150-846-8 (hardcover)

EatingWell in Season: The Farmers' Market Cookbook
(The Countryman Press, 2009) ISBN: 978-0-88150-856-7 (hardcover)

EatingWell Comfort Foods Made Healthy: The Classic Makeover Cookbook
(The Countryman Press, 2009) ISBN: 978-0-88150-829-1 (hardcover) | ISBN: 978-0-88150-887-1 (softcover, 2009)

EatingWell for a Healthy Heart Cookbook: A Cardiologist's Guide to Adding Years to Your Life
(The Countryman Press, 2008) ISBN: 978-0-88150-724-9 (hardcover)

The EatingWell Diet: 7 Steps to a Healthy, Trimmer You
150+ Delicious, Healthy Recipes with Proven Results
(The Countryman Press, 2007) ISBN: 978-0-88150-722-5 (hardcover) | ISBN: 978-0-88150-822-2 (softcover, 2008)

EatingWell Serves Two: 150 Healthy in a Hurry Suppers
(The Countryman Press, 2006) ISBN: 978-0-88150-723-2 (hardcover)

The EatingWell Healthy in a Hurry Cookbook: 150 Delicious Recipes for Simple, Everyday Suppers in 45 Minutes or Less
(The Countryman Press, 2006) ISBN: 978-0-88150-687-7 (hardcover)

The EatingWell Diabetes Cookbook: 275 Delicious Recipes and 100+ Tips for Simple, Everyday Carbohydrate Control
(The Countryman Press, 2005) ISBN: 978-0-88150-633-4 (hardcover) | ISBN: 978-0-88150-778-2 (softcover, 2007)

The Essential EatingWell Cookbook: Good Carbs, Good Fats, Great Flavors
(The Countryman Press, 2004) ISBN: 978-0-88150-630-3 (hardcover) | ISBN: 978-0-88150-701-0 (softcover, 2005)